Case Studies
in Business,
Society,
and Ethics

SECOND EDITION

Case Studies in Business, Society, and Ethics

Tom L. Beauchamp
Georgetown University

Prentice Hall, Englewood Cliffs, New Jersey 07632

Library of Congress Cataloging-in-Publication Data

Beauchamp, Tom L.
    Case studies in business, society, and ethics / Tom L. Beauchamp.
  -- 2nd ed.
        p.   cm.
    ISBN 0-13-119355-4
    1. Industry--Social aspects--United States--Case studies.
  2. Industry and state--United States--Case studies. 3. Trade
  regulation--United States--Case studies.   I. Title.
  HD60.5.U5B38   1989
  658.4'08'0973--dc19   88-31572
                                                              CIP

Editorial/production supervision: Betsy Keefer
Cover design: Wanda Lubelska Design
Manufacturing buyer: Peter Havens

© 1989, 1983 by Prentice-Hall, Inc.
A Division of Simon & Schuster
Englewood Cliffs, New Jersey 07632

Printed in the United States of America
10 9 8 7 6 5 4 3 2 1

ISBN 0-13-119355-4

Prentice-Hall International (UK) Limited, London
Prentice-Hall of Australia Pty. Limited, Sydney
Prentice-Hall Canada Inc., Toronto
Prentice-Hall Hispanoamericana, S.A., Mexico
Prentice-Hall of India Private Limited, New Delhi
Prentice-Hall of Japan, Inc., Tokyo
Simon & Schuster Asia Pte. Ltd., Singapore
Editora Prentice-Hall do Brasil, Ltda., Rio de Janeiro

Contents

Expanded Contents

This alternative listing of cases is an expansion of the basic Contents. It is offered as a guide for teachers and students. It should be especially useful for teachers who plan a large segment of a course around a restricted range of topics. Thus, for example, a teacher who devotes a major part of a course to the topic of business and government can easily locate below the large number of cases relevant to this subject. (The headings in the basic Contents are unchanged, but a much larger set of cases is included under most headings.)

chapter 5 The Government

chapter 6   The Multinational **230**

Preface

This volume contains thirty-four cases that have a common focus on ethical and social issues in business. This second edition contains fourteen new cases not found in the first edition. Fifteen of the twenty cases retained from the first edition have undergone revisions, which range from minor updates to complete rewritings. Thus, twenty-nine of the thirty-four cases differ from those found in the first edition. The chapter introductions have been expanded, and more material on the nature and use of the case method in business has been added to the book's general introduction. There is entirely new material on topics in accounting practices, insider trading and investment, internal ethical review mechanisms, trade secrets and due diligence, commissions on sales, fair competition, corporate social policies, conflict of interest, and confidentiality of information.

The objective of this volume is to make students aware of situations that require moral reflection, judgment, and decision, at the same time revealing the complexities that often surround moral choices and the framing of public policies. The book has not been produced to create a platform for moralistic criticism of the behavior of individual persons, corporations, or governmental agencies that play leading roles in the cases. Some cases do contain dramatic instances of professional irresponsibility or of conduct that is distinctly immoral, illegal, or unprofessional; but it should not be inferred from these cases that their purpose is to condemn a person or profession. Irresponsible actions are occasionally featured because more can sometimes be learned from wrongful behavior than from rightful. However, learning through the study of wrongful or negligent behavior is not the primary orientation of this volume. The focus is generally on circumstances in which hard choices must be made under complex conditions of uncertainty or disagreement. More is to be learned, in my judgment, from reasoning under circumstances of controversy, personal quandary, incompleteness of information, and predictive uncertainty than from paradigmatic cases of irresponsibility.

There are also reasons for the length and structure of the cases. Many cases that now circulate in the general literature of business, society, and ethics are too short to contain enough detail for discussion or contain so much detail that discussion is retarded by the particulars and their connections. Most of us encounter severe limitations on the amount of information we can study and remember about any sequence of events. We thus prefer tidy cases that come to the essence of the matter without a massive body of descriptions and data. Most cases in this book conform to this model.

However, any experienced executive or policymaker will rightly insist that the situations under which decisions are made in business are multifarious, perplexing, and short of desired information. Executives and policymakers thus tend to see cases as too intricate for quick summaries. This point of view has its merits. Every student should appreciate that cases almost always contain imbroglios beyond the mentioned facts. Much remains to be said even when cases are described at book length—as, for example, the Love Canal and Reserve Mining cases reported in this volume have been described. Moreover, judgments about the cases sometimes become progressively more difficult as the description of the case is enriched by detail.

Nevertheless, discussion of cases is facilitated by a brief and orderly display of the pertinent materials. I have therefore tried to write and collect cases that contain sufficient detail to facilitate discussion in the classroom without becoming mired in detail. Cases of this length also make it possible to produce a book with a variety of issues at an affordable cost to students.

Many teachers of the subject matter found in this book prefer cases that take an "inside" view of a corporation or institution under investigation in the case. They are interested in discussing the managerial decisions that must be made on the firing line. The reasons behind this preference for an inside view are set forth in the Introduction to this volume. I endorse this form of pedagogy, and several cases in this book are so oriented. However, this approach incorporates only one profitable form of study. An outside look at corporate activities is sometimes valuable and perhaps even the only perspective obtainable. Moreover, it can be the best approach to cases that involve the formation of public policy. A variety of approaches to case writing is therefore used in this book; some cases take an inside look, some use an outside perspective, and a few employ a mixture of perspectives.

Some teachers and students are enthusiastic about questions for discussion placed at the end of each case, under the belief that these questions focus reflection and discussion on particular features of the cases. I believe this practice is an editorial disservice rather than a service. A teacher may profitably circulate questions in a class, but the problem with this approach *in a text* is twofold: (a) teachers teach the cases with very different approaches, purposes, and problems; (b) students can easily be impeded from their own thinking and from taking novel approaches by being channeled in a particular direction. For these reasons, no questions or aids other than general introductions to chapters accompany the cases in this volume.

Virtually all cases in this book report actual rather than hypothetical events. That is, they are based on authentic sequences of events that occurred in a business or public-policy circumstance. Generally the corporations involved are identified by their correct names. However, in several cases confidential material was used or adequate documentation of some claims was impossible. In these cases names, dates, and locations have been changed, and no identification occurs of the corporations and persons originally involved. In a few of these cases some hypothetical elements have been added to highlight the problem and focus the reader's understanding of the situation. In two instances a composite case has been formed by integrating the features of several individual cases.

T. L. B.

Acknowledgments

A talented research staff has assisted me for several years in the collecting and writing of these cases, and we have in turn been generously supported through two editions of the book by grants. Support came initially from the Exxon Educational Foundation and the Landegger Program in International Business Diplomacy at Georgetown University. The Kennedy Institute of Ethics also supported this work. Through the Institute, work on several cases in the second edition was supported in part by BRSG SO7 RR 0713616, awarded by the Biomedical Research Support Grant Program, Division of Research Resources, National Institutes of Health. I also acknowledge with due appreciation the support provided by the Kennedy Institute's library and information retrieval systems, which kept me in touch with the most important literature and repeatedly reduced the burdens of library research.

Special research unique to this volume was undertaken by Jeffrey Kahn, Kelley MacDougall, Anna Pinedo, R. Jay Wallace, Martha Elliott, Nancy Blanpied, William Pitt, Barbara Humes, Louisa W. Peat O'Neil, Andrew Rowan, Linda Kern, Cathleen Kaveny, and Sara Finnerty Kelly. Ted Moran and John Kline of the Landegger Program steered me in a number of important directions, as did Ed Epstein, Ruth Faden, Norman Bowie, Theodore Purcell, Carl Kaufman, Lisa Newton, Robert Cooke, William H. Hay, Thomas L. Carson, Archie B. Carroll, George Lodge, Henry W. Tulloch, Vivian Weil, Michael Hooker, Deborah G. Johnson, David P. Boyd, Richard E. Wokutch, Burton Leiser, Homer B. Sewell, Stephen Klaidman, and John H. Bubar. Some useful and substantive suggestions for improving the Introduction were made by Terry Pinkard, Norman Bowie, Ruth Faden, Judith Areen, and Alex Capron. In the final stages of the second edition Denise Brooks managed the preparation of the manuscript, ably assisted by Tanja Hens.

A number of corporations discussed in the cases in this volume also provided vital materials and criticisms. I am pleased to be able to name the following sources and constructive critics: Tom Behan of IBM; Ralph L. Halpern, attorney for Iroquois Brands, Ltd.; William A. Tabbert of

New York State Electric and Gas; David W. Barry of the Burroughs Wellcome Co.; James M. Green of Occidental Chemical Corporation; Robert Jeffrey of AT&T; Kathryn Ribbey of Ruder Finn & Rotman; Thomas J. Moore of Tampax; Robert M. Palmer of Polaroid; Aracelia Garcia-Vila of Warner Lambert; John T. Sant of McDonnell Douglas; Frank Tomlinson of McDonnell Douglas; Craig Shulstad of General Mills; Susan K. Hartt of Kellogg Cereals; Carl Kaufman and Bruce W. Karrh of Du Pont; Martha Beauchamp of the American Petroleum Institute; Don Price of the Lakewood Bank & Trust; Tom McCollough of Abbott/Ross Industries; C. L. Scarlott of Exxon; A. A. Gioia of Gulf Oil; J. Lee Bailey of the Cleveland Electric Illuminating Co.; Sydney L. McHugh (and Carol A. Boyd in the first edition) of the Procter & Gamble Co.; and Roger Shelley of Revlon.

I was also aided by several persons in organizations other than corporations, including a number of officials at federal agencies in Washington. I express gratitude in particular to Peggy Charron of Action for Children's Television (ACT); Robert B. Choate of the Council on Children, Media, and Merchandising (CCMM); and unknown sources of The Coalition for Environmental-Energy Balance. Several law firms enabled me to obtain (with permission) confidential papers from corporations. I regret that I am not at liberty to mention these law firms and corporations by name.

T. L. B.

Case Studies
in Business,
Society,
and Ethics

Introduction: The Uses of Cases

The cases collected in this volume emerge from the intersection of professional practice in business, economics, law, and government. The cases can be profitably read from each of these disciplinary perspectives. The purpose of this first chapter is to explore (1) how the perspectives inherent in certain disciplines can structure the problems located in the case, (2) the nature and history of "case methods," (3) whether there exists more than one case method, (4) pitfalls in case analysis, and (5) reservations about the "facts" found in cases.

DIFFERENT PERSPECTIVES ON CASE STUDY

Many students and teachers who profit from the study of cases agree that cases help focus and dramatize problems and, at the same time, locate problems in real-life situations. Beyond this point of initial agreement, diverse orientations and styles of case analysis are plentiful. For example, orientations provided by the disciplines of economics, management, and philosophy direct a reader to pick out different elements in the cases as problematic and deserving of careful reflection. This pluralism of approaches occurs in the general area of "business, society, and ethics" most often as a result of two distinct, although not incompatible, orientations: (1) the perspective of *ethics*, and (2) the perspective of *business*.

The ethics orientation regards its endeavor as "business ethics" and therefore analyzes cases using ethical categories such as justice, utility, and rights. Cases about reverse discrimination in hiring, for example, are studied in light of theories of justice and what these theories demand or permit. Moral decisions and quandaries found in cases are taken to be fundamental to a proper understanding of the case. Ethical theories may not be studied in detail and may not be called on for the analysis of each case, but such theories are generally regarded as having a central role in ethical analysis. A common presumption is that without some

1

understanding of ethical theory one is ill-equipped for the critical examination of the cases.

The business orientation tends to categorize its endeavor as "business and society" and analyzes cases in terms of various relationships between business and industry, on the one hand, and government and society, on the other. Cases about environmental pollution, for example, are studied by detailing empirical facts about pollution and disease and by examining social processes that have tended to diminish the scope of decisionmaking in business and have created new responsibilities through government requirements. The economic aspects of pollution control are central to this approach. The responses of corporations to changing legal and regulatory situations as well as the importance of skillful management are often heavily emphasized, as are the considerations of what has been and may become public policy. Tax policies and the economic consequences of proposed public policies may be studied in detail, and are likely to be viewed as central to the analysis of cases. Here ethical principles may not be mentioned at all—just as those who examine the cases with an ethical interest may wholly ignore questions of good and bad management.

There is no reason to suppose that these different orientations are mutually exclusive or that one orientation is preferable to another. A more constructive approach is to admit that cases invite multiple forms of analysis that can all be profitable. They can be analyzed from many points of view, and increased complexity increases the possibilities for different forms of analysis.

THE CASE METHOD IN LAW

Just as different *perspectives* on cases lead us to look for different ingredients, so different *strategies* in analyzing cases yield different outcomes. The oldest and most extensive body of thought on strategies for analyzing cases (apart from religious traditions) is found in law, where the case method has long been a staple of legal training and where "case law" establishes precedents of evidence and justification. It is instructive to look first to the history of and problems in legal case analysis, which has had a deep impact on the case method in business.

The birth of the case method in law occurred shortly after 1870 when Christopher Columbus Langdell became dean of the law school at Harvard. Upon his ascent he immediately revolutionized previous academic standards and teaching techniques by introducing the case method. He intended this method to replace the prevailing textbooks and lecture methods, which he condemned as promoting rote learning and worthless acumen for passing examinations. Langdell's idea was to use casebooks rather than textbooks for the entire law school curriculum. The casebooks were composed of cases selected, edited, and arranged to reveal to the student the pervasive meanings of legal terms, as well as the "rules" and "principles" of law. This approach used a Socratic manner of teaching to reveal how concepts, rules, and principles are found in the legal reasoning of judges as exhibited in the cases. The skillful teacher presumably could extract the embedded nuggets that are the fundamental principles of law, much as a skillful biographer extracts the true principles of a person's reasoning by studying his or her considered decisions over a lifetime.

Langdell was not a disenchanted teacher who disliked conventional methods of lecturing. He had theoretical reasons for his reforms. In his view the law was no perfunctory profession that any clerk could learn by boning up on textbook wisdom. Langdell believed that the law was a science, resting on an inductive method modeled on the "scientific method" of the natural sciences. Teachers and students developed hypotheses in their dissection of cases, and landed on principles just as any scientist did. In law, he argued, one extracted from cases a select body of principles that framed the English common law.[1] Even though the many particulars in cases varied and their judicial conclusions were sometimes at odds, the principles of judicial reasoning need not vary. Also, one could study by this method exactly how far a principle extended, including where its employment was invalid. In the process the student presumably could acquire a facility and sophistication to move from particular circumstances to generalizations and back.

At Harvard students were horrified at Langdell's innovation, and they cut classes in massive numbers. They disliked criticism by questioning and the preparation required for every class. There was also a faculty revolt, and the school's enrollment slipped noticeably. But in the end Langdell was victorious: The method was adopted and spread quickly to other echelons of American legal education. Eventually every American law school of renown succumbed in some measure to the new method of pedagogy. This outcome was in some ways unfortunate because there were many unexamined problems and pretentious claims in the Langdell vision, not the least of which was the odd notion of making the law a science and making its essence a few abstract principles. This vision tended to suppress such integral aspects of law as legislation, the politics of legislation, particular historical circumstances, jurisdictional variations, and legal practice.

There were, however, important reasons why this method, with appropriate modifications, ultimately prevailed in American law schools and still persists as the basic model. By making analysis of case law a basic source of legal education, teachers had a powerful and attractive tool

---

[1] Langdell's first casebook, *Contracts,* is treated in Lawrence M. Friedman, *A History of American Law* (New York: Simon and Schuster, 1973), pp. 531 f. The general account of the case method in this section is indebted to this source, and also to G. Edward White, *Tort Law in America: An Intellectual History* (New York: Oxford University Press, 1980).

for generalizing from cases. Spanning the tangled web of details in particular cases were "the principles of law." Legal theory and its fundamental doctrines could thus be both *found in and applied to cases.* Moreover, training in the case method was believed to sharpen skills of legal reasoning—both legal analysis and legal synthesis. One could tear a case apart and then construct a better way of treating similar cases. In the thrust-and-parry classroom setting, teacher and student had to *think through* a case and its rights and wrongs; they could no longer simply memorize a section of a textbook that transmitted general wisdom about the right answer. The method prepared the student for the practice of law, not merely for theoretical wisdom about it.

The case method was the soul of American legal education from roughly 1880 until 1910, and leading legal texts and practices today provide evidence that its legacy endures. However, since 1910 the case method has been less grandiosely conceived than it was in the Langdell era. Its minor decline, in retrospect, was inevitable.[2] The principles did not prove to be as uniform across courts or time as had at first been thought, because incompatible and even rival legal theories were found in the precedent cases. The method was also isolationist in the context of the modern university, making law a specialty without connections to other professions and undercutting interdisciplinary investigation.

Ultimately the theory of law as a *science* waned and suffered a natural death. However, it left as its substantial legacy not only the extensive use of legal casebooks, but also an allied belief in the importance of case analysis and synthesis in the training of the legal mind. Its most enduring value is probably found in the way it teaches students to distinguish the nature of principles and evidence at work in one case as opposed to another. By examining cases students learn which courts are considered adept at legal reasoning, how to assemble facts, and where "the weight of the evidence" lies so as to transfer that weight elsewhere in new cases. It is generally (although not uniformly[3]) agreed that it offers substantial benefits in the training of lawyers, whatever its pitfalls and shortcomings.

THE CASE METHOD IN BUSINESS SCHOOLS

Historical Development. When the case method at the Harvard Law School enjoyed its peak of influence, it spawned a new infant across campus at the Harvard Business School, which opened its doors in 1908. The first dean of the school, Edwin F. Gay, determined that courses on

---

[2] See White, *Tort Law in America,* esp. pp. 154 ff.

[3] For a sharp criticism of the method and its milieu in the training of lawyers, see the *Report of the Dean* of the Maryland Law School, Michael J. Kelly, "The Scandal of American Legal Education" (Baltimore: University of Maryland School of Law, 1979).

commercial law would use only the case method, whereas other courses would use it in conjunction with lectures and reports. Dean Gay specifically stated that "the example of the Harvard Law School," greatly prized in academic business circles, was responsible for this decision.[4] Cases and reports were introduced gradually into the business policy and marketing courses. Because the faculty was acclimated to lecturing, Gay had to push hard for more extensive use of the case system, though he never used the method in his own courses, which were in economic history.

The method began to flourish throughout the curriculum under Dean Wallace B. Donham, who took office in 1919. His training in law was instrumental, as the following account by a later dean of the business school, Donald K. David, makes clear:

> Dean Donham's training in the law and his own wide business experience gave him the conviction that the case method was the sound approach for instruction. . . . Dean Donham recognized that the development of the case system for teaching business would be a slow and expensive process. The law schools had the decisions of the courts, the medical schools had hospital cases and clinical records, and the scientific schools had their laboratories and records of experiments. In contrast, there were nowhere any records of the process of making business decisions. Therefore the development of the case system in the Business School had to take the slow and hard way; . . . those who gathered cases had to go out to the businesses themselves to record the actual situations.[5]

Following Langdell's example, Donham pushed his faculty members to develop casebooks for use in courses. These cases were gradually collected from sources in government, business research, and journalism. After a donation was made to the school, faculty began collecting materials through systematic and comprehensive searches, at first emphasizing industrial management. People engaged in business were actively pursued and persuaded to provide accounts of their practices and experiences. This pursuit was called "fieldwork" done on "field trips."[6] There was no attempt to present either good or bad, successful or unsuccessful practices; rather, the intent was to present the typical and significant problems faced by business administrators. During the period from 1920 to 1940, over $2 million was spent for the purpose of case development. It seems that Dean Donham had achieved the same level of commitment to the case method as Langdell.

It was never anticipated, however, that the case method in business

---

[4] Melvin T. Copeland, "The Genesis of the Case Method in Business Instruction," in M. P. McNair, ed., *The Case Method at the Harvard Business School* (New York: McGraw-Hill, 1954), p. 25.

[5] Donald K. David, "Foreword," in McNair, ed., *The Case Method*, p. 11.

[6] Copeland, "The Genesis of the Case Method," in McNair, ed., *The Case Method*, p. 32.

schools would be a science, or even that the cases would be treated in a uniform way. The more typical view has emphasized a broad common-sense perspective: "The case method is so varied, so diverse, so adaptable to the nature of the individual course and to the personality of the individual instructor, that no single person can portray it accurately. Indeed, the only discernible common thread . . . is the emphasis on student participation in the educational process . . . —assessing the facts, making the analysis, weighing the considerations, and reaching a decision."[7] Under this model, the cases collected for courses are chosen with two criteria in mind: (1) that the case requires reflection and administrative decisionmaking under circumstances of instructive complexity, and (2) that the case can be expected to promote vigorous classroom discussion. As the first criterion suggests, cases that involve difficult dilemmas are preferred. As both the first and second suggest, a case that promotes mere passive recounting rather than reflective involvement in a problem is not acceptable. Accordingly, the presuppositions of teachers in business schools often stand in sharp contrast to those of teachers in law. Cases in business are not used primarily to illustrate principles or rules. The whole idea is to develop a capacity to grasp problems and reason effectively toward their solutions.

As at the law school, so at the Harvard Business School, the innovations required for a case-based curriculum generated considerable controversy, even hostility. At stake was the future of two clashing educational philosophies. On one hand were those who believed in distilled wisdom and facts through lecturing. When done well, lecturing can be a highly efficient way of transmitting valuable material to students, who feel comfortable in the controllable facts and safe orientation such a system provides. On the other hand, a different ideal of learning views education as a medium that affords the student an understanding of an environment, usually under constant change and innovation, in which *decisions* must be made. To invoke a distinction of Gilbert Ryle's, the difference in training and educational philosophy is in knowing *that* as distinct from knowing *how*.[8] The direct purpose of the case method in business has long been to train students in how to think and act in highly complex and shifting business environments. The pioneers who pushed hardest for the case method accepted that facts and general principles were sacrificed in order to train thought and decision. Thus, one might know little about probability theory but a great deal about how to think under circumstances of merely probable outcomes.

The Essence of the Case Method. Despite the above warnings about diversity in approaches to cases, there is an essence to the technique of the case

[7] McNair, "Editor's Preface," in McNair, ed., *The Case Method*, p. 11.

[8] Gilbert Ryle, "Knowing How and Knowing That," *Proceedings of the Aristotelian Society* 46 (1945–46), pp. 1–16.

method as practiced in business schools. This is accurately recounted in a classic article on the case method by Charles I. Gragg:

> A case typically is a record of a business issue which *actually* has been faced by business executives, together with surrounding facts, opinions, and prejudices upon which executive decisions had to depend. These real and particularized cases are presented to students for considered analysis, open discussion, and final decision as to the type of actions which should be taken. Day by day the number of individual business situations thus brought before the students grows and forms a backlog for observing coherent patterns and drawing out general principles. In other words, students are not given theories or hypotheses to criticize. Rather, they are given specific facts, the raw materials, out of which decisions have to be reached in life and from which they can realistically and usefully draw conclusions. . . .
>
> There is no single, demonstrable right answer to a business problem. For the student or businessman it cannot be a matter of peeking in the back of books to see if he has arrived at the right solution. . . .
>
> The instructor's role is . . . to provoke argumentative thinking, to guide discussion, . . . and if he chooses, to take a final position on the viewpoints which have been threshed out before him. . . . But *authoritarian* use of the cases perverts the unique characteristics of the system. The opportunity which this system provides the students of reaching responsible judgments on the basis of an original analysis of the facts is sacrificed.[9]

One conviction underlying this pedagogical viewpoint is that students have generally been trained in universities as if they were immature children. Implicitly transmitted in the lecture-based university is the assumption that students do not know enough to think until they have been given a thought apparatus; they are not equipped to make decisions, because they lack basic facts and principles. Decisionmaking is treated as an adult function into which students will gradually grow, upon first learning accepted theories and techniques. Those who initiated the case method thought this an entirely wrong-headed assumption about student abilities and training. As they saw it, a school of business administration has as one of its premiere functions "to achieve the transition from what may be described as a childlike dependence on parents and teachers to a state of what may be called dependable self-reliance."[10] The case method was envisioned as the cornerstone of this shift and advance in pedagogy. It is still so regarded by many of its practitioners.

No assumption is made in this method that there is a right answer to any problem that is presented, but only that there are more or less successful ways of handling problems. Understanding argument and analysis are thus more important than understanding substantive theories. These forms of understanding need not be seen as antagonistic

[9] Charles I. Gragg, "Because Wisdom Can't Be Told," as reprinted in McNair, ed., *The Case Method*, pp. 6–7, 11–13 (italics added).

[10] *Ibid.*, p. 8.

or even competitive, but the case method in business has always placed the premium on the problem-based form of analysis rather than on analysis by use of theory. The student is confronted with a body of facts and data that cannot be dealt with except by thinking through problems and solutions. Just as a medical student must not only learn to *diagnose* a patient's problem but also to exert a *clinical judgment* about its alleviation, so a student who properly uses the case method must not only *understand* a problem situation in business, but also must exert a *judgment* about its alleviation. If, by previous systems of education, a student has become accustomed to passive understanding rather than active judging, the role of the case method is to nullify this conception and to teach habits of active engagement instead.

However, the method has never convinced everyone in the business community that it is *solely* sufficient as a mode of instruction. Many believe that business is too diverse and requires detailed knowledge unobtainable from case studies alone. For example, in 1982 CBS decided to sell Fawcett Books and the Popular Library. CBS had not done well in the mass market paperback book industry with these subsidiaries. When it came time to lay blame for failure, the case method suffered much of the criticism. "Fawcett and Popular were ruined by Harvard MBAs," said Patrick O'Connor, who had moved from Fawcett to Pinnacle Books. He added, "Book publishing is a unique business; it can't be done with case studies."[11]

TWO CONCEPTS OF THE
CASE METHOD

The analysis thus far suggests an important difference between case analysis in law and business. Cases in law are based on the reasoning of judges. A court's reasoned opinion is the *form* of the case, the facts the mere *matter*. In any attempt to extract evidence or other useful parallels from the case, the facts alone are sterile and entirely substitutable; but in business, the cases present no parallel form, no reasoned opinion or precedent case to be studied for its controlling principles and weight of evidence. The cases themselves are nothing but "the facts of the case." Any reasoned opinion is an additional overlay; therefore it could not reasonably be hoped that from a study of the facts, even in related cases, principles could be generalized. There are no principles or predictability because there is no set reasoning and no common law. To this extent legal methods are peculiar to law and impossible to transfer to other professional school contexts.

[11] John F. Berry, "CBS Decides It Wants Out of the Paperback Business," *Washington Post,* February 7, 1982, sec. G, pp. 1, 4.

Thus, there are at least two concepts of the "case method," both deriving historically from Langdell. Let us call these two methods the "problem-based case method" and the "authority-based case method." The former is the governing ideal in business, though it is used by teachers of both ethics and law. This method focuses critical thinking on a problem; it stimulates reflection on what ought to be done, and the problems provoke personal and social decisionmaking. In the use of this method there is (usually) no ultimate authority, and disagreements are expected to abound without final resolution.

The "authority-based case method" contrasts noticeably. Here the facts of the case are merely instrumental; how the judge reasons is essential. Students learn how judges think, and it is this thinking they must master—not the social or moral problems presented by the case. Of course these same cases *can* be examined by the problem-based method; and some of the best cases in this volume derive from court opinions. But to employ a problem-based approach is to abandon the authority-based approach. In the latter, predictability in transferring the reasoning from one case to another is a virtue, for what one seeks to learn in using the authority-based method is what *will happen* in the courts.

THE CASE METHOD IN PHILOSOPHY AND ETHICS

The philosopher R. B. Perry once tendered the following reflection on education in the humanities:

> [I]n subjects such as philosophy and literature, in which it is likewise respectable to entertain different opinions, teachers hesitate to teach their students how to choose among them, and hesitate to choose themselves to choose.
> But thought is applied to action through *decision*. Giving students ideas without enabling them to draw conclusions is like giving them sharpened tools without teaching them what to do with them.[12]

Perry's perspective has become influential but not ascendant in philosophy. Until recently this ambition had never been connected to the case method or to professional practice in fields such as business. The field of philosophy is oriented toward a problem-based approach to learning, but the idea of personal decision by case analysis has not traditionally been a part of the orientation. There has been little detailed discussion paralleling that in law and business as to whether case-based teaching more adequately prepares a student for judgment and practice than conventional textbook, lecture, and seminar approaches.

---

[12] R. B. Perry, *The Citizen Decides: A Guide to Responsible Thinking in Time of Crisis* (Bloomington: Indiana University Press, 1951), Ch. 6.

This hiatus is modestly surprising. Socrates, the first great philosopher, practiced some aspects of the case method with consummate skill. He taught ethical theory by using a method in which he served as a midwife by eliciting from the student reflection, insight, understanding, and both theoretical and practical judgment. He never lectured about ethics, but rather engaged the student in a dialogue that often eventuated in discovery and mutual decisionmaking. His method started with a profession of ignorance (*not* a parading of theory) and proceeded to pointed questions that eventuated in proposed principles or universal definitions. The latter were tested by hypotheses, then modified and tested further until theoretical insight into principles or definitions was achieved. Modifications specifically involved repeated appeals to cases, which, although short, were constantly used in shaping his conclusions.

Another tradition in the use of cases dates from Aristotle, who discussed the role of "practical wisdom" and "practical judgment" in directing human activities. The goal of ethics, he maintained, is to engage in practical reasoning. He depicted a person of practical wisdom as one who envisions what should be done in particular circumstances, using a capacity he thought distinguishable from intellectual abstraction and cleverness. Centuries later Immanuel Kant discussed the study of "cases" and "examples" in the training of practical judgment. Kant did not make comments as flattering as Aristotle's about a person merely of good practical judgment, but Kant did argue that the study of case examples is important for the training of practical decisionmaking.

The case method has also had an interesting history in philosophical and theological traditions now commonly referred to as "casuistry." This tradition is skeptical of rules and principles: One can make actual moral judgments of agents and actions only when one has an intimate understanding of particular situations and a backlog of similar cases. Apart from an acquaintance with both a situation and a "case history" of similar and relevant cases—like case histories in the courts that contain authoritative decisions—one is in no position to try to resolve moral problems. The argument is that until there is a case history rich enough that a cultural unit is able to agree it is normatively adequate, there cannot be moral reasoning applied to new cases within that cultural unit.[13] Just as the courts could not function without the case histories of case law, so from this perspective we could not be moral reasoners without a similar case history that for us is authoritative.

The methods of Socrates, Aristotle, and Kant have long been routine parts of an education in philosophy. Recently in philosophy there has

---

[13] This casuistical tradition was prominent among Jesuits in the seventeenth century when it came under attack by Blaise Pascal in his *Provincial Letters*. The rather negative characterization of casuistry found in contemporary ethics dates from Pascal's attack.

been some stirring of interest specifically in the use of case studies (and some small revival of interest in casuistry as a constructive moral theory). Philosophers have come to insist that we must deal with moral and social problems at the level of both abstract theory and concrete decision-making. For these reasons some have maintained that "case studies are employed most effectively when they can readily be used to draw out broader ethical principles and moral rules . . . [so as] to draw the attention of students to the common elements in a variety of cases, and to the implicit problems of ethical theory to which they may point."[14] The analogy to some legal uses of the case method is obvious; but, as in the case of law, it is not obvious how this goal might be accomplished.

Possibly the best use of cases in both philosophy and business is not as a *source* of generalizations, but rather as a *test* of generalizations. By this criterion cases help sharpen and refine theoretical claims, especially by pointing out the applications, inadequacies, or limitations of theories. As one business-school faculty member expresses this point of view, "In discussing [basic ethical concepts such as] Justice or Freedom, relevant cases or incidents should be introduced to make clear how the principle looks in real world situations."[15] From this perspective, cases illustrate the application of fundamental ethical notions, rather than serving as a medium from which they can be extracted. Cases illustrate principles at work and exhibit how informed judgments are expressed. Case analysis, then, brings a general principle, proposal, or procedure under scrutiny to see how well it applies to one or more particular circumstances. A related maneuver is the use of cases as counterexamples to proposed general principles.

A somewhat grander vision of case analysis is found in John Rawls's proposal that in developing a normative ethical theory it is appropriate to start with the broadest set of our considered moral judgments about a subject such as justice, and then erect principles that reflect our judgments. These principles can then be pruned and adjusted by bringing cases under them. Suppose, for example, that some problems of deceptive advertising and environmental responsibility are selected for examination. Some widely accepted principles of right action might be taken, as Rawls puts it, "provisionally as fixed points," but also as "liable to revision."[16] Paradigm cases of what we all agree are right courses of

[14] Daniel Callahan and Sissela Bok, *The Teaching of Ethics in Higher Education* (Hastings-on-Hudson, N.Y.: Hastings Center, 1980), p. 69.

[15] Henry Eilbirt, "Evaluation of Experimental Courses in Business Ethics," in *Report of the Committee for Education in Business Ethics,* a monograph sponsored by a grant from the National Endowment for the Humanities (Newark, Dela.: CEBE–American Philosophical Association, 1980).

[16] John Rawls, *A Theory of Justice* (Cambridge, Mass.: Harvard University Press, 1971), pp. 20 f.

action might be listed and examined, and a search could then be undertaken for principles consistent with our judgments about these paradigm cases. These principles could be tested by reference to other paradigm cases, and other considered judgments found in similar cases, to see if they yield counterintuitive or conflicting results. The hope is that through this process moral theories and principles can be made to cohere with all our considered judgments about particular cases. That is, general ethical principles and particular judgments could be brought into equilibrium. Principles and theory are justified by the case process. Presumably the more complex and far-reaching the cases that force revisions, the richer the resultant theory will be. Traditional ethical theory would then have as much to learn from applied contexts as the other way around. From this perspective, moral thinking is like other forms of theorizing in that hypotheses must be tested, buried, or modified through experimental thinking.

The point of a more theoretical orientation to the study of cases is that "the case method" in business can become an unrewarding exposure to the unreflective prejudices of others unless controlled by some framework of moral principles. As valuable as cases are, they do not transmit moral understanding merely by a recounting of facts. Good training in case analysis needs supplementation by relevant materials in ethical theory.

HARD CASES: THE PROBLEM
OF DILEMMAS

We have noted that cases may be examined not to extract general principles, but rather to have a concrete forum for testing the authority or "weight" of principles when they conflict. Such testing can be highly illuminating when a dilemma is present and a hard choice must be made. Despite the saying "hard cases make bad law," bad law is not always made from legal dilemmas, and hard choices need not entail tragic choices. Such cases can improve and clarify the application of principles in law and in other fields. Because this volume is filled with cases involving moral and social dilemmas—decisions that one hopes do not make for bad outcomes or confusing generalizations—it is important to understand the nature of dilemmas and their analysis.

First, it is misleading to assume that the only dilemmas of importance in these cases are moral and social. Many involve personal dilemmas, especially where one is confronted with moral reasons for performing acts that may not be in one's self-interest. Whistle-blowing cases often have this character—as, for example, an engineer named Dan Applegate discovers in the DC-10 case in Chapter 1. Similarly, in the Interscience

Publishing case, a manager must make a decision that pits the financial interests of a small company against the privacy rights of employees by introducing a lie-detector examination for all employees. In such dilemmas two or more conflicting but reasonable judgments can often be made—as anyone who makes hard choices, managerial, moral, personal, or whatever, will understand.

As we reflect on disagreements, we may be increasingly tempted to declare them *irresolvable* dilemmas. Even if rational deliberation plays a critical role in our argument, reason alone is generally insufficient to resolve dilemmas. It is thus understandable why there seem to be intractable social controversies over many cases. Nevertheless, we must not make too much of this intractability. Many apparent dilemmas turn out to be at least partially resolvable, and many cases can be studied with an eye to ways in which dilemmas can be *avoided*. Perhaps the majority of dilemmas found in this volume could have been avoided or minimized through more skillful management. Good management is rarely present in situations where, for example, persons face agonizing dilemmas about whether to blow the whistle or pledge allegiance. A study of these cases in order to reveal actual steps that management could have taken can be profitable, as can reflection on procedures that might have deflected or defused a problem. For example, as the cases on conflict of interest illustrate, many problems arise because a manager failed to consult with others or because no peer or employee review committee existed.

This point about sound management and sound procedures suggests the need to examine cases in terms of alternative strategies and actions. There will invariably be many alternatives that might have been employed. Indeed, there is such a rich possibility of alternatives that it is often not feasible to reach agreement on a single best solution. Such agreement need not be the goal of case analysis, any more than reaching consensus or agreement on an exact analysis of the problem in a case should be the goal. *Learning how* to spot problems and create alternative maneuvers may be of chief importance.

In ethics as elsewhere it is difficult to escape the view that reasonable and informed persons differ concerning both actions that should be taken and justifying principles invoked as grounds for such actions. They can disagree vigorously over the proper interpretation of cases, and nowhere will they disagree more than in dilemmatic cases. Moreover, argument from analysis of cases may not stem from shared evaluative beliefs, and hence is not simply a matter of systematically bringing general intuitions into harmony. Often such argument is revisionary of our beliefs. Cases shock intuition and alter belief. Disagreements, then, may turn into discussions concerning why some beliefs and principles ought to be *readjusted*.

In short, even if intractable disagreement does set in, learning how to spot problems and resolve or deflect them may turn out to be as important as the substantive moral issues themselves.

"THE 'FACTS' OF THE CASE"

The majority of cases in this volume are factual rather than hypothetical, and most use actual rather than fictitious names. What is reported about the role of management at IBM in handling its employees or about Kellogg Cereals in advertising its product are presumably the facts of the case. It is prudent, however, to have reservations about this notion. What happened at IBM or Kellogg may not have been exactly as it is reported here for several reasons.

First, analysis of the notion of a fact has itself proved an elusive task. A fact is generally assumed to be an empirically confirmable or falsifiable statement that describes some event or object. Factual statements are thus either true or false. A value, by contrast, is presumably an evaluative statement or judgment concerning what is or is not good, right, or virtuous. Evaluative statements appraise and assess events, while factual statements describe some concrete aspect of the event and do not appraise or assess. Unfortunately, this noble ideal of the neutrality of fact can quickly dissipate at the level of personal reports of facts. In criminal trials, for example, different eyewitnesses report the facts differently, but often not because of biases or prior opinions. Similarly, journalists often provide substantially different accounts of a press conference or an athletic event. Even scientists operate with different theories that direct them to see the facts differently.

Second, the facts as presented are always selected for a purpose. From an infinity of events in a given day, the nightly national news is condensed to less than thirty minutes. Such selectivity does not itself entail a distorting bias; selection is necessary and may be an intelligent and revealing structuring of an otherwise massive and baffling array of events and relationships. The Love Canal case in this volume is an example of a case that requires careful historical selection of data due to the immense amount of data accumulated. Moreover, the goal of a *complete* set of facts is a mythical ideal. Whole volumes have been written on some of the cases in this text, and yet these volumes omit many possible descriptions of what occurred. On the other hand, selectivity and sheer lack of available information *can* introduce bias in the writing of cases. The cases in this volume have been carefully scrutinized to keep the problem of bias to a minimum, but the cautious reader will never forget the likelihood that circumstances will be commonly described and evaluated in starkly different terms by different individuals.

This reminder is especially important when companies and individuals are named. The picture of management at McDonnell Douglas, for example, is not favorable in the DC-10 case, but we also lack many facts about what transpired at that company over a multi-year period. What is emphasized in these descriptions may be de-emphasized or even ignored in other accounts. In the end there is no neutral mirror of history; rather, there are human actors interpreting the actions of others. A useful rule of thumb is to try to put aside the identities of individuals and companies while *assuming* the correctness of the facts. One can then more easily criticize decisions and strategies rather than individuals or corporate groups. That is, a charitable approach analyzes cases *as if* they occurred in the way described, but without fervent commitment to the precision of the account as reality.

Third, in cases such as those presented in this volume, corporations have often been treated harshly by journalists who first present the facts of the case to the public. As a result, corporations have become leery of opening their office doors to journalists. Indeed, at present there is something of a cold war between the two groups. Journalists tend to view corporations as inherently secretive and as presenting facts with the same objectivity with which they prepare advertising for public consumption. Management, in turn, regards journalists as biased and even sensationalistic distorters of the truth who investigate cases with the thoroughness of someone who picks horses on a friend's tips. They also see reporters as unqualified for the range of issues their newspapers commission them to study, since news coverage by a single reporter can cover such diverse matters as new products, embezzlement schemes, plant relocations, labor relations, securities, investments, price hikes, company growth, salaries, profits, and so on.

This is not the place to arbitrate their dispute, but it is the place to note that the press is frequently a major source of information about the "facts of the case." The reports of journalists alone are rarely used in this volume, and attempts to incorporate divergent views of corporate officials have been maximized in cases where there has elsewhere been a reliance on the press. However, the use of investigative journalism in researching and writing cases is common and provides one more reason to place some distance between "the facts of the case" and the actual circumstances from which they arose. "The facts as reported" or "the facts as they have thus far emerged" are more guarded but fairer descriptions.

There is a final reason for caution about the facts of the case: Those who study them invariably want more facts. They believe that if only more facts were known, dilemmas and uncertainties would disappear. A temptation is to doctor the case by adding hypothetical facts, usually prefaced by someone saying, "But what if . . . ?" These retreats to new or different facts are understandable reactions, but it is desirable to suppress them in the analysis and discussion of cases in this volume, which have been selected *because* of the way they present difficult problems. It is a vital part of the process of case analysis to come to grips with the problems as presented, not to alter the circumstances or shelve the problems on grounds of an insufficiency of facts. Understanding the dilemmatic nature of situations faced in professional practice is a prime reason for studying the cases. Moreover, presenting more facts may not waive the problem; it may only increase the complexity of the situation, which in turn increases the problems in case analysis.

This position does not imply that it is never a useful exercise to modify the conditions and then think through problems under new conditions. To the contrary, this method can be valuable, and skillful teachers use it with profit. Furthermore, these warnings are not intended to discredit the careful reader who looks for pertinent missing facts. One should sleuth for missing facts as well as for facts subject to alternative description. But just as persons in business must make decisions every day on incomplete and uncertain information, so must cases in this volume be studied under conditions of uncertainty. To do otherwise would be to distort "the 'facts' of the case."

CHAPTER 1

The Employee

INTRODUCTION   The dominant model of the employee-employer relationship in business has long been "labor and management." This model has typically been understood as adversarial, placing conflicting goals and interests at the center of the relationship. Traditionally this model has awarded the balance of power to management. Therefore, as with a member of the military, an employee must be loyal, obey the orders of superiors, and keep confidential information secret—unless some overriding moral wrong or illegal act is involved.

Of special importance has been a body of law governing corporations known as the "law of agency." This law, fashioned largely from legal precedent, deals with the duties of loyalty and obedience of an employee and generally has functioned to protect corporations. For example, in conflicts of obligation, corporate executives and lawyers owe their allegiance and legal duty to the corporation and *not* to stockholders, the public, or other employees. In some influential cases it has been held that disloyalty by an employee to the corporation or to its interests is in effect "private treason."

Recently this model of the employer-employee relationship has been under careful scrutiny, with much discussion focusing on the rights of employees. Rights of employees to privacy, to information about hazards in the workplace, to "blow the whistle," to security, to avenues of complaint, and to due process have all been under examination. There is now considerable ferment over the nature and strength of these claims to rights. Some corporations have taken up the challenge and have invested heavily in plans of increased worker participation, including reorganization to give employees more say about their jobs and about company fringe benefits. Corporations have, for example, established explicit standards for hiring, firing, merit evaluation, retirement, grievance proceedings, and participative management by workers.

But the corporation also retains important rights against the disloyal and even the feckless employee. Virtually no one would deny that employers themselves have rights, one of which, for example, is to be able to protect their business interests and investments. Employees can function as spies, can use company resources for private gain, and can easily secure confidential information (information they possess only because of their relationship with an employer) when moving from one firm to another. Because employers have a right to the protection of property, and employees a right to accept new positions, the protection of "trade secrets," for example, has become a sticky problem—as illustrated in this chapter by the case of venture capital for Rubbernex. This case invites reflection on the fact that, under law, it is not a breach of any obligation owed to an employer to plan for a new competitive venture while still employed, even though the employee has an opportunity to observe (what will later be) a competitor's secrets, and even though the employee may leave with a wealth of experience in and knowledge about the competitor's processes, products, research, and financial matters.

The traditional rule in law and industry is that a former employer is entitled to retain proprietary information for purposes of competition. However, some have begun to look closely at the relative weights of the competing interests in many cases. A few courts have adopted what might be called a "balancing model" of trade secrets protection, according to which the employee's interest in mobility and opportunity should be weighed against the employer's rights in determining the scope of protection afforded to confidential information. These courts have attempted to weigh a public policy favoring the protection of trade secrets against a competing public policy favoring the interest of an employee to use skills and knowledge acquired in a field in order to earn a livelihood. Trade secrets have come under discussion similarly because a corporation can shield information from the public about harmful products. For example, under current American law a manufacturer can market a trade name chemical that is known by the company to be a carcinogen and not label it a carcinogen because of the privilege of trade secrets.

Another issue of current interest about employee rights—raised in this chapter in the Du Pont female exclusion case—is increased protection for workers in hazardous environments. Flimsy scaffolding, exposed saw blades, careless dynamiting, and thousands of similar dangers in the workplace have long been known, and precautions have been taken to minimize these hazards. However, many have argued that an unprecedented and unanticipated situation now prevails—namely, we are beginning to understand the dangers of various toxic agents and airborne dangers in the work environment, and yet do not have enough information to assess the actual seriousness of the threat. This raises questions about the nature of a "safe workplace" and about the notion of an "acceptable risk."

Obviously a workplace cannot be guaranteed safe, but what constitutes an adequate precaution? Can a company treat employees paternalistically by protecting them against their decisions to assume risks? And what counts as providing adequate information to employees so that they can protect themselves against or assess the dangers of their workplace? This last question plays a central role in the Du Pont case, which features a policy to prevent fertile women employees from exposure to certain chemicals by banning them from the environment.

A series of important issues also surrounds conflicts among the roles or obligations an employee must assume. The best known among these is "whistle-blowing," whether employees ought to blow the whistle on presumed corporate wrongdoing by revealing information to or encouraging inspections by responsible parties outside the corporation. Although a whistle-blower may believe that his or her conscience compels action in "the public interest," this rationale could be a self-protective cover. Whistle-blowers may be trying to seize more power within the company or trying to cover up personal inadequacies that represent a legitimate reason for discipline or dismissal.

On the one hand, management has generally denounced whistle-blowing as a practice involving despicable acts of disloyalty. On the other hand, loyalty to the corporation is no more an absolute obligation than is loyalty to the military. Thus, cases of whistle-blowing generally involve balancing the duty of loyalty with the duty to protect the public interest by revealing presumably wrongful actions. Such cases also raise interesting questions of management practices that could have avoided this kind of conflict. The reluctant security guard and DC-10 cases in this chapter feature the issue of whistle-blowing. They stimulate reflection on whether, by whom, and, very centrally, when the whistle should be blown.

Also found in this chapter are two cases featuring the employee's right to privacy. Questions of rights of privacy and confidentiality (or, correlatively, duties to respect privacy and confidentiality) have appeared in many areas of business, including, for example, in screening employees in the workplace for genetic diseases or for use of illicit drugs. "Privacy" may be defined as "a state or condition of limited access to a person." A person has privacy if others do not have access, or do not use their access, to him or her. A loss of privacy occurs when others gain any form of access to a person, *e.g.,* by intervening in zones of secrecy, anonymity, and solitude. Privacy obviously extends to that person's intimate relationships, *e.g.,* with friends, lovers, spouses, and physicians and other health care professionals.

Although employee privacy is a treasured value, tough corporate rules that intrude on privacy may still be justifiable. For example, the managers of day care centers have an obligation to their customers to determine whether a potential employee has ever been convicted of child molesting, and an airline company has a right to know if its pilots are taking narcotics. Polygraph testing might be appropriate in such cases—the primary issue raised in the case of polygraph tests at Interscience Publishing. But even if an employer has a right to invade an employee's privacy in obtaining such information, there is always a question of appropriate means. For example, an employer might ask the employee if he or she takes drugs, might require that the employee submit to urinalysis, or might hire a private investigative firm to poke into intimate aspects of the employee's personal life. And there are also questions of appropriate disclosures, perhaps the primary issue in the case of the open door at IBM.

As for restricting conduct off the job, the response of an employee tends to be that private life is absolutely private. But this response may be unrealistic in many situations that might embarrass or otherwise negatively affect the company. Many employees cannot shed their company identity the way they shed their clothing. For example, what the president of the bank does in a private club off hours may affect the profits of the bank. How businesses should respond to employee conduct that reduces or is likely to reduce profit presents an unavoidable problem.

To affirm a right of privacy also does not rule out the possibility of criticisms of various exercises of the right. A person may exercise the right with poor judgment or choose a loss of privacy in a degrading or cheapening manner. A company may be justified in overriding rules of privacy in order to protect other moral objectives. Usually it is possible for society to handle such conflicts by protecting zones of privacy that cannot be invaded, while distinguishing other zones where conduct that would offend in a public setting is prohibited. But, as both the IBM and Interscience cases indicate, the line between these zones is often fragile.

Polygraph Tests at Interscience Publishing

Dick Snell, President of Interscience Publishing Company of La Jolla, California, faces a difficult decision about the control and monitoring of his employees. Increasing dishonesties and thefts of office materials—complicated by declining sales and profits in the college textbook market—now threaten the publishing business that he had founded (originally as a largely independent subsidiary of a major publisher located in the eastern United States). His company is on such shaky financial ground that its parent company is considering absorbing it into their larger editorial and marketing operations.

In order to combat the employee dishonesties, Snell is considering instituting a polygraph (lie-detector) examination for all employees. The test is relatively simple and works as follows: The person to be screened is seated next to the polygraph. He or she is connected to the machine by a set of wires that measure respiration, blood pressure, and perspiration. The person is asked a series of questions, and the machine monitors the body's responses. Physiological responses such as respiration are used to attribute psychological events. The common name "lie detector" can be misleading, because the test measures fear and anxiety rather than lies. There is no one physiological response unique to deception.

Polygraph testing has spread through much of the nation's private sector, and use of the polygraph is already routine in a number of California companies of comparable size to Interscience. In recent years as many as one million tests have been given annually, and approximately 20 percent of Fortune 500 companies now use some form of polygraph tests. However, polygraph usage by the private sector is also surrounded by controversy. Over 40 percent of the states in the United States have made the use of polygraphs on employees illegal.

The success of the testing in decreasing corporate costs has been documented to Snell's satisfaction. Nonetheless, Snell still resists initiating this technology. He finds himself paradoxically horrified at the idea and attracted to its benefits. He has read about a serious strike at the Adolph Coors Brewery in Golden, Colorado, in which 1,000 workers left their jobs in a bitter walkout partially caused by the use of lie detectors for screening job applicants. He has also watched a television documentary on "the new era" of industrial spying that examined the new wave of polygraph examinations and so-called "monitoring devices," which were principally wiretaps placed on office phones. The documentary showed supervisors listening to long-distance private calls placed clandestinely by employees to friends, parents, and, sometimes, rival firms to which they were passing information as "industrial spies." The documentary pitted the private interests of employees against the company's interest. Employees who were interviewed in the documentary expressed strong reservations about wiretaps and polygraph examinations on grounds that their privacy was invaded and their personal integrity challenged without cause. The executives interviewed (all of whom had instituted polygraph testing) denied that there had been violations of privacy rights; they reasoned that *company* time and phones, not *private* resources, were at stake. As one executive put it, "We would never tap an employee's home phone, even if we thought the person was spying on us; but during working hours you are not a private person."

Snell was struck by the powerful feelings displayed by employees and management alike. The documentary made an excellent case that the use of wiretaps and polygraph examinations raised productivity, cut costs, and reduced waste. Thus far no one had been able to show that employee morale was lowered, as long as executives and employees at all levels were treated similarly. Still, employees *complained* of lower morale, and some court cases were pending. Snell felt sick to his stomach watching the president of one company listening to tape recordings monitored by a supervisor, as a happy employee on Christmas Eve morning spoke to the man to whom she was engaged. This long-distance call had cost the company $25.94, and when a consistent pattern of such calls from the employee was detected, she was fired. Snell was so bothered by the idea of wiretapping that he had ruled out its use. But he saw polygraph tests as a different matter. He viewed them as less invasive; everyone could be treated similarly, and it would all be out in the open.

Interscience Publishing had never been involved in any form of employee inspection program. The company had been established in 1963 as a venture into science textbook publishing, a market then rapidly expanding. Snell had been made president of the new satellite, and under his management the company had slowly grown from a four-editor, one-sales-manager operation to have a large sales staff and separate editors for each scientific field in which it published. There were also a number of production editors, technical and clerical assistants, and secretaries at the main office.

Snell had been a superb editor before becoming president of Interscience, and he had built up the company through long hours of patient training of new editors. He taught them skills of manuscript acquisition and sales, but several editors had left for larger companies as soon as they had experience and could learn nothing further from Snell. He shrugged off these losses as the new way of the industry; but he was shocked at the general lack of employee loyalty, a far cry from his early years with the parent company. Corporate and personal loyalties had been institutionalized in those days, and an employee thought much more about moving up to higher management positions in the company than about moving to a competitor and in some cases taking the entire editorial staff to the new employer.

Nonetheless, the major management challenge in textbook publishing had been, and still is, to attract and develop promising editors with strong individual initiative and the ability to work with the sales staff in the field. This sales staff is composed of a number of company representatives or "travelers" who "work" various science departments in universities and colleges in the region in which they live. "Working" involves calling on professors to promote books, searching for manuscripts in preparation, making phone calls to encourage the adoption of texts, and in some cases gathering data for direct-mail campaigns. The sales force cannot be supervised on a day-to-day basis because its members work independently in distant cities. They tend to move from company to company even more frequently than do editors. Over the years Snell had developed an efficient and effective system of managing editors and sales staff of which he is justifiably proud, but minor thefts and various forms of dishonesty still plague him, and matters are getting worse. Snell had long known about the problem of private long-distance phone calls made at company expense. This had been easy to control when he ran a smaller operation, but now it was almost impossible to trace the calls if an employee was at all clever. Snell had also uncovered some theft of petty cash, and had his suspicions about two computers that had mysteriously vanished at considerable expense to the company. He had also been shocked to discover recently that several members of the sales force had been selling large numbers of promotional copies of new books to campus bookstores as "used books." This doubly affected profits and sales: First, the books did not get in the hands of professors, and second, the bookstores would sell the "used copies" directly to students and would order fewer or no copies from the publishing company.

Snell had also discovered a pattern of "cheating on company time" by members of the sales force. The representative in Tacoma, Washington, for example, had taken the job of apartment manager in the 190-unit apartment house in which he lived. This was allegedly only a "weekend job," but in fact the employee was spending over 80 percent of his time managing the apartment house. The employee had been clever at concealment, and it took over three years to discover why sales had been declining in the region. (In fact, it might never have been discovered had not suspicion been aroused when several phone calls were placed to the publishing company about various apartment disasters while the representative was on vacation.)

While Snell was trying to figure out how to solve this problem, he was confronted with the apparent embezzlement of over $10,000 by his highly trusted sales manager. Because the sales manager was married to the company's accountant, Snell was unsure how aggressively to pursue the matter and how much proof he could muster. He was certain from his examination of the books only that the company was out $10,000 and that it could not be explained.

With this discouraging series of events Snell became convinced over a six-month period that he had to protect the company through new initiatives. He is now generally angry and depressed about the company's future. He has always felt keenly his responsibilities to his employees, but now he feels betrayed by them. He is convinced, however, that he has many conscientious, loyal, honest, hard-working employees, and he knows that they too would be subjected to the polygraph tests should he implement them.

Part of the discomfort he feels about using the polygraph tests is due to the problem of "false positive" results that occur when an innocent party incorrectly tests out as guilty or as being deceptive. While the accuracy of finding *guilty* persons surpasses 95 percent, Snell is concerned about two studies showing that between 37 percent and 55 percent of *truthful* persons were classified by the tests as deceptive. There seems to him a strong bias against the innocent.

Snell has searched for other solutions, but is convinced that the ones he has found would not succeed. His consultants and executives support his hypothesis that the polygraph would be successful. One executive in another publishing company had reported an amazing cost reduction after instituting polygraph tests, as well as no complaints from employees once the examinations had become routine, and no attempts at unionization. The very *threat* of possible detection by a polygraph, he argued, deters most employees.

Snell hired a polygraph consultant from New York who proposed a scheme under which employees would not be tested for past dishonesties.

No question would be asked about any event that might have occurred prior to the time of the tests. Snell would therefore never learn about past dishonesties, and employees would not have to worry about embarrassing disclosures. (Potential new employees would, however, be asked about their records with other companies.) Employees would also not be asked about the behavior of other employees, until some legitimate suspicion had been detected about a specific employee. The tests would be administered to potential employees prior to employment and annually to all employees, including Snell. Only ten questions would be asked, and these questions would be handed out on a typed sheet to the examinee prior to the examination. To Snell, the most offensive of the ten questions are: (1) "Do you believe it is all right to cheat if no law is broken?" (2) "Have you been refused a loan or credit in the past three years?" Yet Snell himself felt it important to answer these questions.

Snell felt strongly attracted to this consultant's program, which had worked effectively elsewhere, but he still had that nauseous feeling in his stomach.

The Open Door at IBM

Robert Bratt has been employed by International Business Machines Corporation (IBM) in Massachusetts since March of 1970. Bratt has sought to resolve several personal grievances through the channel of a company policy known as the open door procedure. This policy is described as follows in the IBM *Manager's Manual:*

A. Employee Appeal
   1. Any employee who has a problem which has not been resolved to that employee's satisfaction by his or her immediate manager may bring the complaint or concern to the attention of higher management.
   2. While the employee will normally choose to address an appeal first at the local level, the Open Door procedure makes available to an employee either direct or progressive access to any level of management in the Corporation. . . .
   4. If the employee is still not satisfied the problem may be reviewed with the IBM Chief Executive Officer by mail or personally if that is appropriate to the resolution.
   5. Management should be sensitive to assure that no action is taken which may appear to be retaliation for an employee's appeal under the Open Door Policy. . . .
B. The Investigation Process . . .
   4c. The investigation cannot be anonymous; however, the discussion will be restricted to those necessary to resolve the issues. Those consulted will be advised to keep the matter confidential.

Bratt used the open door policy approximately four times during the 1971 to 1978 period to complain about company practices. In 1971, Bratt was promised a promotion and a salary raise if he transferred from the Waltham to the Cambridge office. He agreed to the transfer, but he did not receive the promotion or the raise. When Bratt used

This case was prepared by Anna Pinedo and revised by Tom L. Beauchamp. **Not to be duplicated without permission of the holder of the copyright,** © 1989 Tom L. Beauchamp.

the open door procedure, he was granted the promotion. In 1975, Bratt used the policy again, this time with no success, to inquire about a promotion he thought he was due. He was then transferred back to the Waltham office without a promotion or raise.

Bratt made several suggestions to improve control of a cash-fund account while he was working at the Waltham office. His suggestions were implemented with good results, although they had initially been rejected. The cash-fund office was given credit as a unit for the innovations, thus minimizing Bratt's individual contribution. In July 1977, Bratt was given a lower work rating than he thought he deserved, but his immediate manager refused to discuss the rating with him. At the same time, Bratt's wife was undergoing tests for cancer. Bratt was denied time off by his immediate manager, but he went to higher authorities and received the requested time off.

In 1978, Bratt discovered that copies of some suggestions he had made for preventing embezzlement in the Waltham office were not in his files. One of these suggestions had been adopted throughout the company, but this time he had received *no* credit for the innovation. Inquiries to the Suggestions Department revealed that no records existed of any of Bratt's suggestions. Bratt then again invoked the open door process in May or June of 1978, arguing that his manager was discriminating against him.

The investigation of the matter was conducted by a higher level manager, David Blackburn. After failing to receive a response from Blackburn, Bratt brought the open door procedure to the Chairman of the Board of IBM in September of 1978. The chairman appointed Wesley Liebtag, Director of Personnel Programs at IBM corporate headquarters in Armonk, New York, to investigate Blackburn's handling of the open door complaint and to resolve Bratt's grievances. Bratt also asked Liebtag to look into the unfavorable 1977 work rating.

In investigating the open door grievances, Liebtag judged it essential to disclose certain information concerning Bratt's complaints to other IBM personnel. He also had to report the results of the investigation and his recommendation to D. E. McKinney, Vice-President of Personnel, and to T. A. Vadnais, Administrative Assistant to the Chairman of the Board, from whom he received the assignment. Liebtag completed his inquiry on October 3, 1978, at which time he discussed his findings with Bratt and recorded them in a letter, dated October 3, 1978. Liebtag assured Bratt that his suggestions had been *properly* reviewed and evaluated and that the 1977 work appraisal would be destroyed. Liebtag explained in his letter that he was going to receive for review a new "performance plan" for Bratt in thirty days.

After the meeting with Liebtag, Bratt complained about the findings to his supervisor, Rita Lynch, and said he thought Liebtag, Blackburn, and others were involved in a "cover-up." Several days later, on October 13, Bratt complained to Lynch of "bad nerves," headaches, and inability to sleep. He told her that he had seen a doctor, and he agreed at Lynch's suggestion to see an IBM-employed physician. On October 16, Bratt requested a transfer within IBM. He gave as his reasons an unfair management situation, an unfair work situation, and poor health.

On October 18 Bratt saw a general practitioner, Dr. Martha Nugent, who was not part of the IBM in-house medical staff, but was an independent physician retained under contract by IBM. Dr. Nugent reported to Lynch, who had set up the appointment, that Bratt "seemed paranoid," and suggested that he see a psychiatrist. Nugent, who had not been apprised of IBM's policy limiting management access to employee medical records, proceeded to discuss Bratt's presumed medical condition with his managers and with members of IBM's medical staff.

Lynch informed her supervisor, Johanna Crawford, of Dr. Nugent's report, and Crawford communicated this information to Liebtag, who was still considering Bratt's open door complaints and was charged with finding him another work assignment. Crawford told Liebtag that Bratt had seen Dr. Nugent and that the doctor felt Bratt was "paranoid" and suggested that he see a psychiatrist. Dr. Nugent recommended that Bratt receive no changes in assignment, including transfer, until his medical evaluations were complete.

Liebtag made notes on what he was told about Bratt's condition in a memorandum labeled to "File," dated October 18, 1978, and marked "IBM CONFIDENTIAL." The following day Liebtag received a second call from Bratt's branch manager, Crawford, explaining that Bratt was distraught and in tears upon receiving a "close out" letter denying his most recent open door complaint. This call was recorded in a memorandum dated October 19, 1978, also labeled "IBM CONFIDENTIAL." Liebtag wrote in this memorandum that "it appears that the psychiatrist's first reaction, that there is a mental problem that goes beyond IBM, is accurate." Copies of these memoranda were sent to Mr. McKinney and to Mr. Vadnais.

Bratt took a three-month leave of absence beginning on December 14, 1978. Upon his return Bratt was given a temporary position at the Cambridge Center office. Bratt's psychiatrist reported that Bratt was enjoying his job. He was considered for a permanent assignment at this office, but the office manager did not want someone with a history of using the open door policy. Bratt initiated another grievance procedure when this fact came to his attention in September 1979. He complained to Liebtag about not having a permanent position, and he said that he thought the poor work rating from 1977 was still in his files. The rating was, in fact, still in his file, but it was promptly destroyed.

Bratt's dissatisfaction with his working conditions continued. He felt that he had been discriminated against or penalized for his use of the open door policy. Bratt felt that his right to privacy and confidentiality had been violated by IBM personnel. Shortly thereafter Bratt brought a lawsuit against IBM and charged Liebtag and Dr. Nugent with improper disclosure of both his use of the open door grievance procedure and his medical condition.

The case, *Robert Bratt, et al.* v. *International Business Machines Corporation, et al.*, began a long litigation history in the Superior Court of Middlesex County, Massachusetts, in February 1980. The initial complaint charged IBM with intentional infliction of emotional distress and included a claim by Robert Bratt's wife, Carol Lee Bratt, for the loss of her husband's consortium ("the legal right of one spouse to the company, affection, and service of the other"). Bratt later amended his complaints: He added libel and breach of privacy claims, including a count based on Dr. Nugent's alleged publication of his confidential medical information without his authorization. The third amended complaint, as presented to the U.S. District Court, District of Massachusetts, included the charge that Dr. Nugent violated Bratt's right to privacy by disseminating confidential medical information through oral and written communication with IBM employees.

In November 1982, the U.S. District Court entered a judgment in favor of the IBM defendants on all counts of Bratt's third amended complaint and denied Bratt's motion to file a fourth amended complaint. The District Court's decision was based on two grounds. First, the court concluded that Massachusetts courts would not support a breach of privacy claim when an employee alleged that his employer disclosed private information among other employees in the course of their employment. Second, the court concluded that Massachusetts courts would recognize a "qualified privilege for legitimate business communication."[1]

Bratt appealed the District Court's decision to the U.S. Court of Appeals for the First Circuit.[2] The Court of Appeals ruled that there was no clear precedent in Massachusetts concerning the issues of breach of privacy and libel law. The court sent a series of questions to the Massachusetts Supreme Judicial Court, which then ruled on a standard for the employee's right to privacy in the workplace. The court ruled on July 16, 1984, that "the disclosure of private facts about an employee among other employees in the same corporation can constitute sufficient publication under the Massachusetts right of privacy statute" so as to breach

---

[1] *Robert Bratt, et al.* v. *International Business Machines Corporation, et al.*, No. 80-547-K, slip op. at 13–14 (Nov. 10, 1982).

[2] *Bratt*, 467 N.E.2d 126 (1984).

the employee's right to privacy.[3] The court concluded that "no conditional privilege for legitimate business communications exists under the Massachusetts right of privacy statute."[4]

Violations of the privacy statute, according to this opinion, must be determined by balancing "the employer's legitimate business interest in obtaining and publishing the information against the substantiality of the intrusion on the employee's privacy resulting from the disclosure."[5] Finally, concerning the disclosure of medical information, the court found that "when medical information is necessary reasonably to serve a substantial and valid interest of the employer, it is not an invasion of the employee's statutory right of privacy for the physician to disclose such information to the employer."

After the Supreme Judicial Court responded to the legal questions that had been posed, the defendants once again moved for summary judgment on the privacy claims in the U.S. District Court.[6] IBM counsel explained that the company and the parties involved had a legitimate business interest in the disclosures that were made concerning Bratt's use of the open door policy and his medical condition. Liebtag, they maintained, was charged with investigating Bratt's use of the open door procedure, and he was involved in finding a suitable work assignment for Bratt. IBM contended that Liebtag followed the standard practice in investigating and following up on open door complaints. IBM submitted that the two memoranda relied upon most heavily by Bratt[7] were not disseminated beyond managerial employees with a legitimate interest in Bratt's work assignments.

Robert Bratt then narrowed his lawsuit to a few basic complaints. Bratt contends that Liebtag violated his privacy by informing an estimated sixteen other managerial employees not directly involved in the open door process of his assertion of open door rights. He also charged that copies of Liebtag's memos (dated October 18 and 19, 1978) were included in the "Waltham file" kept at the Waltham office, and that these were made available to Waltham employees, including the manager of the Cambridge Center. In addition, Bratt claims that Liebtag violated his right to privacy by distributing the memos dated October 18 and 19, 1978, which stated that Bratt was found "paranoid" by Dr. Nugent and

[3] Ibid., at 134.

[4] Ibid., at 135.

[5] Ibid., at 135–36.

[6] Once the Supreme Judicial Court had defined a standard for deciding an employee's right to privacy claims against an employer, the issue returned to the U.S. Court of Appeals for a ruling. The Court of Appeals affirmed the District Court's dismissal of the libel claims against the defendants; however, the District Court's grant of summary judgment as to the privacy claims was reversed. The case was remanded for additional findings and rulings by the district court on the privacy claims.

[7] Dated October 18, 1978, and October 19, 1978.

that he had "a mental problem beyond IBM." IBM is charged with having intruded upon Bratt's privacy by allowing Dr. Nugent and the IBM medical staff to discuss his medical condition with IBM management without his consent.

The argument made by IBM in response is the following: Liebtag was responsible for conducting an investigation of Bratt's open door complaints and for finding him an appropriate work assignment. Liebtag followed the standard procedure for open door grievances and then made limited disclosures about Bratt's use of the open door procedure. He reported his finding to his superiors, McKinney and Vadnais, from whom he had received the assignment. Liebtag made note of Bratt's medical condition because Bratt's health was pertinent to his job placement. In addition, the defendants explain that Bratt used the open door procedure knowing that some disclosure was necessary for an investigation of his complaints. Bratt, the defendants claim, also volunteered information concerning his own health. For example, he told his manager that he had seen his own doctor because he was having headaches and was unable to sleep.

The IBM defendants assert that Bratt was aware, in accepting IBM's offer of medical assistance, that Dr. Nugent was "being retained by IBM, at its expense, to conduct an examination of Bratt for the purpose of advising IBM concerning his medical condition." Bratt could not have expected the confidentiality of a doctor-patient relationship to have existed. Defendants' counsel cites a precedent from *Hoesl* v. *United States*[8] that when a physician is employed by an employer to evaluate the fitness of employees, the "physician's duties run primarily to [the] employer." Dr. Nugent's assessment of Bratt's medical condition, they argue, was necessary for evaluating his request for transfer (in which Bratt had cited health reasons) and in assigning him to a new position.

District Court Judge Robert E. Keeton found in favor of the IBM defendants on the breach of privacy issues. Keeton stated, "It is clear that the defendants had a legitimate interest in disclosing the information at issue. I conclude that a fact finder, weighing all of the factors discussed above and applying the balancing test set out by the Supreme Judicial Court in *Bratt,* could not, with support in the evidence, find that the defendants unreasonably interfered with Bratt's right of privacy."

Robert Bratt appealed the District Court ruling of June 1985 to the U.S. Court of Appeals, First Circuit. The court considered whether the District Court erred in saying that no rational fact finder could conclude that IBM had violated Bratt's right to privacy in communicating his use of the open door grievance procedure and his medical problems with IBM personnel. In considering the alleged violation of privacy by

[8] 451 F. Supp. 1170, 1176.

Liebtag's disclosure of Bratt's use of the open door procedure, the court observed that the open door process at IBM necessarily involves disclosure of a complaint for a thorough investigation. Disclosure was limited to approximately sixteen persons, most of whom were directly involved in or had a legitimate business interest in the process. The court concluded, "There can be no question that these individuals had a legitimate business need for this information and that Bratt's voluntary use of the open door process essentially waived any claim of breach of privacy *vis-à-vis* these persons."

Concerning the allegation that Liebtag violated Bratt's privacy by disclosing memoranda making mention of Bratt's medical condition, the court again applied a balancing standard. The nature of this intrusion was at once more substantial and more personal; however, the employees to whom the disclosure was made had a legitimate business interest in the information. The Court of Appeals affirmed the District Court's judgment for the defendants.

Bratt has argued that Dr. Nugent owed him a duty of confidentiality, regardless of her contract with IBM. He testified that he believed that everything he said to Dr. Nugent would be held in confidence. Dr. Nugent did not inform Bratt that she would report the results of his examination to IBM personnel, nor did she ask Bratt to sign a disclosure form. The defendants assert that Dr. Nugent was employed by IBM to assess its employees' health and provide an evaluation for the company.

The Court of Appeals referred to the Massachusetts Supreme Judicial Court's statement in *Bratt* that "[w]hen an employer retains a physician to examine employees, generally no physician-patient relationship exists between the employee and the doctor."[9] However, the Massachusetts court later ruled in another case, *Alberts* v. *Devine,* that "in this Commonwealth all physicians owe their patients a duty, for violation of which the law provides a remedy, not to disclose without the patient's consent medical information about the patient, except to meet a serious danger to the patient or to others."[10] Consequently, the Massachusetts Court has not conclusively addressed the conditions under which a physician-patient relationship is established. Nor have the other issues in the Bratt case been finally resolved in the courts.

---

[9] 467 N.E.2d at 136, n. 21.
[10] 479 N.E.2d 113, at 119 (Mass. 1985).

Du Pont's Policy of Exclusion from the Workplace

In January 1981 the *New York Times* reviewed a new and startling development in the workplaces of the nation. Some fertile women workers chose
to undergo voluntary sterilization rather than give up high-paying jobs
that involved exposure to chemicals potentially harmful to a developing
fetus. Disclosure of this practice precipitated discussion of a new civil
rights issue with "questions . . . raised about whether a company should
be allowed to discriminate against a woman to protect her unborn child,
or whether the practice of keeping a woman out of certain well-paying
jobs because she was fertile was simply another form of sex discrimination
in the workplace."[1]

Some background information is necessary to understand this issue.
The causes of congenital (or "birth") defects in humans are not well
understood. Four to six percent are caused by specific drugs and environmental chemicals, but the causes of at least 65 to 70 percent are unknown.
It is known, however, that of the 28,000 toxic substances listed by the
National Institute of Occupational Safety and Health (NIOSH), 56 are
animal mutagens (that is, they cause chromosomal damage to either
the ova or the sperm cells), and 471 are animal teratogens (that is,
they cause deformations in a developing fetus).[2]

Fetuses must be protected from potential harm due to the mother's
exposure to a teratogenic substance. The 1960s thalidomide tragedy
showed the devastating effects that a teratogenic substance, which is
perfectly harmless to the mother, can have on the developing fetus.

---

[1] Philip Shabecoff, "Industry and Women Clash over Hazards in the Workplace," *New York Times*, January 3, 1981.

[2] Earl A. Molander, "Regulating Reproductive Risks in the Workplace," in his *Responsive Capitalism: Case Studies in Corporate Social Conduct* (New York: McGraw-Hill Book Co., 1980), p. 9.

Doctors had prescribed thalidomide for pregnant women as a tranquilizer, but found that the drug caused such fetal defects as missing or deformed arms, legs, hands, and feet, in addition to many soft tissue malformations. Fetal defects could be either physical or functional alterations, including the possibility of growth retardation, deformities, behavioral problems, genetic alterations, or a higher than normal tendency to develop cancer.[3]

Exposure of workers to toxic substances in the workplace is complicated by the fact that chemicals usually do not occur singly, but in combination. Also, the average worker does not have knowledge of the chemical makeup of many products. Fetal exposure to teratogenic drugs is even more complex. The human embryo is most sensitive to toxic agents during the gestation period of day 18 to day 60, which is often before the pregnancy is detected. Pregnancy tests are not accurate during these early stages when the fetus is most susceptible to the damaging toxins.

The U.S. government (the FDA and the EPA, in particular) requires animal testing of drugs to insure that any new product to which pregnant women may be exposed is harmless to the fetus. Animal testing is a costly and lengthy process; it involves the testing of more than one species for a 3- to 6-month period. The results are uncertain. Dr. Charles Reinhardt, Director of Du Pont's Haskell Laboratory for Toxology and Industrial Medicine, notes that "the absence of teratogenic effect in two species, or even a dozen more, does not mean that the substance won't be hazardous to human fetuses." It is also easier to calculate the permissible levels of exposure for adults than for fetuses. The tests are still the best available means of establishing the toxicity of new substances.

Industries such as chemical plants and zinc smelters with high concentrations of lead have dealt with this potential threat to the fetus in a number of ways. The most common strategy is simply to make jobs that involve the risk of exposure "off limits" to women "of child-bearing potential." That is, fertile women in their late teens to their forties are banned from those particular positions. Department of Labor statistics show that 60 percent of all women between the ages of 18 and 54 are currently working. Since a woman is assumed fertile until proven otherwise, this sweeping policy affects a large portion of the female workforce.[4]

This "protective exclusion" policy has aroused the ire of the women's movement and of civil libertarians, who see it as one more form of sex discrimination. Their charges of discrimination are made credible for several reasons. Jobs that are open to "women of child-bearing potential"

---

[3] Bruce W. Karrh, "Reproductive Hazards: Evaluation and Control of Embryotoxic Agents" (1983), p. 4, available from Du Pont.

[4] Albert Rosenfeld, "Fertility May Be Hazardous to Your Job," *Saturday Review* 6 (9), p. 12.

are almost always lower-paying jobs. In addition, women's groups have noted a lack of well-supported evidence about exposure to certain alleged toxic hazards and a general lack of consensus in government and industry about proper levels of unsafe exposure.

The most significant charge of discrimination rests on evidence of the male's contribution to birth defects. As noted earlier, mutagenic substances affect the sperm as well as the egg. Exposure to these toxins can result in sterility for the man, but it can also produce mutated sperm and ultimately a malformed fetus. (See p. 39 for a table of chemicals known to affect the male reproductive system.) Thus, any policy designed to protect the fetus must include considerations of the sperm and egg that form it. This would logically require a more expansive protective policy than the mere exclusion of women from the workplace.

E.I. Du Pont de Nemours and Company, the largest chemical manufacturer in the world, has long been concerned with issues of chemical toxicity and exposure. Du Pont uses only four hazardous chemicals that require special controls. Over the years, the company has promulgated a number of policies dealing with reproductive hazards, including one that focuses on fetal damage from chemical exposure.

If a chemical is found to be or is suspected of being a developmental toxin (toxic to the fetus), the first step is to use engineering and administrative procedures to eliminate the risk of exposure or to reduce it to an acceptable level. Engineering procedures might, for example, involve special ventilation equipment; administrative procedures might involve management of the length of exposure time or the required use of protective clothing. However, where no "acceptable exposure level" has been determined or where engineering and administrative procedures are inadequate to control exposure to the acceptable level, the Du Pont policy reads: "females of child-bearing capacity shall be excluded from work areas."[5]

Du Pont has rejected the suggestion that a woman be apprised of the health risk and sign a waiver if she chooses to accept the risk. The Du Pont position is that the exclusionary policy is to protect the fetus, not the woman. Bruce W. Karrh, Vice President for Safety, Health, and Environmental Affairs of Du Pont, holds that "the issue with exposure to embryotoxic chemicals is one of protecting the susceptible embryo or fetus from chemical substances which can cross the placenta and cause damage to the developing embryo or fetus at concentrations which would have no adverse effects on the female or male adult."[6] Du Pont

---

[5] Bruce W. Karrh, "A Company's Duty to Report Health Hazards," *Bulletin of the New York Academy of Medicine* 54 (September 1978), esp. pp. 783, 785, and Molander, "Regulating Reproductive Risks," p. 16.

[6] Karrh, "Reproductive Hazards," p. 7.

has developed a specific procedure for managing the issue, upon determination that a substance presents a risk to the fetus:

1. Employees who may be affected shall be informed of the possible consequences of exposure to such substances and appropriate handling procedures shall be established and communicated.

2. Engineering controls shall be used to the extent practical to reduce and maintain exposure to embryotoxins to acceptable levels. Such controls shall be augmented by administrative controls as appropriate.

3. Whenever engineering and administrative controls are not practical to keep exposure at or below acceptable levels, personal protective equipment, where appropriate, and training for its proper use shall be provided to and required to be used by employees who may be affected by such compounds.

4. Females of child-bearing capacity shall be excluded from work areas where:
   a. there is potential for exposure to an embryotoxin for which an acceptable level cannot be set, or
   b. whenever engineering and administrative controls augmented as appropriate by personal protective equipment, are determined to be inadequate to insure acceptable levels of exposure.[7]

Du Pont also holds that ". . . the waiver of subsequent claims by the female worker would be of no legal significance because the deformed fetus, if born, may have its own rights as a person which could not be waived by the mother."[8] A recent ruling by the Illinois State Supreme Court upheld this position. The court ruled that a child injured at birth had the right to sue the hospital for damages resulting from the mother's transfusion with the wrong blood type.

Women's groups continue, however, to view "protective exclusion" as sex discrimination, especially since there is growing evidence that the reproductive systems of men are also adversely affected by certain industrial chemicals that can affect a future fetus.[9] A discussion between Dr. Donald Whorton, one of the first scientists to study testicular toxins in the workplace, and Dr. William N. Rom illustrates the problem many women's groups find with policies of female exclusion:

[7] Bruce W. Karrh, "Women in the Workplace," an address on May 2, 1978, as quoted in Molander, "Regulating Reproductive Risks," p. 16.

[8] Molander, "Regulating Reproductive Risks," p. 16.

[9] Sources: M. Donald Whorton, *et al.*, "Testicular Function among Carbaryl-Exposed Employees," *Journal of Toxicology and Environmental Health* 5 (1979), pp. 929–941; H. Northrop, "Predictive Value of Animal Toxicology," a paper presented at the "Symposium on Reproductive Health Policies in the Workplace," Pittsburgh, Penna., May 10, 1982; Vilma R. Hunt, "The Reproductive System Sensitivity through the Life Cycle," a paper presented at the American Conference of Governmental Industrial Hygienists, "Symposium: Protection of the Sensitive Individual," Tucson, Ariz., November 9, 1981.

DR. WHORTON: . . . In a situation in which there is testicular toxicity, why would you be removing women?
DR. ROM: Because it may affect both sexes.
DR. WHORTON: But you would remove the men before the women, wouldn't you?
DR. ROM: Somebody has to work there.[10]

The Coalition for the Reproductive Rights of Women, a group organized to fight discrimination against women of child-bearing age, points out that exclusionary protections are unusually broad, especially since not all women want or plan to have children. An attorney for the women's rights project of the American Civil Liberties Union has criticized the notion that women should be protected "against their wishes" and states that "we insist that the cost of safety cannot be equality. Another solution should be found."[11]

Du Pont considers the sex of the excluded party as irrelevant, on the grounds that the sole issue is that of protecting the susceptible fetus. Du Pont notes that "the complexity of the issue lies in the separate, but not separated, nature of the affected groups—fetuses and females." Women are excluded only because they are capable of becoming pregnant and then bringing the fetus into the workplace.[12] The difficulty of determining pregnancy during the early stages when the fetus is most vulnerable to damage necessitates the policy of exclusion.

The company also notes that implementation of the above four-step procedure is far more costly to the company than a policy that would allow women to make their own choices. However, women's advocates take the view that companies such as Du Pont are simply remiss in developing technological solutions for the control of embryotoxins. A common union complaint is that industry makes the worker safe for the workplace, even to the point of exclusion, rather than making the workplace safe for the worker. Management contentions that acceptable levels of exposure cannot be achieved are viewed with suspicion.

Policy formulation is further complicated by a lack of sufficient or accurate data concerning the developmental toxicity of substances. For example, Du Pont was informed by a supplier in March 1981 that a chemical it used in some resins and elastomers was possibly teratogenic. The data was preliminary and needed corroboration by a study designed

---

[10] M. Donald Whorton, "Considerations about Reproductive Hazards," in Jeffrey S. Lee and William N. Rom, eds., *Legal and Ethical Dilemmas in Occupational Health* (Ann Arbor: Butterworth Group), p. 412.

[11] Shabecoff, "Industry and Women Clash."

[12] Karrh, "Reproductive Hazards," p. 1.

to show if teratogenicity occurs. Instead of waiting for the study to be completed, Du Pont immediately determined a level of exposure considered to pose "no risk." Du Pont then promptly advised all employees working with the chemical of the preliminary findings and determined that the jobs of about fifty women involved unacceptable levels of exposure. About one-half were found to be of child-bearing capability and were excluded. All excluded were moved to comparable positions without penalty in wages or benefits.

Du Pont's Haskell Laboratory simultaneously conducted an animal study to corroborate the preliminary work. The supplier's follow-up study and the Du Pont study both found no teratogenic effect in the animals studied. The supplier's earlier study results apparently contained experimental error. Du Pont notified its employees of the new findings and no longer excluded women of child-bearing capability. Return preference was given to women formerly removed from these jobs. During this period, Du Pont made its plant physicians available for counseling employees and for consultations with the personal physicians of employees.[13]

With the increasing sophistication of manufacturing processes, more workers will face the possibility of exposure to toxic substances. An adequate response is needed to protect workers and their offspring from the potential dangers of mutagenic and teratogenic substances. The lack of accurate scientific data about the embryotoxicity of chemicals used in the workplace and the conflicting opinions concerning the preventive measures necessary to protect workers aggravate the problem. Cooperation between the disputing parties, private industry and the workers, is essential in formulating a satisfactory policy; however, this issue is not likely to prove amenable to simple solutions.

[13] Recent developments at Du Pont were provided by Bruce W. Karrh in correspondence of April 5, 1988 with Tom L. Beauchamp. The final two paragraphs are based on personal correspondence of August 24, 1982, from Nancy K. Tidonia of Du Pont's Public Affairs Department to Tom L. Beauchamp.

TABLE 1. MALE REPRODUCTIVE EFFECTS: ENVIRONMENTAL AGENTS, HUMAN STUDIES

Agent	Exposure Conditions	Species	Type of Study	Effects
Anesthetic gases	Occupational	Male workers	Reproductive history	Increased incidence congenital anomalies offspring
Chloroprene	Occupational	Male workers	Semen analysis; reproductive history	Decreased motility and number of sperm; threefold excess miscarriages in wives
Dibromochloropropane	Occupational	Male workers	Semen analysis; reproductive history	Decreased sperm count; infertility
High altitude	14,000 ft.	Male	Semen analysis	Decreased sperm count and motility; increased number abnormal sperm
Hydrocarbons	Occupational	Male workers	Reproductive history	Twofold increased incidence childhood cancer with occupational hydrocarbon exposure of father
Kepone	Environmental	Male	Reproductive history	Decreased fertility males
Lead	Occupational	Male workers	Semen analysis	Decreased sperm count and motility; increase abnormally shaped sperm
Microwaves	Occupational	Male workers	Semen analysis; reproductive history	Decreased libido; decreased sperm count and motility, increase abnormally shaped sperm
Carbon disulfide	Occupational	Male workers	Semen analysis; reproductive history	Impotence, loss of libido
Irradiation	Occupational	Male workers	Gonadotropic hormone and semen analysis	Depression gonadotropic hormone levels; alterations in spermatogenesis
Oral contraceptives	Occupational manufacture	Male workers	Reproductive history, physical exam, blood analysis	Gynecomastia, decreased libido, infertility
Vinyl chloride	Occupational	Male workers	Reproductive questionnaire	Adverse pregnancy outcome wives; excess fetal loss
Cigarette smoking	Environmental	Male	Semen analysis	Increase in abnormally shaped sperm
Elevated temperature	Occupational, environmental ($30 \rightarrow 37°C$)	Male	Semen analysis; histology	Inhibition spermatogenesis, testicular pathology

Source: Vilma Hunt, *Work and the Health of Women* (Boca Raton, Fla.: CRC Press, Inc., 1979), pp. 158–159.

The DC-10's Defective Doors

The Douglas Company had always held the lead in commercial aviation until the Boeing Company captured a significant portion of the jet market in the late 1950s with its 707. (The 707 was actually similar to Douglas's DC-8, which was already in service.) The Douglas Company, keenly aware of new and stiff competition, hoped to manufacture a wide-bodied jet that would be attractive in international markets. Management viewed an "airbus" as crucial to long-term economic well-being (although no wide-bodies were actually produced for another ten years).[1]

Douglas was taken over by McDonnell Aircraft in 1967. By this time, pressure to produce a wide-bodied jet had intensified. The Boeing Company had already introduced its 747, and neither Douglas nor the Federal Aviation Administration (FAA) wished Boeing to have exclusive control over this aspect of the air travel market. The McDonnell Douglas firm then searched for a structural design subcontractor capable of sharing short-term financial burdens of a program building wide-bodied jets that would realize long-term profits. The Convair Division of General Dynamics was a subcontractor with an excellent reputation for structural design. The understanding between the two companies was that McDonnell Douglas had the primary authority to furnish design criteria and to amend design decisions. Convair's role was to create a design that would satisfy the stipulated criteria.[2]

---

[1] This paragraph profited from three unpublished sources: Fay Horton Sawyier, "The Case of the DC-10 and Discussion" (Chicago: Center for the Study of Ethics in the Professions, Illinois Institute of Technology, December 8, 1976), mimeographed, pp. 2–3; correspondence with John T. Sant of the McDonnell Douglas Corporation's Legal Department in St. Louis; and correspondence with Professor Homer Sewell of George Washington University (see his article in footnote 5).

[2] See Paul Eddy, Elaine Potter, and Bruce Page, *Destination Disaster: From the Tri-Motor to the DC-10* (New York: Quadrangle Books, New York Times Book Co., 1976); John Newhouse, "A Reporter at Large: The Airlines Industry," *New Yorker*, June 21, 1982, pp. 46–93.

In August 1968, McDonnell Douglas awarded Convair a contract to build the DC-10 fuselage and doors. The lower cargo doors became the subject of immediate discussion. These doors were to be outward-hinging, tension-latch doors, with latches driven by hydraulic cylinders—a design already adequately tested by DC-8 and DC-9 models. In addition, each cargo door was designed to be linked to hydraulically actuated flight controls and was to have a manual locking system designed so that the handle or latch lever could not be stowed away unless the door was properly closed and latched. McDonnell Douglas, however, decided to separate the cargo door actuation system from the hydraulically actuated primary flight controls. This involved using electric actuators to close the cargo doors rather than the hydraulic actuators originally called for. Fewer moving parts in the electric actuators presumably made for easier maintenance, and each door would weigh 28 pounds less.

However, the Convair engineers had considered the hydraulic actuators critical to safety. They were not satisfied with these changes, and they remained dissatisfied after further modifications were introduced. As Convair engineers viewed the situation, the critical difference between the two actuator systems involved the way each would respond to the buildup of forces caused by increasing pressure. If a hydraulic latch was not secured properly, the latches would smoothly slide open when only a small amount of pressure had built up in the cabin. Although the doors would be ripped off their hinges, this would occur at a low altitude, so that the shock from decompression would be small enough to land the plane safely. By contrast, if an electric latch failed to catch, it would not gently slide open due to increasing pressure. Rather, it would be abruptly and violently forced open, most likely at a higher altitude where rapid decompression would dangerously impair the structure of the plane.

Convair's Director of Product Engineering, F. D. "Dan" Applegate, was adamant that a hydraulic system was more satisfactory. However, McDonnell Douglas did not yield to Convair's reservations about the DC-10 cargo door design.

Once a decision had been made to use an electrical system, it was necessary to devise a new and foolproof backup system of checking and locking. In the summer of 1969 McDonnell Douglas asked Convair to draft a Failure Mode and Effects Analysis, or FMEA, for the cargo door system. An FMEA's purpose is to assess the likelihood and consequences of a failure in the system. In August 1969, Convair engineers found nine possible failure sequences that could result in destruction of the craft, with loss of human lives. A major problem focused on the warning and locking-pin systems. The door could close and latch, but without being safely locked. The warning indicator lights were prone to failure, in which case a door malfunction could go undetected. The

FMEA also concluded that the door design was potentially dangerous and lacked a reliable failsafe locking system. It could open in flight, presenting considerable danger to passengers.[3]

The FAA requires that it be given an FMEA covering all systems critical to safety, but no mention was made of this hazard to the FAA prior to "certification" of the DC-10 model. McDonnell Douglas maintains that no such report was filed because this cargo door design was not implemented until all defects expressed in the FMEA were removed. The FMEA *submitted*, they contend, was the *final* FMEA, and did not discuss past defects because they had been removed.[4]

As lead manufacturer, McDonnell Douglas made itself entirely responsible for the certification of the aircraft and, in seeking the certification, was expressing its position that all defects had been removed. Convair, by contrast, was not formally responsible because its contract with McDonnell Douglas forbade Convair from reporting directly to the FAA.

During a model test run in May 1970, the DC-10 blew its forward lower cargo door, and the plane's cabin floor collapsed. Because the vital electric and hydraulic subsystems of the plane are located under the cabin floor (unlike in the 747, where they are above the ceiling), this collapse was doubly incapacitating.[5] A spokesperson at McDonnell Douglas placed the blame for this particular malfunction on the "human failure" of a mechanic who had incorrectly sealed the door. Although no serious design problems were contemplated, there were some ensuing modifications in design for the door, purportedly to provide better checks on the locking pins. As modified, the cargo door design was properly certified and authorities at McDonnell Douglas believed it safe. Five DC-10s were flight tested for over 1,500 hours prior to certification of the craft.

Certification processes are carried out in the name of the FAA, but the actual work is often performed by the manufacturers. As a regulatory agency, the FAA is charged with overseeing commercial products and regulating them in the public interest. However, the FAA is often not in an independent position. The FAA appoints designated engineering representatives (DERs) to make inspections at company plants. These are company employees chosen for their experience and integrity who have the dual obligations of loyalty to the company that pays them as design engineers and of faithful performance of inspections to see that

---

[3] Eddy, *et al.*, *Destination Disaster*; see also Martin Curd and Larry May, *Professional Responsibility for Harmful Actions* (Dubuque, Iowa: Kendall/Hunt Publishing Co., 1984), pp. 11–21, and Peter French, "What Is Hamlet to McDonnell-Douglas or McDonnell-Douglas to Hamlet: DC-10," *Business and Professional Ethics Journal* 1 (Winter 1982), pp. 1, 5–6.

[4] John T. Sant, personal correspondence.

[5] See Homer Sewell, "Commentary," *Business and Professional Ethics Journal* 1 (Winter 1982), pp. 17–19.

the company has complied with federal airworthiness regulations. The manufacturers are in this respect policing themselves, and it is generally acknowledged that conflicts of interest arise in this dual-obligation system.[6]

During the months surrounding November 1970, a number of internal memos were written at both McDonnell Douglas and Convair that cited old and new design problems with the cargo door. New structural proposals were made, but none was implemented. McDonnell Douglas and Convair quarreled about cost accounting and about pinning fault for remaining design flaws. The FAA finally certified the DC-10 on July 29, 1971, and by late 1971 the plane had received praise for its performance at virtually all levels. Under rigorous conditions its performance ratings were excellent. The company vigorously promoted the new aircraft.

But on June 12, 1972, an aft bulk cargo door of a DC-10 in flight from Los Angeles to New York separated from the body of the aircraft at about 11,750 feet over Windsor, Ontario. Rapid cabin decompression occurred as a result, causing structural damage to the cabin floor immediately above the cargo compartment. Nine passengers and two stewardesses were injured. A National Transportation Safety Board (NTSB) investigation found that the probable cause of the malfunction was the latching mechanism in the cargo door and recommended changes in the locking system. The NTSB's specific recommendations were the following:

1. Require a modification to the DC-10 cargo door locking system to make it physically impossible to position the external locking handle and vent door to their normal locked positions unless the locking pins are fully engaged.
2. Require the installation of relief vents between the cabin and aft cargo compartment to minimize the pressure loading on the cabin flooring in the event of sudden depressurization of the compartment.[7]

The administrator of the FAA, John Shaffer, could have issued an airworthiness directive that required immediate repairs. He elected not to issue the directive, choosing instead a "gentleman's agreement" with McDonnell Douglas that allowed the company to make the necessary modifications and recommend new procedures to affected airlines. All actions by the company were to be voluntary.

Fifteen days *subsequent* to the blowout over Windsor (June 27, 1972), Dan Applegate wrote a stern memo to his superior at Convair that

---

[6] Eddy, *et al., Destination Disaster*, pp. 180–81.

[7] National Transportation Safety Board, Aircraft Accident Report no. NTSB-AAR-73-2 (February 28, 1973), p. 38.

expressed his doubts about the entire project and offered some reflections on "future accident liability." The following excerpts from the memo reveal Applegate's anguish and concerns:[8]

> The potential for long-term Convair liability on the DC-10 has caused me increasing concern for several reasons.
>
> 1. The fundamental safety of the cargo door latching system has been progressively degraded since the program began in 1968.
> 2. The airplane demonstrated an inherent susceptibility to catastrophic failure when exposed to explosive decompression of the cargo compartment in 1970 ground tests.
> 3. Douglas has taken an increasingly "hard-line" with regards to the relative division of design responsibility between Douglas and Convair during change cost negotiations.
> 4. The growing "consumerism" environment indicates increasing Convair exposure to accident liability claims in the years ahead. . . .
>
> In July 1970 DC-10 Number Two was being pressure-tested in the "hangar" by Douglas, on the second shift, without electrical power in the airplane. This meant that the electrically powered cargo door actuators and latch position warning switches were inoperative. The "green" second shift test crew manually cranked the latching system closed but failed to fully engage the latches on the forward door. They also failed to note that the external latch "lock" position indicator showed that the latches were not fully engaged. Subsequently, when the increasing cabin pressure reached about 3 psi (pounds per square inch) the forward door blew open. The resulting explosive decompression failed the cabin floor downward rendering tail controls, plumbing, wiring, etc. which passed through the floor, inoperative. This inherent failure mode is catastrophic, since it results in the loss of control of the horizontal and vertical tail and the aft center engine. We informally studied and discussed with Douglas alternative corrective actions including blow out panels in the cabin floor which would accommodate the "explosive" loss of cargo compartment pressure without loss of tail surface and aft center engine control. It seemed to us then prudent that such a change was indicated since "Murphy's Law" being what it is, cargo doors will come open sometime during the twenty years of use ahead for the DC-10.
>
> Douglas concurrently studied alternative corrective actions, in house, and made a unilateral decision to incorporate vent doors in the cargo doors. This "bandaid fix" not only failed to correct the inherent DC-10 catastrophic failure mode of cabin floor collapse, but the detail design of the vent door change further degraded the safety of the original door latch system by replacing the direct, short-coupled and stiff latch "lock" indicator system with a complex and relatively flexible linkage. (This change was accomplished entirely by Douglas with the exception of the assistance of one Convair engineer who was sent to Long Beach at their request to help their vent door system design team.)

[8] Eddy, *et al., Destination Disaster,* pp. 183–85.

This progressive degradation of the fundamental safety of the cargo door latch system since 1968 has exposed us to increasing liability claims. On June 12, 1972 in Detroit, the cargo door latch electrical actuator system in DC-10 number 5 failed to fully engage the latches of the left rear cargo door and the complex and relatively flexible latch "lock" system failed to make it impossible to close the vent door. When the door blew open before the DC-10 reached 12,000 feet altitude the cabin floor collapsed disabling most of the control to the tail surfaces and aft center engine. It is only chance that the airplane was not lost. Douglas has again studied alternative corrective actions and appears to be applying more "band-aids." So far they have directed to us to install small one-inch diameter, transparent inspection windows through which you can view latch "lock-pin" position, they are revising the rigging instructions to increase "lock-pin" engagement and they plan to reinforce and stiffen the flexible linkage.

It might well be asked why not make the cargo door latch system really "fool-proof" and leave the cabin floor alone. Assuming it is possible to make the latch "fool-proof" this doesn't solve the fundamental deficiency in the airplane. A cargo compartment can experience explosive decompression from a number of causes such as: sabotage, mid-air collision, explosion of combustibles in the compartment and perhaps others, any one of which may result in damage which would not be fatal to the DC-10 were it not for the tendency of the cabin floor to collapse. The responsibility for primary damage from these kinds of causes would clearly not be our responsibility, however, we might very well be held responsible for the secondary damage, that is the floor collapse which could cause the loss of the aircraft. It might be asked why we did not originally detail design the cabin floor to withstand the loads of cargo compartment explosive decompression or design blow out panels in the cabin floors to fail in a safe and predictable way.

I can only say that our contract with Douglas provided that Douglas would furnish all design criteria and loads (which in fact they did) and that we would design to satisfy these design criteria and loads (which in fact we did). There is nothing in our experience history which would have led us to expect that the DC-10 cabin floor would be inherently susceptible to catastrophic failure when exposed to explosive decompression of the cargo compartment, and I must presume that there is nothing in Douglas's experience history which would have led them to expect that the airplane would have this inherent characteristic or they would have provided for this in their loads and criteria which they furnished to us.

My only criticism of Douglas in this regard is that once this inherent weakness was demonstrated by the July 1970 test failure, they did not take immediate steps to correct it. It seems to me inevitable that, in the twenty years ahead of us, DC-10 cargo doors will come open and I would expect this to usually result in the loss of the airplane. [Emphasis added.] This fundamental failure mode has been discussed in the past and is being discussed again in the bowels of both the Douglas and Convair organizations. It appears however that Douglas is waiting and hoping for government direction or regulations in the hope of passing costs on to us or their customers.

If you can judge from Douglas' position during ongoing contract change negotiations they may feel that any liability incurred in the meantime for loss of life, property and equipment may be legally passed on to us.

It is recommended that overtures be made at the highest management level to persuade Douglas to immediately make a decision to incorporate changes in the DC-10 which will correct the fundamental cabin floor catastrophic failure mode. Correction will take a good bit of time, hopefully there is time before the National Transportation Safety Board (NTSB) or the FAA ground the airplane which would have disastrous effects upon sales and production both near and long term. This corrective action becomes more expensive than the cost of damages resulting from the loss of one plane load of people.

F. D. Applegate
Director of Product Engineering

If this memo had reached outside authorities, Applegate conceivably might have been able to prevent the occurrence of events that (to some extent) he correctly foresaw. However, this memo was never sent either to McDonnell Douglas or to the FAA. Applegate received a reply to his memo from his immediate supervisor, J. B. Hurt. By now it was clear to both Applegate and Hurt that such major safety questions would not be addressed further at McDonnell Douglas. Hurt's reply to Applegate pointed out that if further questions were now raised, Convair, not McDonnell Douglas, would most likely have to bear the costs of necessary modifications. Higher management at Convair subsequently agreed with Hurt. Without taking other routes to express his grave misgivings about the DC-10, Applegate filed away his memo.

In July 1972, Ship 29 of the DC-10 line was inspected by three different inspectors at the Long Beach plant of McDonnell Douglas. All three certified that the ship had been successfully altered to meet FAA specifications. Two years later, Ship 29 was owned by Turkish Airlines. This ship crashed near Paris in 1974, killing all 335 passengers and 11 crew members—the worst single-plane disaster in aviation history. Experts agreed that the immediate cause of the crash was a blowout of the rear cargo door, at approximately twelve minutes after lift-off. Decompression of the cargo bay caused a collapse of the cabin floor, thereby severing control cables. It was alleged by Sanford Douglas, President of McDonnell Douglas, that the Turkish airline involved in the crash had attempted to "rework" the door rigging or latching mechanism, was working with an inadequately trained ground crew, and failed to follow specified procedures for proper latching. The Turkish airline denied the charges. Recovery of a flight recorder indicated that there was no explosion, fire, or evident sabotage, and that the cargo door blew because it was not securely sealed.

In 1980 the McDonnell Douglas Corporation issued a special report addressing the public's growing fears about the design of the DC-10. The facts presented in the corporation's report were aimed at proving "that the DC-10 meets the toughest standards of aerospace technology."[9] The report does not mention the problems with the cargo doors. This omission is perhaps understandable in that a cargo door malfunction did *not* cause the American Airlines DC-10 crash at Chicago's O'Hare Airport on May 25, 1979, which killed 275 people and was then the worst air disaster in U.S. history. Subsequent examination by the FAA revealed that this DC-10, whose floor-venting problems (mentioned by Applegate) had been corrected, suffered from different defects.[10]

---

[9] McDonnell Douglas Corporation, *The DC-10: A Special Report* (Long Beach, Calif.: McDonnell Douglas Corporation, 1980).

[10] Newhouse, "A Reporter," p. 89; *New York Times*, June 7, 1979, sec. B, p. 13, and *New York Times*, June 19, 1979, sec. D, p. 19; see also "New Testing Methods Could Boost Air Safety," *Science* 205 (July 6, 1979), pp. 29–31.

The Reluctant Security Guard

David Tuff, 24, is a security guard who has been working for the past seventeen months for the Blue Mountain Company in Minneapolis, Minnesota. Blue Mountain is engaged in the management and operation of retail shopping malls in several midwestern states. The company has a security services division that trains and supplies security guards for the malls, including the Village Square Mall, at which Tuff has been employed.

Minnesota state and local laws require that security officers be licensed and approved by the county police department. Security officers are bound to obey the rules ordained by this police unit. Tuff completed the required training, passed the compulsory examination for security guards, and was duly issued a license. Tuff has always carried out his duties as a security guard conscientiously. He had completed a distinguished four-year tour of duty in the U.S. Marine Corps, serving as an MP, before taking the security job with Blue Mountain. His commanding officer had praised both his service and integrity.

As part of his job training at Blue Mountain, Tuff was required to learn the procedures found in the *Security Officer's Manual*, which uses military regulations as a model. Two sections of this manual are worded as follows:

Section V, subsection D.

Should a serious accident or crime, including all felonies, occur on the premises of the licensee, it shall be the responsibility of the licensee to notify the appropriate police department immediately. Failure to do so is a violation of the provisions of this manual.

Furthermore, the manual provides for the following action to be taken if the provisions are violated:

This case was prepared by Anna Pinedo and Tom L. Beauchamp. **Not to be duplicated without permission of the holder of the copyright,** © 1989 Tom L. Beauchamp.

Section XI—disciplinary and deportment

    A. General
        1. The Private Security Coordinator may reprimand a licensee as hereinafter provided. In cases of suspension or revocation, the licensee shall immediately surrender his identification card and badge to the County Police Department. . . .
    B. Cause for Disciplinary Action
       13. Any violation of any regulation or rule found in this manual is cause for disciplinary action.

The reverse side of a security officer's license bears this inscription:

Obey The Rules And Regulations Promulgated By The Superintendent of Police.
    We will obey all lawful orders and rules and regulations pertaining to security officers promulgated by the superintendent of police of the county or any officer placed by him over me.

Given the above language, Tuff believed that his license could be revoked or suspended for any failure to report illegal behavior such as drunk driving and selling narcotics. He had sworn to uphold these rules and regulations at the end of his training and had later signed a statement for the police acknowledging that he knew a police officer could ask for his badge in a situation of conflict.

After he had been employed for fourteen months, the Blue Mountain Company issued new rules of procedure outlining certain assigned duties of its security guards. These rules required security officers "to order and escort intoxicated persons, including persons driving under the influence of alcohol, off its parking lots and onto the public roads." The security officers were instructed not to arrest the drivers and not to contact or alert the police.

Tuff immediately expressed his opposition to the new company policy. During the ensuing months, he expressed his dissatisfaction to every officer of the company he could locate. He complained to his immediate superiors several times a day that he was being asked to set a drunk out on the road who might drive for a mile and kill an innocent pedestrian. He would also describe imagined scenarios in which a law was clearly being violated by a drunk and ask what he was supposed to do in these circumstances under the new rules.

His immediate supervisor, Director of Security Manuel Hernandez, told him that if any such situation were to arise he should contact the supervisor in charge and the supervisor would make the decision. Hernandez noted that most drunks do not weave down the road and hit someone. Tuff was not satisfied and used abusive language in denouncing the rules. Hernandez became angry and told Tuff that his supervisors were becoming irritated with his complaints and could tolerate only so much of this behavior. Hernandez also told him that he should worry less about his license and more about the source of his paycheck. Neither man put any complaint in writing. Tuff was in fact never given a written warning or reprimand by any company official. Tuff maintained that he felt the policy was against the rules he had sworn to uphold, was illegal, and would subject him to loss of his license. Neither his supervisor nor the company manager agreed with his interpretation and they encouraged him to continue his job as usual, but under the new rules.

Tuff then contacted a volunteer organization working to prevent drunk driving. At first he simply sought the organization's interpretation of the law, but later, he voiced a specific complaint about the Blue Mountain policy. His supervisors were approached by representatives of the organization who expressed strong opposition to Blue Mountain's policy for security guards and treatment of drunk drivers.

In the following weeks, Tuff discussed the company policy with several other concerned security guards. He met with security officers Fred Grant and Robert Ladd at a restaurant after work, where they discussed the company procedure and its conflict with their licensing requirements and sworn commitments. They talked of going to the local newspaper with their grievances against the company policy.

Tuff took the initiative by contacting the local television news station and a local newspaper. He talked to four reporters about several drunk driving incidents on the parking lots. The reporters followed up Tuff's complaint by talking to company officials about the policy. The reporters proved to their editors' satisfaction that Tuff's complaints to the media were not given in reckless disregard of the truth and were entirely truthful.

Tuff was called into his supervisor's office to discuss his disclosures to the newspaper. He was asked to sign a document acknowledging that he had spoken with news reporters concerning Blue Mountain company policies, but he refused to sign. Tuff's supervisor reminded him of a company policy prohibiting an employee from talking to the media about company policies. This policy is mentioned on a list of "company rules" distributed to all employees which states that violation of the rule results in dismissal or in disciplinary procedures. Tuff was aware of the company rule, but he did not believe that he had violated it because he had not talked to the press *on company time.*

Hernandez considered this interpretation of the scope of the rule ridiculous. He consulted that afternoon with the company's Council of Managers. Every manager agreed that Tuff's interpretation of the rule showed a blatant disregard for company policy and that Tuff's excuse was an ad hoc rationalization. They also agreed that Tuff had shown himself to be a complainer and a man of poor judgment, which could not be tolerated in a security guard. The discussion of this problem at the meeting took little more than five minutes. Council members instructed Hernandez to give Tuff a few days off to think over this situation. Hernandez duly reported this conclusion to Tuff, who then departed for home. The number of days of leave he should take was not specified, but both men agreed in an amicable although tense setting that they would "be in touch."

Three days later an article on the company's policies appeared in the local newspaper, along with a picture of Tuff in the mall, about to report for work. This story prompted an editorial on a local television station critical of the company. The story was based entirely on data provided by Tuff, some of which had been copied from his sheets of nightly reports to the company.

The newspaper had also interviewed Sergeant Shriver of the county police department. He corroborated Tuff's interpretation that any failure by a security guard to report those driving while intoxicated or those under the influence of drugs constituted a violation of the security manual and the specific terms of the officer's license. He also confirmed Tuff's statement that police officers routinely inspect the activity of security officers and that the police have instructions to look for failures of compliance with license requirements.

After the television editorial, Blue Mountain began to receive phone calls at a rate of fifteen per hour, over 90 percent of them in opposition to the company's policies. Several callers indicated that they shopped in the malls mentioned in the newspaper story and that they would no longer patronize them.

The Council of Managers immediately reconvened to consider this escalation of the problem. The members quickly agreed that Tuff had to be fired and that the sole reason to be given to him and to the public was that he violated the company rule against disclosures to the news media. The managers took this to be an unforgivable act of disloyalty. They discussed whether the proper and precise reason for Tuff's dismissal was disclosure of confidential information or his approach to the media. Their decision on this point entailed a sharpening of the vaguely formulated corporate rule: They decided that an approach to the media is grounds for dismissal even if no disclosure of confidential information is made.

Five working days later, Tuff was called into the company manager's office and dismissed. He was informed that the reason for his dismissal was his violation of company policy by talking to the press.

Tuff then issued a public statement. He explained that his complaints against Blue Mountain Company's procedures had proceeded from his concern to protect the public and other security officers. Tuff had discussed the policy with all the company security guards, who had all expressed some degree of concern over the policy because it forced them to violate their licensing requirements and subjected them to possible suspension or revocation of their licenses. Based on these encounters, Tuff believed that he was acting on their behalf as well as on his own.

Tuff also disclosed a legal argument he wanted to pursue: He contended that his admissions to the media and his complaints about company policy were protected activities. The company interfered with, restrained, and coerced its employees in the exercise of their rights, as protected by the National Labor Relations Act of 1935, by suspending and eventually dismissing Tuff for his disclosures to the press, which violated company policy.

Tuff brought his case to the National Labor Relations Board (NLRB), where it was determined that Blue Mountain was within its legal rights to fire him. The Board found that "whistle-blowers" are legally protected only if they engage in "concerted activity" together with their fellow workers. Because Tuff had acted substantially alone, he was not protected. However, a spokesperson for the NLRB said the board was making no moral judgment on either the employer's or employee's conduct. The moral behavior of the parties, he said, was not at stake in the decision.

Venture Capital for Rubbernex

On a Saturday morning in April 1987, five good friends met in the basement of John Kleinig's house near Palo Alto, California. They saw each other frequently because they carpooled to work at the Globe Coating Company, one of the world's largest manufacturers of fine paints and varnishes. Globe had long been ahead of other manufacturers in the development of several new products and had the finest research staff in the world. The five commuters and friends were all members of this crack research staff, although only two were research scientists. The other three were in administration and computer records.

Kleinig was manager of the research division, a job he had obtained five years ago after fifteen years with the company. He was also the clear leader of this group of five. Each of the other four had more than ten years of experience with the company. They all believed Kleinig was more responsible than anyone else for making their research division the best in the world. Between the five men was virtually everything known about research, administration, secret formulas, the competition, suppliers, and so forth. Along with thirteen other key figures in the division, these five men had helped develop several products vital for Globe's leading position.

During their commute, the five had ample opportunity to criticize their peers and to discuss how cumbersome and slow a huge operation can be. Gradually over the months they became convinced that they could do more advanced research on new coatings in upcoming years than could Globe.

They met, therefore, on this Saturday morning in Kleinig's basement to put the final touches on a business plan for which they hoped to find funding. Kleinig and another group member, Jimmy Liang, had already drafted a tentative plan and had taken it through several drafts.

Their idea for a new business venture was based on the strategy of constructing a plant that would manufacture "thin film" coatings. These coatings are new products pioneered and brought to the market by Globe, which devoted ten years of research to the development of three forms of the coating. The film coating is so thin that it is invisible to the eye and allows various forms of electrical and adhesive contact as if there were no coating at all. Yet it provides all the protection of traditional clear coatings. The technology has a marvelous potential for everything from oak floors to computer parts, and yet production costs are only 68 percent of the costs of polyurethane coatings. It is the most exciting new product in the coating industry.

Between July and the end of August 1987, a friend of Kleinig's, Jay Ewing, offered several critiques of the evolving business plan and helped develop a number of contacts for Kleinig with venture capitalists. He also arranged for a meeting with the specialty law firm of Lion and Lion in Los Angeles to provide legal counsel.

In early September contacts were made with various venture capitalists, and the meeting on September 9, 1987, proved to be decisive. Kleinig hit it off beautifully with a representative of a large east coast venture capitalist, HH Ventures of Philadelphia. This representative was already convinced that there is a major potential in the industry and that these five men represent the epitome of coating knowledge. Their discussion of personnel and business plans lasted approximately two and a half hours, and both were sold on each other's integrity and capability by the end of the meeting. Between September 10 and 18, fifteen phone calls were placed in the evening hours between Kleinig and HH representatives to build the basis for an agreement between HH and what was to be Rubbernex Industries.

On September 19, 1987, Kleinig resigned from Globe. He was nearing an agreement with HH Ventures and felt he could no longer in good conscience remain a loyal employee of Globe. The other four members of his group did not resign at this point because they were not holding *direct* discussions with HH. At his "exit interview" with his supervisor and a lawyer at Globe, Kleinig encountered a hostile and intimidating environment in which he was told in straightforward terms that if he were to put his skills to work with another company by utilizing the trade secrets he had learned at Globe, he would face a massive lawsuit. His supervisor told him that Globe was seriously concerned that its trade secrets and confidential business information would be misappropriated. Kleinig was asked to sign a letter that enumerated 168 broadly worded "trade secrets" that he could not transmit or use. He refused to sign it, but assured Globe that there would be no misappropriation. The discussion nonetheless focused heavily on moral and legal questions about trade secrets.

At the end of the exit interview those present negotiated the following very tentative arrangement: In advance of taking a new job or developing any product, Kleinig would consult with his ex-supervisor at Globe to insure that there would be no trade secret violations. He also would submit a plan to show that any market he wished to explore would not conflict with already established Globe markets. Neither the nature of trade secrets nor trade secrets specific to thin film technology were discussed at the exit interview.

On September 21, 1987, in a meeting between Kleinig, three HH representatives, and lawyers representing both, a tentative agreement was signed. Funding was given for one month during which the business plan was to be developed further. HH was given one month to evaluate its position with the choice of dropping its interest at the end of the month or trying to reach a final agreement for major funding. There was included an offer of further financing after one month conditional on what is called "due diligence" in the venture capital industry (as well as elsewhere). In this context due diligence means, in part, that HH has obligations of due care when money is given to assist in launching a business. It is a standard of proper care that requires an investigator to competently and thoroughly investigate the business viability of a proposal as well as to protect against violations of the rights of all affected parties.

At the September 21 meeting there were lengthy discussions about Kleinig's exit interview, about Globe's concerns about trade secrets, and about HH's need for assurances that there was no trade secrets problem. Kleinig reassured them that he could "build thin film coatings using many different alternative chemicals and processes" and that Globe should have no basis for concern by the time the new processes were developed.

The next day, Jimmy Liang and the chief scientist in the group, Jack Kemp, resigned from Globe. One week later the final two members of the group resigned. All four were told during their exit interviews that Globe was considering a suit against Kleinig to protect its trade secrets, and all were warned that if they joined him they could be in the same position. Globe officials stated to all four that they could prove Kleinig had conspired with other individuals to steal Globe's secrets as early as nine months before leaving the company. These officials would not, however, specify the trade secrets when requested by Kemp to do so.

Whether this package called a "tentative agreement" between venture capitalist HH and the five entrepreneurs will be rewritten and result in a new manufacturing company now rests in the hands of Henry Hardy, the man whose massive personal fortune constitutes the venture capital that fuels HH. He had at first decided not to fund Rubbernex, based on his lawyer's explicit concern that Globe's threat of a lawsuit was not idle; but Mr. Hardy had left the door open to the possibility that Globe could be pacified or that the trade secrets problem could be otherwise dispatched in an honest and forthright manner.

Mr. Hardy had personally taken charge of the due diligence review at HH, which he usually leaves to subordinate officers. He began by hiring the best firm in New York to do reference checks on the entrepreneurs; these consultants were asked to examine both professional credentials and former or existing employment contracts. Mr. Hardy next commissioned a thorough review of the legal questions surrounding trade secrets by a specialist law firm. He then hired twelve outside consultants at American universities to review the feasibility of the scientific claims made by the entrepreneurs and asked in each case for an evaluation of whether the venture could be successfully launched without using Globe's trade secrets. He then asked for a thorough review of the company's financial and legal position by his in-house lawyer and three of his program directors.

Furthermore, Mr. Hardy examined the business viability of the enterprise by having two of his most trusted consultants check the plan. He commissioned a review by a Wall Street security analyst of the coating industry and held discussions with two other venture capitalists who had in the past been involved with trade secrets issues. He also asked for an appraisal by Kleinig of whether he would need further direct hires from Globe in order to carry out the staffing requirements in his plan.

Mr. Hardy then attempted to contact executives at Globe with the intent of asking them to review the Rubbernex business plan for possible trade secrets problems. Following the course sketched out during Kleinig's exit interview, Mr. Hardy was prepared to propose that engineers and chemists from Globe might spend time in any manufacturing facility built by Rubbernex for observational purposes to insure that there were no trade secrets violations. He was prepared to divulge any formulas used for thin film coatings and allow a neutral inspector to examine Rubbernex's formulas by comparison to Globe's to see if there were any violations. His proposal was examined by Globe's lawyers, who replied only with a warning that the technology of thin film coatings was proprietary to Globe and that if any venture capital was forthcoming from HH, Mr. Hardy would personally be named in a lawsuit.

This response angered Mr. Hardy. He felt that whereas he had been prepared to bend over backwards to insure that there was no moral or legal violation, Globe had taken a hostile position of non-negotiation purely in order to prevent potential competition. At about this time, Mr. Hardy's internal and external legal advisors submitted reports in which it appeared that, with enough chemical and engineering ingenuity and enough venture capital to buy expensive new machinery from West

Germany, there was the potential to introduce modifications to claim a *new* product rather than a mere clone of the Globe product. However, everyone who advised him judged it necessary to qualify his or her report with roughly the following statement: "I cannot insure that there will be no violation of trade secrets unless I am able to examine the trade secrets, and this I am prohibited by law and ethics from doing."

HH Venture's due diligence standards had always equalled or surpassed those of any venture capitalist in the business, and Mr. Hardy cannot imagine a more thorough review than he has done. But this is his first foray into the territory of a trade secrets problem, and he is perplexed by the fact that there is no way to examine whether a trade secrets violation is likely to occur, because it is uncertain both how much ingenuity the entrepreneurs have (although in the past they have not lacked for a wealth of new ideas) and what the trade secrets *are* that cannot be utilized. He is now facing the fact that his consultants could not have known whether a Globe trade secret was being exploited. Every consultant said there was the *potential* for the entrepreneurs to make thin film coatings through—as one recent court opinion put it—"skillful variations of general processes known to the particular trade,"[1] but no one could say for sure whether the potential would be actualized.

Mr. Hardy's legal consultants had supplied him with the standard legal definition and analysis of trade secrets, which his consultant report-sheet summarizes as follows:

> A trade secret consists of any formula, device, pattern, or compilation of information used in business that gives one an opportunity to obtain advantage over competitors who do not know or use it. It is not a secret of any sort, but a process or device for continuous use in the operation of the business. An exact definition of trade secrets is not possible, but there are factors that can be considered in determining whether something is a trade secret: general knowledge, employee knowledge, the adequacy of protective guarding, the value of the information, the amount of money expended in development of the secret, and ease of acquisition or duplication. An employee in possession of confidential information that could damage the economic interests of an employer if disclosed is under an obligation of confidentiality that remains in force when the employee leaves the firm and takes employment elsewhere. However, under common law it is not a breach of any obligation owed to an employer to plan for a new competitive venture while still employed, even though the employee has an opportunity to observe (what will later be) a competitor's secrets, and even though the employee may leave with a wealth of experience in and knowledge about the competitor's processes, products, research, and financial matters.

Mr. Hardy sees that a sharp distinction is made in this legal material between a company that *owns* a formula, device, or process that has

---

[1] *Aetna Building Co.* v. *West*, 39 Cal. 2d 198, at 206.

been *disclosed* in confidence to one or more employees and a company whose formula has been *developed by those employees while employed at the company.* A typical pattern in some of the more innovative industries is that employees are instrumental in creating or advancing a formula, device, or process through their own ingenuity and skills. The more an employee creates or otherwise improves the confidential information or property, the more the employee seems to have a right to use it elsewhere, and the less an employer seems to have a right to claim sole possession. Mr. Hardy's reading is that the entrepreneurs who came to him for funding were, and still are, in precisely this latter circumstance.

Thus, it seems unfair to the entrepreneurs to keep them from starting Rubbernex merely because their former employer is intimidating them from starting a new venture. As Mr. Hardy sees it, these employees have several types of obligation to Globe: contractual obligations based on their employment contracts, avoiding conflicts of interest such as remaining employed by the firm that will become a competitor of the firm being planned, and making sure that the new venture will use independently developed competitive technologies, thus avoiding violations of trade secrets, patents, proprietary designs, and the like.

Although there is some disagreement and ambiguity, Mr. Hardy's reference checks and technical consultants say that these conditions have been at least minimally satisfied in this case. They all point out that the law of trade secrets is amorphous, conceptually muddy, and formed in a patchwork from a number of different areas of law. The law tries to foster innovation and progress without leaving firms the victims of faithless employees or placing employees in a situation of servitude. An employer has a right to its intellectual property, but the employee also has a right to seek gainful employment that requires his or her abilities. If employees could be prevented by the intimidation of lawsuits from moving from one firm to another, the growth and spread of technology could be stilled.

Mr. Hardy is impressed by this argument and conclusion. He is leaning toward funding the entrepreneurs even though he senses that two lengthy lawsuits are now a near certainty, one against the former Globe employees for misappropriation of trade secrets and the second against HH Ventures for a failure of due care. Mr. Hardy denies the latter charge because it implies that he performed an inadequate due diligence review prior to an investment. He is convinced that this charge is groundless.

CHAPTER 2

The Consumer, Customer, Client, and Competitor

INTRODUCTION   The general subject of "business, society, and ethics" reminds us that business has a multitude of social relationships, most of which involve the obligations of some parties and the rights of others. Just as we studied the relationship between business and its employees in the first chapter, so in this chapter we shall explore the relationships between a business and its consumers, customers, clients, and competitors. In particular, we shall encounter cases requiring reflection on the obligations business has to advertise its products truthfully, to sell products at reasonable and clearly identified prices, to market only "quality" products, to provide information about products to its purchasers, to avoid profiting from inside information that gives an unfair advantage, and to avoid sharp practices (shrewd practices bordering on the dishonest) that intrude an unfair advantage in a competitive situation.

The circumstances under which markets are created and goods are sold and delivered are notoriously complex, yet few would deny that advertising is the primary instrument of marketing—unrivalled by the use of sales representatives and by other sales techniques. Misleading or information-deficient advertising has frequently been denounced, but the moral concepts underlying these denunciations have seldom been carefully examined. What is a deceptive or misleading advertisement? Is it, for example, deceptive or misleading to advertise presweetened children's cereals as "nutritious" or as "building strong bodies"? Are such advertisements forms of lying? Are they coercive or manipulative, especially when children are the primary targets or when people are led to make purchases they do not need (or would not have made were it not for the advertising)? If so, is the coercion or manipulation related to the deception? For example, if Listerine advertisements about killing germs manipulate listeners into purchasing the mouthwash, does it follow that consumers have been deceived?

In light of certain theories of the free marketplace, can there be unjustifiable advertising or unjustifiable competition at all: If markets shift in competitive struggles to meet consumer, customer, or client demands, then is not the purchaser king, and is not the role of advertising simply to provide information about the products that consumers demand? Or is this depiction merely a convenient fiction that has crept into beliefs about the market? Similar problems are found in various other marketing practices. Even so simple a problem as the way counter goods are displayed in a grocery store can raise moral problems of deception and manipulation. The case of commissions at Brock Mason Brokerage in this chapter raises deeper and less obvious problems. It is a study of the marketing of investment opportunities. Here we encounter a complex set of relationships that may contain problems of conflict of interest as well as problems of deception and manipulation.

One major question about most advertising and other marketing practices denounced as misleading is whether they can be justified by the "rules of the game" that prevail in business. Some have argued that marketing is analogous to activities in which we all engage—for example, purchasing a house or bargaining over the price of an overpriced rug in a store. Here bluffing, overstatement, and enticement are expected and invite similar countermoves. Whereas abuse and contempt are not tolerated, deception is—so long as the rules of the game are known and the players are in a roughly equal bargaining position. This toleration suggests, on the one hand, that deceptive practices and sharp practices need not be unjustifiable. On the other hand, there clearly are limits to deception, manipulation, and cunning maneuvers that take advantage of a competitor's misfortune. For example, harmful products cannot simply be marketed as if benign—a problem explored in the Rely tampon case in this chapter.

According to the rules-of-the-game model, there are more-or-less established, well-delineated procedures for marketing a product or making a business move; consumers, clients, competitors, and customers are well acquainted with these rules of the game, and they are generally in an equal bargaining position. While ads abusing subliminal persuasion or ads inherently offensive to large segments of the population are not permitted, it might be argued that sexual suggestion in ads pitched to adults, strong pitches to young children in toy advertisements, and sharp practices carried out under open rules of law are simply parts of the game. This defense of prevailing business practice has its advocates, but remains controversial.

The Federal Trade Commission and others take the view that the rules of acceptable advertising encompass more than the mere creation of a market, because advertising is the dissemination of information from which those contacted make an informed choice. If they are misled in the attempt to make an intelligent choice or are enticed into a choice by deception, the advertising cannot be justified—no matter what the implicit rules of the game may be. The FTC has therefore placed strict regulations on some industries that produce potentially harmful products, cigarettes being the best known example, as explored in Chapter 4 in the case of banning cigarette ads.

The two cases in the advertising section of this chapter show how the government and consumer protection groups focus on the consumers' *response* to advertising and on its social effects, rather than on the *intention* of those who create the advertising. By contrast, those who defend controversial advertising focus more on the intentions of advertising agencies and manufacturers in marketing a product—*viz.*, the intent to sell a "good product." These different emphases complicate the issues, especially since a product marketed with good intentions can nonetheless be misleading or have bad effects.

Another complicating factor is that not everyone has the same threshold of deception: What deceives one person can be laughed off by another. As federal agencies have pointed out, the so-called "reasonable person" and the "ignorant person" are both persons to whom business relates with its advertising and marketing techniques. The rules-of-the-game defense of advertising and marketing practices has this same problem, because how skillfully a person understands and deals with the rules of a game is also relative to individual resistance and acceptance. The abilities of children to grasp the nature of advertising and to distance themselves from its appeal is a celebrated issue featured in the Kellogg cereals case.

One related and widely discussed issue is the extent to which a consumer's, customer's, or client's desires and needs originate with the person, and the extent to which those desires and needs are *created* by advertising. Debates on this subject are hard to assess, because our desires and needs commonly derive from social causes and conventions. Moreover, even if a desire or need for a product does not *originate* from a person's choice, it does not follow that it is an *unfortunate* desire or that it has not been *freely* accepted. One who trades in an old car and buys a new Chrysler because of the advertised rebate may have had a desire stimulated, or even created, but this cause may be neither manipulative nor regrettable. These debates are especially heated when a product is thought to be harmful—as some have alleged presweetened children's cereals, cigarettes, risky forms of investment, and various automobiles are.

A different but important perspective on all the issues thus far discussed is that *quality control* is the true problem with products. If cereals and cupcakes were certified as nutritious and free of harmful artificial coloring before being allowed on the market, then we would care much less about what is conveyed by advertisements or sales representatives. This is a call for higher qualitative standards in industry and regulatory branches of government as a means to resolve these issues of consumer protection. ("Consumerism" and "consumer advocates" have generally focused more on quality control than on marketing practices.) Higher standards would also protect manufacturers who produce quality products in the first place from those who produce inferior ones. There are, however, liberty issues at stake—*e.g.,* the freedom to put a new "junk food" on the market may be jeopardized (in theory there would no longer be junk foods), the freedom to buy cheap but substandard products would be lost (because they could not be marketed), and risky forms of investment might be banned altogether.

Finally, on occasion, a consumer, client, customer, member of a board of directors, or officer of a corporation obtains "inside information" about developments in a company and begins to trade in the stock of the company. Insider trading is regulated by the Securities and Exchange Commission, which operates on the principle that it is illegal to trade on nonpublic, financially useful information that has been misappropriated or secured by a breach of fiduciary duty. It is forbidden by law for a person to use information obtained on the inside to buy or sell securities or to pass the information on to others so that they might benefit. However, there is moral ambiguity surrounding insider trading, and not every authority considers it unfair. Several scholars have argued that permitting insider trades would actually make the securities markets more efficient and would involve no moral violation. The small-time insider trading case in this chapter provides a common circumstance in which this thesis might be tested.

Kellogg Cereals and Children's Television Advertising

> It is both unfair and deceptive . . . to address televised advertising for any product to young children who are still too young to understand the selling purpose of, or otherwise comprehend or evaluate, the advertising. . . . The classical justification for a free market, and for the advertising that goes with it, assumes at least a rough balance of information, sophistication and power between buyer and seller. . . . In the present situation, it is ludicrous to suggest that any such balance exists between an advertiser who is willing to spend many thousands of dollars for a single 30-second spot, and a child who is incapable of understanding that the spot has a selling intent, and instead trustingly believes that the spot merely provides advice about one of the good things in life.[1]

The above quotation from a 1978 Federal Trade Commission (FTC) staff report presents the heart of an argument advanced by the FTC staff and others against televised advertising directed to children for presweetened, ready-to-eat cereals. This report accompanied a set of proposed regulatory rules that would:

(a) Ban all televised advertising for any product which is directed to, or seen by, audiences composed of a significant proportion of children who are too young to understand the selling purpose of, or otherwise comprehend or evaluate, the advertising;

(b) Ban televised advertising directed to, or seen by, audiences composed of a significant proportion of older children for sugared food products, the consumption of which poses the most serious dental health risks;

(c) Require that televised advertising directed to, or seen by, audiences composed of a significant proportion of older children for sugared food products not included in paragraph (b) be balanced by nutritional and/or health disclosures funded by advertisers.[2]

[1] FTC, "Staff Report on Television Advertising to Children" (February 1978), pp. 27, 29.

[2] *Ibid.*, pp. 345–346.

This case was prepared by Linda Kern, Martha W. Elliott, and Tom L. Beauchamp and revised by Anna Pinedo. **Not to be duplicated without permission of the holder of the copyright,** © 1989 Tom L. Beauchamp.

This proposal on children's advertising was triggered by a petition with a specific intent. In 1977, Action for Children's Television (ACT) and the Center for Science in the Public Interest (CSPI) jointly petitioned the FTC. They proposed a ban on the advertising of sugary, in-between-meal (snack) foods for children. ACT and CSPI got more than they requested when the above-mentioned 1978 staff report called for a ban on all children's advertising. This discussion, however, has a prior history.

HISTORY

Circa 1970. A U.S. Senate consumer subcommittee opened hearings on the nutritional value of ready-to-eat cereals in 1970 that reflected a growing national concern about nutrition. Two separate issues then under discussion set the context of later debate: First, does the food industry have an obligation to market a nutritious product? Second, even if a product is highly nutritious, what limits should be placed on advertising this product to children?

Robert Choate, Jr., President of the Council on Children, Media, and Merchandising, figured prominently in the 1970 hearings. He made headlines with his nutritional ranking of sixty leading cold cereals. He said, "I watch TV commercials on Saturday morning and get really mad. The image projected for these cereals is that they give kids muscles and energy so they can catch every football pass. But read the nutrients on the boxes, and there is little to support these claims."[3] Although his criteria for ranking the nutritional value of cereals rested on *vitamin fortification* and not on *sugar content* (later a central concern), his ranking system may have had significant impact. Top executives of the cereal companies consulted their technologists, who had already advocated nutritionally improved formulae. Within eighteen months of Choate's first Senate testimony, twenty-six of forty criticized cereals had been reformulated.

At these 1970 Senate cereal hearings, Dr. Frederick Stare, Chairman of the Department of Nutrition, Harvard University School of Public Health, and Dr. W. H. Sebrell, Jr., of the Institute of Human Nutrition at Columbia University, gave testimony. They agreed with the cereal industry that cereal with "milk and sugar" is a nutritionally adequate food and that evaluating the nutritional content of cereal without milk is unfair.[4] Dr. Jean Mayer, then Harvard Professor of Nutrition, agreed with industry experts that "taken in the whole breakfast context, cereals did make an important contribution." Nevertheless, Mayer continued, "There are wide differences in nutritional value between various types

---

[3] "A Gadfly Buzzes around the Table," *Business Week* (September 26, 1970), p. 116.

[4] Earl A. Molander, "Marketing Ready-to-Eat Breakfast Cereals at the Kellogg Company," in *Responsive Capitalism: Case Studies in Corporate Social Conduct* (New York: McGraw-Hill Book Co., 1980), p. 130.

of cereals, and these differences could be easily avoided if modern technology and nutritional knowledge were used to upgrade weaker products."[5] Later Mayer was quoted as saying that "the nutritional value of a food varies inversely with the amount of money spent to advertise it."[6]

1973–1977. In 1973, a second Congressional investigation focused on children's presweetened, ready-to-eat cereals. This time the Senate Select Committee on Nutrition and Human Needs addressed the twin issues of nutritional value and advertising fairness. Some of the 1970 testimonies were reiterated. Action for Children's Television presented evidence that a child watching a particular Boston station from 7:00 A.M. to 2:00 P.M. on Saturday, October 28, 1972, would have seen sixty-seven commercials for sugary foods, including ready-to-eat cereals. Representatives of the cereal companies, including Kellogg and General Mills, testified at the hearings.[7] Executive Vice-President of the Kellogg Company William E. LaMothe stated: "Our company is very conscious of the fact that social responsibilities go hand-in-hand with business responsibilities. The steps that we are taking to contribute to the improvement of the understanding of the need for breakfast and a complete and adequate breakfast reflect this consciousness."[8]

In March of 1973, the FDA introduced the standards for recommended daily allowances, replacing the older minimum daily requirement. The cereal companies had to reset their standards at this more stringent level. Also in 1973, FTC Chairman Louis Engleman set up a task force in the Division of Special Projects to investigate the issues of children's advertising further. During his term of office, the FTC staff was granted the use of a compulsory process that gave them the right to subpoena cereal companies for access to their market research data and thus to examine their advertising strategies.

In 1974, the FTC staff proposed a guide for advertising that was rejected in 1976. However, in 1977, the debate flourished again. Renewed interest in children's advertising, especially in regard to presweetened, ready-to-eat cereals, was sparked by the FTC's unexpected reaction to the ACT and CSPI petitions.

1977–1978. In April of 1977, ACT and CSPI presented their petitions to the FTC. These proposals included the call for a ban on the advertise-

---

[5] *Ibid.,* p. 131.

[6] John Culkin, "Selling to Children: Fair Play in TV Commercials," *Hastings Center Report* 8, no. 3 (June 1978), p. 7.

[7] Molander, "Marketing Ready-to-Eat Breakfast Cereals," p. 135.

[8] Part 5—TV Advertising of Food to Children, Hearings before the Senate Select Committee on Nutrition and Human Needs, 93rd Cong., 1st sess., 1973, p. 258, as quoted by Molander, "Marketing Ready-to-Eat Breakfast Cereals."

ment of sugary, in-between-meal (snack) foods to children. Arguments were also presented against *all* foods with a high sugar content, including some cereals, and also against the practice of advertising to children *in general*. Shortly after the publication of these two petitions, in November 1977, Kellogg ran a newspaper advertisement countering the implication that presweetened cereals are not nutritious, or are possibly harmful for young children. A series of "facts" for which it claimed empirical support included:

1. Ready-sweetened cereals are highly nutritious foods.
2. Ready-to-eat cereals do not increase tooth decay in children.
3. Ready-to-eat cereal eaters skip breakfast less than non–ready-to-eat cereal eaters.
4. There is no more sugar in a one-ounce serving of a ready-sweetened cereal than in an apple or banana or in a serving of orange juice.
5. The sugars in cereals and the sugars in fruit are chemically very similar.
6. Ready-to-eat cereals provide only 2 percent of the total consumption of cane and beet sugars in the U.S.
7. On the average, when children eat ready-sweetened cereals as a part of breakfast, the nutritional content of that breakfast is greater than when they eat a non–ready-to-eat cereal breakfast.
8. Most ready-to-eat cereals are consumed with milk.
9. On the average when children eat ready-sweetened cereals as part of breakfast, consumption of fat and cholesterol is less than when they eat a non–ready-to-eat cereal breakfast.
10. The per capita sugar consumption in the U.S. has remained practically unchanged for the last fifty years.[9]

Three months later, in February of 1978, the FTC staff issued the aforementioned report, proposing an all-encompassing ban on children's advertising. This 350-page document included concerns about the effects of advertising on children, and about the nutritional value of the product advertised. This report described the preparation of commercials directed to children and the selling techniques they employ. The following approaches were mentioned:

1. Magical promises that a product will build muscles or improve athletic performance.
2. The chase or tug of war sequence in which one character tries to take a product away from another.
3. The use of magic, singing, and dancing.
4. The use of super heroes to entice children.
5. The voice of authority.

[9] Molander, "Marketing Ready-to-Eat Breakfast Cereals," App. 11-1.

6. The voices of children agreeing with the announcer.
7. Depictions of children outperforming adults.
8. Animation.
9. Peer group acceptance appeals.
10. Selling by characters who also appear in programming.

The report attacked eighteen commercials in particular. Half of these were for presweetened, ready-to-eat cereals. The following is a list of those cereals:

1. Count Chocula and Frankenberry
2. Lucky Charms
3. Cookie Crisp
4. Crazy Cow
5. Post Pebbles (Fruity and Cocoa)
6. Cocoa Puffs
7. Corny Snaps
8. Super Sugar Crisp
9. Honeycomb

This first staff report effectively argued for a complete ban on children's advertising. Three years later, in 1981, the FTC staff issued a second staff report. The interim period consisted of hearings, exchanges of papers, interviewing of witnesses, and—when the process was completed—600,000 pages of records.

1980. Public attention shifted away from regulation of children's television advertising in 1980. The FTC Improvements Act passed in May 1980 effectively prohibited the FTC from promulgating children's advertising rules on any basis other than that of preventing deceptive advertisement. But on March 31, 1981, the FTC issued its (presumably) final staff report and recommendations concerning children's advertising. Their recommendation was "that the [Federal Trade] Commission terminate proceedings for the promulgation of a trade regulation rule on children's advertising." They called for a halt on any further attempt to ban children's advertising. The following excerpt from this second report illustrates the degree to which they revised their initial statements:

> The record developed during the rulemaking proceeding adequately supports the following conclusions regarding child-oriented television advertising and young children six years and under: (1) they place indiscriminate trust in televised advertising messages; (2) they do not understand the persuasive bias in television advertising; and (3) the techniques, focus and themes used in child-oriented television advertising enhance the appeal of the advertising message and the advertised product. Consequently,

young children do not possess the cognitive ability to evaluate adequately child-oriented television advertising. Despite the fact that these conclusions can be drawn from the evidence, the record establishes that the only effective remedy would be a ban on all advertisements oriented toward young children, and such a ban, as a practical matter, cannot be implemented. Because of this remedial impediment, there is no need to determine whether or not advertising oriented toward young children is deceptive.[10] Staff's recommendation for this portion of the case is that the proceeding be terminated.[11]

This statement was actually a reiteration of findings put forth in the initial report. Most of the original *claims* were again accepted. For "practical" reasons, however, they recommended that "the proceedings be terminated." The "practical matter" that prohibited the FTC from banning children's advertising was two-fold. First, dental research has not been able to positively identify which foods are cariogenic, or cavity producing. There are too many unknown factors involved in cavity formation to place a ban on any particular product or set of products. Second, although children *under* six cannot understand the intent of a commercial message, children *over* six often can. To ban the advertising to one group would automatically affect the other older group. For these practical reasons, then, the FTC terminated all investigative proceedings associated with children's advertising.

In 1984 the Federal Communications Commission (FCC) eliminated its guidelines on children's advertising. The FCC had maintained "voluntary" guidelines that limited the number of advertisements during children's shows to 9.5 minutes each hour on Saturday and Sunday and 12 minutes an hour on other days. Stations that failed to comply with the guidelines were subject to FCC review.

A three-judge panel of the U.S. Appeals Court later reopened the issue of regulating children's advertising. In June 1987 the court ruled that the FCC had not sufficiently justified its policy change eliminating the established guidelines. The FCC announced in October 1987 that it was conducting new inquiries on the issue of regulating children's advertising to assess the need for new guidelines. It planned to consider new developments such as cartoon action shows based on popular children's products and interactive video and television programs.

Representative Edward Markey (D., Mass.), Chairman of the House Commerce Committee's telecommunications subcommittee, has begun hearings on children's television and is pressing for a bill to reimpose advertising guidelines. The FCC has been petitioned for a reconsideration of this issue by Action for Children's Television. The agency is actively

---

[10] Consumers Union of the U.S., Inc., and Committee on Children's Television, C-9, pp. 1–46, quoted in *FTC Final Staff Report and Recommendation in the Matter of Children's Advertising,* 43 Fed. Reg. 17,967, TRR No. 215-60 (1981), p. 3.

[11] *FTC Final Staff Report,* p. 3.

considering the promulgation of time limits on advertising or, as an alternative, the creation of "advisory boards" comprised of educators and psychologists to "elevate the consciousness of broadcasters as to the impact of commercials on children."[12]

TWO MAJOR ISSUES

Two issues have been present throughout the debate between the FTC and the cereal companies. The first is whether the product (for our purposes, cereal) has significant nutritional value. But even if a product ranks high on a nutritional scale, a second consideration remains: Is the practice of advertising to children inherently unfair?

1. The Adequacy of Nutrition. The ACT and CSPI petitions, along with the FTC staff reports, all attacked children's cereals on the basis of high sugar content. Quoting the staff of the Senate Select Committee on Nutrition and Human Needs, the ACT petition states:

> [Sugar calories] increase requirements for certain vitamins, like thiamin, which are needed [for the body] to metabolize carbohydrates. They may increase the need for trace minerals . . . as well. Thus, a greater burden is placed on the other components of the diet to contribute all the necessary "nutrient density" to compensate for the emptiness of sugar calories.[13]

The initial 1978 staff report presented expert testimony from several fields on the nutritional value of ready-to-eat cereals. The following statement from this report illustrates its general conclusions:[14]

> Dr. Juan Navia, a nutritional biochemist who is senior scientist at the Institute of Dental Research, University of Alabama at Birmingham, has observed that: "Foods compete for space in the stomachs of mankind. Every time a person selects a sugar rich food, he does it at the expense of other foods, and these other foods are *always* better as a source of vitamins and minerals than the sugar that replaces them."[15]

These other foods are "always better" because sugar contributes calories to the human diet, but is not otherwise nutritious.[16] This is the point

[12] Bob Davis, "FCC Is Planning to Launch an Inquiry into Tougher Rules for Children's TV," *Wall Street Journal,* October 8, 1987, p. 34, and "FCC Takes Second Look at Children's Advertising," *Broadcasting,* October 26, 1987, p. 54.

[13] Senate Select Committee on Nutrition and Human Needs, 93rd Cong., 2d sess., *National Nutrition Policy Study, Report and Recommendation* 9 (1974), quoted in ACT petition to the FTC (1977), p. 4.

[14] FTC, "Staff Report on Television Advertising to Children," *loc. cit.*

[15] Senate Select Committee on Nutrition and Human Needs, 93rd Cong., 1st sess., *Hearings on Nutrition Education, Part 3, TV Advertising of Food to Children,* Mar. 5, 1973.

[16] U.S. Department of Agriculture, *Nutritional Value of Foods, Home and Garden Bulletin* no. 72 (April 1977), p. 24.

of the phrase "empty calories." The energy content of a calorie of sugar is, by definition, the same as the energy content of a calorie of any other food.

While children need calories, they have no need to get them in a form devoid of other nutrients. Ivalee McCord, Chairman of the Child Development and Family Relations Section of the American Economics Association, has put the matter as follows:

> At a time when a body is growing at a more rapid rate and body structures are developing, the need for quality food is crucial. There is no room in the diet for "empty calories"—those represented by most sugar-coated and snack foods. At this time children need balanced diets providing the nutrients needed for growth.[17]

The Life Sciences Research Office (LSRO) of the Federation of American Societies for Experimental Biology has warned, in a report to the Food and Drug Administration, that at present levels of sugar consumption, "It is likely that some individuals may eat enough to exclude adequate amounts of other foods that furnish required nutrients."[18]

That warning has to be read in conjunction with the theory that sugar consumption is high and rising fast among children. As Dr. Jean Mayer has observed: "Particularly when you consider that a large part of the population eats relatively small amounts of sugar, it means we have a lot of children where sugar becomes a gigantic proportion [of the diet]."[19]

With a few exceptions, it is not claimed by manufacturers that the sugared snack foods and candies promoted to children on television have any nutritional value apart from calories. But claims are made that presweetened cereals are "highly nutritious."[20] Manufacturers point out that most, if not all, of their cereals have been fortified by adding vitamins and minerals. This was not always the case. Fortification began in the early 1970s, following congressional hearings in which it was pointed out that the nutritional value of the unfortified cereals was

---

[17] Letter to ACT, Feb. 23, 1972. To similar effect, *see* Arlen, *The Science of Nutrition* 253 (2d ed. 1977).

[18] The *LSRO Report* (*Dextrose*) and the *LSRO Report* (*Sucrose*) were commissioned by the Food and Drug Administration and submitted within the past two years by the LSRO of the Federation of American Societies for Experimental Biology. The full titles are *Evaluation of the Health Aspects of Sucrose as a Food Ingredient* (1976) and *Evaluation of the Health Aspects of Corn Sugar (Dextrose), Corn Syrup and Invert Sugar as Food Ingredients* (1976).

[19] Senate Select Committee, *Hearings on Nutrition Education, Part 3, TV Advertising of Food to Children.*

[20] This phrase was used by the president of the Kellogg Company in threatening to sue the American Dental Association for defamation of these products. See *Washington Post*, December 2, 1971.

essentially nil.[21] The manufacturers contend that some children are reluctant to eat breakfast at all, and that some sugar in these cereals is a necessary attraction in order to get them to swallow the now-added vitamins and minerals.[22]

In contrast to the manufacturers' position, Mayer has argued that "in spite of their being enriched with some vitamins and iron, the total effect [of these cereals] is one of inadequate nutrition (deficient, in particular, in trace minerals . . .)."[23] Dr. Mayer added to this assessment that: "Cereals, some of which are extremely highly processed so that their *intrinsic nutrient content is very low,* particularly when combined with sugar, which is the prototype of 'empty calories,' are *not a complete food even if fortified with eight or 10 vitamins.*"[24]

2. *Fairness of Advertising.* Advertisers and their critics agree that children's advertising should not be deceptive. However, they disagree over their classification of material as deceptive or misleading to young children. The dispute is complicated by the many unanswered questions that remain. For example, there are questions about the *effect* of television advertising on children; about the ability of children to *process cognitively* the advertising information; about the ability of children to *discriminate* between the content of the program and the commercial; and about the ability of children to *resist* persuasive appeals even if they understand them to be commercial in character. While research in this area is relatively recent and still somewhat sparse, a 1977 National Science Foundation (NSF) study, *Research on the Effects of Television Advertising on Children,* came to two major conclusions on these questions. The first conclusion was that television commercials *do* affect children:

> Children have been shown to acquire specific product information presented in food commercials. There is also preliminary evidence indicating that information about the nutritional content and value of food products can be effectively communicated to children both within commercials and in brief (5-second) slide presentations. Studies have also demonstrated shifts in children's beliefs about advertised foods following their exposure to specific commercial messages. These may include incorrect as well as correct beliefs about promoted food products.

[21] *Hearings on Dry Cereal before Consumers Subcommittee, Senate Commerce Committee,* 91st Cong., 2nd sess. (1970); Robert Choate, "The Sugar Coated Children's Hour," *Nation* (January 31, 1972), p. 146.

[22] Kellogg's data, however, show that fewer children (5%) than adults (9%) skip breakfast, and that fewer consumers of *non*sugared cereals (5%) than of sugared cereals (7%) skip breakfast. See Kellogg, *Breakfast and Nutrition* (undated pamphlet), and the presentation of Dr. Gary Costley, Kellogg's Director of Nutrition, before the Commission on November 22, 1977.

[23] Senate Select Committee, *Hearings on Nutrition Education, Part 3, TV Advertising of Food to Children.*

[24] *Ibid.,* emphasis added.

The second conclusion of the NSF study is that specific advertising practices—such as wording—affect the child's ability to understand and remember the message. Some have argued that these problems of comprehension are at the center of the problem:

> The important question . . . is not so much whether children are influenced by commercials, as whether whatever influence there is occurs because of failure to comprehend the commercial appeal. For example, there is little evidence that children comprehend typical commercial disclaimers much before the age of 7. . . .
> However, the relationship between comprehension of intent to persuade and resistance to persuasive appeals remains uncertain.[25]

Advertisers and critics also dispute the extent of an advertiser's responsibility to the child viewer. Both parties recognize that children are not "capable of acting as rational self-interested consumers" because they lack a complete understanding of the "concepts of time, money and self" necessary to evaluate the information being presented to them by advertisers.[26] However, advertisers deny any obligation to take the child's limitations and inclinations into account in formulating their marketing approaches.

John Culkin concentrates on the unfairness of manipulating children as a means of selling to their parents. Culkin quotes an advertisement that appeared in *Broadcasting* magazine soliciting advertising for a Boston television station. The ad was entitled "Kid Power is Coming to Boston." It read as follows:

> If you're selling, Charlie's mom is buying. But you've got to sell Charlie first.
> His allowance is only 50 cents a week but his buying power is an American phenomenon. He's not only tight with his Mom, but he has a way with his Dad, his Grandma and Aunt Harriet, too.
> When Charlie sees something he likes, he usually gets it.[27]

Culkin questions the morality of an industry that would spend half a billion dollars a year on TV advertising directed at children in order to sell to their parents. "Quite apart from the question of the real value of the advertised product, what is the propriety of the sponsor contesting the parent for control of the child? . . . Parents have enough difficulty

[25] Donald F. Roberts and Christine M. Bachen, "Mass Communication Effects," *Annual Review of Psychology* 32 (1981), section on effects on children and adolescents, pp. 336, 338.

[26] Lynda Sharp Paine, "Children as Consumers: An Ethical Evaluation of Children's Advertising," *Business and Professional Ethics Journal* 3, nos. 3 and 4 (Spring/Summer 1984), pp. 123–125.

[27] Culkin, "Selling to Children," p. 7.

in helping their children make wise choices without skewing the process by $500 million worth of counter-persuasion."[28]

There is empirical evidence that children influence their parents' purchases. A study done by the Harvard Business School found that "5 to 7 year olds successfully influenced parental purchases of cereals (88% of the time), snack foods (52%), candy (40%), and soft drinks (38%)." A survey of almost 600 mothers found that 75 percent of the women chose products and brands requested by their children.[29] However, there is still no evidence directly linking food commercials to the actual nutritional status of children.

Culkin points out that in fairness to the cereal industry, the broadcasters, and the advertising agencies, it should be acknowledged that parents and schools have a responsibility to prevent the abuse of television by children, as well as the abuse of children by television. Culkin maintains that "even the best of all possible programming does not justify the four hours a day spent by the average American in front of the TV set. In our less than perfect world, the uncomfortable fact is that we have to reform ourselves as well as the networks."[30]

The cereal industry and its advertising agencies contend that claims of unfair and deceptive practices are unwarranted and that the cereal industry is being singled out for criticism on an issue that involves numerous products, especially candy and soft drinks. In particular, opponents of federal regulation argue:

1. that advertising to children is not unfair or deceptive;
2. that sugar in foods has been directly linked to dental caries, but not to many alleged health problems;
3. that the conflict between parents and children is an inevitable part of growing up and would not disappear if Frosted Flakes and Milky Way bars were banned from TV.[31]

Opponents of proposed constraints on advertising also contend that First Amendment rights are at stake. Peter McSpadden, president of a large advertising agency, sees the primary issue as censorship: "The question is, do we have a right to market a product to a particular group—in this case, children—and does another group have the right to say, 'no, you can't'?"[32] Members of Congress also have taken seriously

[28] *Ibid.,* pp. 8–9.

[29] As quoted from Linda McJ. Micheli, "Kellogg Company: Sugar, Children, and T.V. Advertising" (Boston, Mass.: Harvard Business School, 1979), p. 4.

[30] Culkin, "Selling to Children," p. 9.

[31] See Micheli, "Kellogg Company," p. 6. Craig Shulstad of General Mills helped us formulate the wording here, which modifies Micheli's wording.

[32] *Ibid.,* p. 7.

the censorship issue, with its implied threat to liberty. In 1978 the Senate Appropriations Committee threatened to cut off all FTC funding if the commission continued its inquiry into these issues. The majority report of the Senate committee took the position that "if the question of how many cavities for how much freedom is to be considered seriously at all, then it should be done with full Constitutional process and not as a matter of regulatory rulings."[33]

KELLOGG'S RESPONSE TO THE ISSUE OF CHILDREN'S ADVERTISING

Kellogg is the nation's largest manufacturer of ready-to-eat cereals, with more than 40 percent of U.S. sales and over $1.7 billion in 1978 annual sales (38.9 percent in 1982, with over $3.2 billion in sales). General Foods and General Mills, the next largest producers, have a *combined* total sales figure equal to Kellogg's (37.07 percent in 1982). The Kellogg Company has been active over the years in attempting to refute the charges leveled at its cereals in the areas of nutrition and advertising.

The Nutritional Value of Kellogg Cereals. As early as 1971, the Kellogg Company formally published an ambitious corporate nutrition policy. However, it cautioned in the policy that "consumer acceptability of our products in flavor, texture and appearance is essential if they are to make any nutritional contribution." In early 1973 the Kellogg Company, along with General Mills, testified before the Senate Select Committee on Nutrition and Human Needs. Dr. Gary Costley, Kellogg's Director of Nutrition, argued (1) that "only a small part of a child's sugar intake comes from sweetened breakfast cereals"; (2) that "a normal serving of most canned fruits contained far more sugar" than a serving of cereal; (3) that presweetened cereals do not cause a child to become "hooked" on sugar; and (4) that "research studies show no correlation between new dental caries and the amount of pre-sweetened cereal consumed."[34]

In October 1981, the Consumer Service Department of Kellogg printed and distributed a pamphlet entitled "Cereal Fortification," which followed their 1980 monograph *Ready-to-Eat Cereals and Nutrition.*[35] The pamphlet provided a detailed analysis or "nutrient profile" of their "Corn Flakes" and "Sugar Frosted Flakes." The pamphlet's purpose was to prove that Kellogg cereals, as presently fortified and when used with milk, easily provide the daily nutrient intake recommended by nutritionists.

[33] *Ibid.,* p. 6.

[34] Molander, "Marketing Ready-to-Eat Breakfast Cereals," p. 136.

[35] The pamphlet argued that in 1955, Kellogg's "Special K" was introduced to provide higher levels of essential nutrients, and in 1966 "Product 19" had been introduced for the same reason.

In 1971, Kellogg's nutritional staff and marketing department worked in conjunction on two projects. First, in the process of marketing, Kellogg strove to retain as much as they could of the look, taste, and "mouthfeel" of the original cereal, while continuing to refortify it. Second, the nutritional and advertising staffs carefully examined their advertising to ensure that all nutritional claims were substantiated. In conjunction with these efforts, Kellogg also initiated a "Stick Up for Breakfast" educational program. This included television spots urging children to eat a balanced breakfast. By 1972, Kellogg and all the major cereal companies had introduced 100 percent natural cereals into their product lines.[36]

Kellogg's Advertising Practices. The Kellogg Company has worked tirelessly to refute charges that its advertising makes false nutritional claims. Kellogg issued a pamphlet on "Advertising" in late 1979. In this pamphlet the company argued as follows:

> Kellogg's has been recognized an unprecedented seven times by *Family Health Magazine* for excellence in nutritional advertising. . . .
> For years we have placed great emphasis on creating honest and tasteful advertising for youngsters with messages that convey the inherent nutritional value of our products. We present these messages in a way that is not only informative and interesting, but also appropriate for a child's level of understanding.
> Our advertising serves not only as a product selling tool, it also stresses the importance of starting the day with a nutritious breakfast. Since 1973 Kellogg cereal advertisements for both children and adults have shown cereal and milk being eaten as a part of a complete breakfast. Our advertising improves a child's awareness of the need for a complete, nutritious breakfast.

The Consumer Service Department at Kellogg has not directed the same level of effort at charges that their advertising practices are an *unfair* means of influencing children. The views of Seymour Banks, Vice-President of the advertising agency that handles the Kellogg account, have been widely quoted:

> Even if a child is deceived by an ad at age four, what harm is done? He will grow out of it. He is in the process of learning to make his own decisions. . . . Even if, as many psychologists claim, a child perceives children in TV advertising as friends, not actors selling them something, what's the harm? All a parent has to say is, "Shut up or I'll belt you."[37]

Kellogg believes that the products in question are nutritious and that children would be worse off if they were not available and not advertised.

---

[36] Molander, "Marketing Ready-to-Eat Breakfast Cereals," p. 132.

[37] Micheli, "Kellogg Company," p. 7. Banks is not an officer of the Kellogg Company.

William E. LaMothe, President of Kellogg at the time of the proposed FTC ban on advertising, commented:

> We try to construct our commercials so that they can be entertaining, and have a message. We're convinced that if we could get every youngster in the country to eat a ready-to-eat cereal—the nutritional information we have says they would have a better diet than the mix of things they have now with high cholesterol and high fat, or no breakfast at all. We are almost evangelistic in our thrust to try to convince youngsters to be interested in breakfast.[38]

---

[38] Molander, "Marketing Ready-to-Eat Breakfast Cereals," p. 138.

Listerine Antiseptic, Colds, and Sore Throats

"Listerine will not help prevent colds or sore throats or lessen their severity."[1] From September 4, 1978, through February 1, 1980, all advertisements for Listerine carried this disclaimer. The advertising that carried the disclaimer cost $10.2 million, an amount equal to the sum the manufacturer—Warner-Lambert of Morris Plains, New Jersey—had spent between 1962 and 1972 proclaiming the effectiveness of Listerine in fighting colds and sore throats.

The Federal Trade Commission had ordered the disclaimer statement in 1975 as part of an action (initiated in 1972) against Warner-Lambert for failure to maintain "truth in advertising." According to the original order, the disclaimer was to have read, "Contrary to prior advertising, Listerine will not help prevent colds or sore throats or lessen their severity." Warner-Lambert declared the order unfounded and without legal authority or precedent and appealed the ruling in the federal courts. In 1977 the United States Court of Appeals for the District of Columbia circuit upheld the FTC's position but also ordered the phrase "*Contrary to prior advertising . . .*" deleted, on the grounds that it was not necessary to the purpose of the disclaimer and that there was no need "to humiliate the advertiser."[2] In April 1978 the Supreme Court refused to hear a further appeal and the lower court ruling went into effect.

Listerine antiseptic, which has been marketed since 1879, is the leading mouthwash in U.S. sales. Approximately $275 million is spent annually on mouthwash. Listerine's share of that market varies from about 40

---

[1] "FTC Tells Listerine to Take It All Back," *Consumer Reports* 41 (March 1976), p. 152.

[2] U.S. Court of Appeals for the District of Columbia Circuit, argued March 25, 1977. Judgment entered August 2, 1977: *Warner-Lambert Co.* v. *Federal Trade Commission*, No. 76-1138 (August 2, 1977), p. 26.

percent to 50 percent. Listerine is also the only brand of mouthwash that has consistently kept its "medicine bottle" shape and has continually focused its advertisements on the product's effectiveness as a remedy for colds and sore throats.[3]

From 1938 to 1972 Listerine labels proclaimed:

LISTERINE
Antiseptic
Kills Germs
By Millions
On Contact
For Bad Breath, Colds and
Resultant Sore Throats

For Colds and Resultant Sore Throats—Gargle with Listerine Antiseptic Full Strength at the First Sign of Your Cold.[4]

In print advertisements, Listerine's effectiveness as a cold fighter was a constant theme:

FIGHT BACK—The colds-catching season is here again! Nothing can cold-proof you . . . but Listerine Antiseptic gives you a chance to fight back!

Fight back with Listerine Antiseptic. Gargle twice a day—starting now—before you get a cold. You may find the colds you do get will be milder, less severe. That's why more people use Listerine during the colds-catching season than any other oral antiseptic. Why don't you?

Colds-catching season is here again! Nothing can cold-proof you—but Listerine Antiseptic gives you a fighting chance! For fewer colds, milder colds, try this:
Get plenty of rest.
Watch your diet.
Gargle twice a day with full-strength Listerine.[5]

Television commercials also used the fight-back-against-colds-and-sore-throat message. Two such advertisements are the following:

(1) In a commercial entitled "Rubber Stamp–Boy," a woman and young boy (obviously mother and son) are shown. The words "Cold Proof" appear on the boy's forehead. The following announcement covers the action that takes place: "Wouldn't it be great if you could make him cold-proof? Well, you can't. Nothing can do that [boy sneezes]. But there is something

---

[3] Robert Young, "The FTC and Listerine," *Harvard Business School Case Services*, Harvard Business School, 1978, p. 3.

[4] FTC, *In the Matter of Warner-Lambert, Federal Trade Commission Decisions* 86, July 1, 1975 to December 31, 1975 (Washington, D.C.: Government Printing Office), p. 1399.

[5] *Ibid.*, p. 1400.

you can do that may help. Have him gargle with Listerine Antiseptic. Listerine can't promise to keep him cold-free, but it may help fight off colds. During the cold-catching season, have him gargle twice a day with full-strength Listerine. Watch his diet, see he gets plenty of sleep, and there's a good chance he'll have fewer colds, milder colds this year [the words "Fewer Colds, Milder Colds" are superimposed on the picture]. It's a fact that more families use Listerine during these cold-catching months than any other oral antiseptic. So be sure your family gargles regularly with Listerine Antiseptic. We can't promise to keep your family cold-free, but Listerine may help you fight off colds" [the words "Fight Colds" are shown with a bottle of Listerine].

(2) In a commercial entitled "Boxer," a boy wearing boxing gloves is shown as the announcer says, "Can a 12 year old boy . . . wage a one-boy fight against the common cold? Well, he can give it a good try if right behind him there's a mother armed with Listerine Antiseptic [Mother appears]. We can't promise that Listerine will keep him cold-free, no product can do that. But Listerine may help him fight off colds [the words "Fight Colds" are superimposed on the picture]. If you have him gargle twice a day with full-strength Listerine, if you watch his diet and see that he gets plenty of sleep, there's a good chance that he'll have fewer colds, milder colds this year [the words "Fewer Colds, Milder Colds" are superimposed on the picture while the boy gargles]. Many mothers see that their families gargle regularly with Listerine. In fact, during the cold-catching season, more people use Listerine than any other oral antiseptic. We can't promise to keep your family cold-free, but Listerine may help you fight off colds." [The words "Fight Colds" are superimposed on the picture.][6]

The Federal Trade Commission evaluated these and several other advertisements and concluded that they deceptively portrayed Listerine as a cure for colds and sore throats. The FTC complaint and Warner-Lambert's response are summarized in the initial decision by Alvin L. Berman, the FTC Administrative Law Judge:

The Commission's complaint charges respondent Warner-Lambert Company ("Warner-Lambert") with having engaged in unfair methods of competition and unfair and deceptive acts and practices in violation of Section 5 of the Federal Trade Commission Act by virtue of various statements and representations made in connection with, and to induce the sale of, its "Listerine" mouthwash preparation. More specifically, it is charged that, through various advertisements, including product packaging and labels, respondent has represented that the use of Listerine will cure colds and sore throats, will prevent colds and sore throats and will cause colds and sore throats to be less severe than they otherwise would be; that these representations are false, misleading and deceptive. . . .

Another allegation of the complaint is that respondent misrepresented that the most recent tests conducted by or for it, or available to it, prove that children who use Listerine have fewer or milder colds and miss fewer days of school than children who do not use Listerine. Still another allegation is that respondent has misrepresented that the ability of Listerine to

[6] *Ibid.*, p. 1410.

kill germs is of medical significance in the prevention, cure or treatment of colds and sore throats.

Respondent, by its answer, admitted that it has represented that the use of Listerine as directed, in conjunction with a regimen of proper rest and diet, will cause fewer colds and will help reduce the severity of colds. It denied representing that the use of Listerine would cure or would totally prevent colds or sore throats. It admitted that Listerine would not cure colds or totally prevent colds or sore throats, but averred that the use of Listerine as directed, in conjunction with a regimen of proper diet and rest, had been demonstrated to result in fewer colds, milder colds and milder symptoms thereof and less severe colds and sore throats.

Respondent admitted that the severity of a cold is judged or measured by its accompanying symptoms, and that the representation that the use of Listerine would make colds less severe constituted a representation that such use would relieve or lessen the severity of cold symptoms to a significant degree. It denied, however, that the use of Listerine as directed will not have a significant beneficial effect on cold symptoms. Respondent denied other material allegations of the complaint.[7]

In developing its case against Warner-Lambert, the FTC relied heavily on medical evidence that colds are caused by viruses (not by bacteria or "germs"), that there are no treatments that cure a cold or shorten its severity, and that "catching cold" is not related to diet, rest, or exposure to the elements. The FTC did allow that gargling could relieve the uncomfortable symptoms of a cold, but held that warm water was as effective as Listerine for this purpose. The FTC also found the claim "Listerine kills millions of germs on contact" to be essentially irrelevant, because "germs" do not cause colds.

A number of the studies relate to the alleged antibacterial properties of Listerine. Since a cold is an infection caused by virus particles inhaled into the nose which enter into and damage the cells there, the antibacterial properties of Listerine are, for all practical purposes irrelevant. Bacteria play no part in the common cold, and the ability of Listerine to kill millions of bacteria in the oral cavity is of no medical significance in the prevention, cure or treatment of colds or sore throats. Listerine does not reach the site of infection or manifestation of symptoms in medically significant concentration and the tests and writings relied upon by respondent do not tend to show otherwise.[8]

In its defense Warner-Lambert executives noted that the company position was that Listerine would help prevent colds and sore throats only when conjoined with proper rest and diet. They denied their advertisements claimed that Listerine alone would *prevent* colds and sore throats. The company also relied on expert witnesses and on two clinical studies of the frequency and severity of colds. The first study, the Reddish test, was done between 1932 and 1942, using employees of Warner-

[7] *Ibid.*, pp. 1405–1406.
[8] *Ibid.*, p. 1456.

Lambert as subjects; the second study was done between 1967 and 1971 at the St. Barnabas Elementary School. The first study supposedly showed that the group that gargled with Listerine did in fact have fewer colds and sore throats than the control group and that the colds they did have were of lesser severity and shorter duration. From the results of the second study, it was again concluded that Listerine users had milder colds than nonusers (although the data can be interpreted to suggest that they also had more colds than nonusers and that their colds lasted longer).[9]

The FTC faulted both studies for their poor experimental design. It further alleged that the method of selection in the first test and the fact that neither study was blind indicated that the experiments were biased from the start. The FTC criticisms of the two supporting studies are summarized as follows:

1. The St. Barnabas Test

Students in an elementary school and a high school were randomly selected to participate in this study which spanned four years (the high school was dropped at the end of the third year). During the first two years, the participating students were assigned either to the treatment group, which gargled with Listerine twice a day, or to a control group which used no mouthwash at all. During the last two years the control group gargled with water colored to resemble Listerine's amber hue. Since it did not have Listerine's taste or odor, the ALJ concluded that this amber-colored water was not a true placebo, and that the absence of a true placebo biased the test results in favor of the tested agent, Listerine. . . . In order to determine whether the product has efficacy, the bias of the placebo effect should be removed. This bias can be neutralized by "blinding" the participants, *i.e.*, dispensing to the control group a placebo which simulates in taste, smell and appearance the product being tested. This practice of blinding the control group through the use of a placebo is a generally-accepted procedure today. Use of an adequate placebo becomes even more important where the evaluation of symptoms involves subjective judgments. The record demonstrates that a cold is a self-limiting infection, and evaluation of cold symptoms tends to be quite subjective.

We are not requiring in this case that the placebo duplicate the taste, smell, texture, color, etc. of the tested product. There may well be degrees of simulation short of duplication which would neutralize the placebo effect.[10] However, the use of caramel-colored water was patently inadequate.

[9] Young, "The FTC and Listerine," pp. 7–8.

[10] Dr. Vernon Knight, a witness for respondent, identified an alternative that may have proved adequate. A new study would have to be of the "double blind" type. This might be arranged by completely avoiding use of the word "Listerine." Listerine colored another color or conceivably flavored slightly differently as well could be compared with a colored, flavored, 25% alcohol solution. A third group could be given a non-alcoholic, non-germicidal solution of a different color and flavor.

Respondent urges that the absence of a true placebo can be counter-balanced by factors which tend to reduce the impact of the placebo effect, such as conducting the study over a long period of time, permitting the use of concomitant medication, and maintaining the "blindness" of the examining physician—precautions which respondent claims were taken in the St. Barnabas study. Perhaps in some drug studies other factors could compensate for the absence of a placebo but so many uncertainties permeate the St. Barnabas test that we cannot place any reliance in it. For example, it is unclear whether the examiner was properly blinded. We note that blinding the examiner is not merely a device for counter-balancing the absence of a proper placebo; it is essential that a properly administered test avoid bias on the part of the investigator. Whatever bias he may consciously or subconsciously possess can be neutralized by preventing him from knowing which subjects used the purported medication and which received no medication. In this sense, the examiner is "blinded." . . .

The ALJ concluded that the examiner, Dr. Benjamin W. Nitzberg, was not properly "blinded" because the test protocol required that the children gargle at 9:00 A.M., and he began examining them at 10 A.M. Although Dr. Nitzberg denied that he knew which children were in the test group or that he smelled Listerine on the students' breath except on rare occasions (*i.e.*, three or four children in six months), the ALJ concluded that Dr. Nitzberg must have detected the odor of Listerine on the students' breath because other witnesses for respondent testified, on the basis of their own experiences with Listerine, that Listerine can be smelled on the breath for 1½ to 2 hours after gargling.

The record offers support for the ALJ's concern. It establishes that Dr. Nitzberg knew that the test was being conducted for Warner-Lambert, that it involved Listerine and that the data would be used to determine the effect on colds of gargling with Listerine daily. Thus, if he knew which children used Listerine, he might have biased the results in favor of Listerine. The students gargled at 9:00 A.M.; Dr. Nitzberg arrived at 10:00 A.M. and left within an hour during the first two years of the study and within 1½ hours during the last two years. Therefore, many students were examined one to two hours after gargling. Two physicians who testified for respondent stated that, on the basis of their own experience with Listerine, it can be detected on the breath for 1½ to 2 hours after gargling. . . .

Three additional infirmities heighten our concern about the study's probative value. Students were instructed to report to the medical examiner, usually Dr. Nitzberg, at the first sign of a cold. The medical examiner would evaluate and record the overall severity of the cold plus the severity of fourteen cold-related symptoms (only eight during the first two years of the study). The student returned to the examiner each day for the duration of the cold episode, and the physician examined and questioned the student about each symptom, recording the severity of the symptoms on the same sheet that he used the previous day (a rating scale of 0–4 was used during the first two years and 0–7 for the last two). Dr. Nitzberg allotted himself only 1½ to 2 minutes to examine and question each child. This procedure detracts from the probative value of the test in three respects. First, by using the same score sheet day after day Dr. Nitzberg would know how he evaluated a child's symptoms the previous day. As the ALJ found, Dr. Nitzberg's knowledge of what he had done previously would tend to bias his scores, and therefore he would not make an independent judgment each day. Second, given the number of symptoms which Dr. Nitzberg had to evaluate and the fine gradations he had to make in his evaluation, we question whether he spent an adequate amount of time on each subject. In addition to asking each child for historical data on every item on the report form, he would "examine the upper respiratory tract, the eyes, the ears, the nose, and the throat, the sinuses by palpitation and the neck for cervical adenopathy." During the last two years of the study the examiner checked for six additional symptoms. On Mondays he often had to fill in the form for Saturday and Sunday. Third, even if Dr. Nitzberg had been properly blinded the scores he recorded could have been biased to the extent the scores were based upon the non-blinded child's subjective evaluation.

All of the foregoing defects have the cumulative effect of rendering the St. Barnabas study unreliable for evaluating the efficacy of Listerine. In view of this conclusion, we find it unnecessary to consider the parties' disagreement over the meaning of the results.

2. The Reddish Cold Tests

During the winters of 1932 to 1942 respondent conducted tests, mainly using its own employees, to determine whether Listerine has the ability to fight colds. These tests, which respondent claimed established Listerine's efficacy against colds and sore throats, have such grave deficiencies in design and execution that their results are meaningless. Of foremost concern, no placebo was used. (During some winters control groups gargled with a saline solution or tap water. These liquids cannot qualify as adequate placebos.) Moreover, employees were allowed to choose which group they preferred, thereby further biasing the results because those who thought that gargling was an effective method for fighting a cold would most likely join the test group. In addition, the ALJ found that the investigators themselves had predetermined beliefs that Listerine was good for colds. Finally, the investigators were not provided with a uniform definition of a "cold." Common colds last no longer than 10 days, yet illnesses lasting up to 69 days were counted as "colds" in the Reddish study. Even respondent's own expert, Dr. Knight, said that "present opinion would hold that satisfactory evidence for efficacy is no longer provided by these early studies."[11]

Expert witnesses introduced by Warner-Lambert relied heavily on these two studies to support the Listerine claims and to refute FTC charges. Warner-Lambert executives felt victimized by the regulatory system, since the Administrative Law Judge who settled the dispute between the FTC and the company was himself located at the FTC. The executives believed that the judge had cavalierly dismissed their scientific studies, in addition to data indicating customer satisfaction with Listerine and a substantial repurchase rate for the product. They

[11] FTC, *In the Matter of Warner-Lambert.*

also maintained that the decision reached by this judge was without precedent.

The FTC, however, had found the studies so faulty that the additional testimony in favor of Listerine was of little positive significance. Consequently it held that Warner-Lambert had failed to support the Listerine advertising claims. In December 1975, the FTC concluded its case against Warner-Lambert and ordered the company to cease and desist from:

> Representing, directly or by implication, that any such product will cure colds or sore throats;
>
> Representing, directly or by implication, that any such product will prevent colds or sore throats;
>
> Representing, directly or by implication, that users of any such product will have fewer colds than nonusers;
>
> Representing, directly or by implication, that any such product is a treatment for, or will lessen the severity of, colds or sore throats;
>
> Representing that any such product will have any significant beneficial effect on the symptoms of sore throats or any beneficial effect on symptoms of colds;
>
> Representing that the ability of any such product to kill germs is of medical significance in the treatment of colds or sore throats or the symptoms of colds or sore throats.[12]

At the same time that the FTC issued its "cease and desist" order, it also issued the "corrective advertising" order, holding that "mere cessation" of the "false" advertising would not erase the beliefs that people had developed about the effectiveness of Listerine against colds.[13] The commission held that the corrective advertising was necessary because "consumer beliefs tend to continue once they are created," and "future representation of Listerine as a germ killer, without corrective advertising, would automatically constitute, or remind the public of cold claims even in the absence of reference to colds":[14]

> Listerine has been on the market since 1879. Throughout its history, the product has been represented as being, *inter alia,* beneficial in certain respects for colds, colds symptoms and sore throats. Listerine has been advertised directly to the consuming public as a cold remedy since 1921. Since prior to 1938, Listerine labeling has included claims regarding colds and sore throats. . . .
>
> The record shows that over the past ten years, respondent has spent large sums of money in all major media for advertising Listerine as a remedy for the prevention and cure of colds and sore throats and as an

---

[12] *Ibid.,* pp. 1513–1514.

[13] "FTC Tells Listerine to Take It All Back," p. 152.

[14] Young, "The FTC and Listerine," p. 10.

ameliorative for cold symptoms. The vast majority of these expenditures were spent on network and spot television, covering all parts of the day and evening but particularly on prime time network television. Spot television commercials covered practically all the major media centers in the United States. Listerine "colds" print advertising was disseminated in major magazines and newspapers throughout the country.

Advertising acts both in creating a belief in consumers and in reinforcing a belief once it has been created. It has a large role in creating and shaping beliefs with respect to a new product. Its role with an older, established product such as Listerine is more to reinforce established beliefs and act as a reminder. It serves to keep people from changing their attitudes. It still influences some new beliefs. There are always new people coming into the market, *e.g.*, people who were not users who grow up and form households.

Advertising plays a relatively more important role for packaged goods, such as a mouthwash, than for items such as automobiles. Listerine having been advertised as a cold preventative, cure and symptom ameliorative for so many years, it is clear that it has acted both to create and reinforce beliefs in consumers corresponding with respondent's representations concerning that product. It is not plausible that respondent would have spent the millions of dollars that it has over such a long period of time to create and reinforce beliefs about Listerine's use for colds unless it were convinced that the advertisements were effective.[15]

Ironically, Warner-Lambert's own market research gave some support to the thesis that people think that Listerine is effective against colds and sore throats (and therefore lent support to the thesis positing a need for corrective advertising in addition to cessation of misleading claims). Between 1964 and 1971 the percentage recall of Listerine advertising claims showed that between 65 and 75 percent of the subjects tested held Listerine to be effective in killing germs and between 67 and 80 percent thought it effective for colds and sore throats.[16] Another poll conducted for Warner-Lambert showed that "nearly two-thirds of the shoppers polled thought Listerine was a help for colds but that fewer than one-fifth thought other mouthwashes were good cold antidotes."[17] The J. Walter Thompson Company, Warner-Lambert's advertising agency, reported that the major distinctive phrases remembered were "effective for colds and sore throats" and "effective for killing germs":[18]

> Although recall of Listerine's "colds" advertising is at all times very high, such advertising is recalled to an even greater degree during the winter months' "cold season" when Listerine "colds" advertising is disseminated. This indicates that the advertising is especially effective during the months

[15] FTC, *In the Matter of Warner-Lambert*, pp. 1468–1469.

[16] Young, "The FTC and Listerine," p. 11.

[17] "Back on the Warpath Against Deceptive Ads," *Business Week* (April 19, 1976), p. 151.

[18] FTC, *In the Matter of Warner-Lambert*, pp. 1472–1473.

in which it is disseminated. At the same time, it is important to recognize that the "colds" theme is highly recalled as recent advertising even during the 6-month period when there is no such advertising. This is most significant in considering the propriety of requiring corrective advertising, particularly in view of the fact that the subjects are being asked to recall the major themes of recent advertising, not of advertising 3, 4, 5 or 6 months ago. It shows the lasting impression of the non-current advertising.[19]

What do consumers now think about Listerine? In October 1981 the FTC released the results of a mail survey which found that even at the end of the "corrective advertising" campaign about 39 percent of the Listerine users surveyed reported that they used the mouthwash to relieve or prevent a cold or sore throat: "While 22 percent of Listerine users associated the corrective message with Listerine advertising, . . . 42 percent still believed colds and sore throat effectiveness is a principal Listerine advertising theme."[20]

Warner-Lambert faced the possibility of federally mandated modifications of Listerine again in 1982. The "Oral Cavity Advisory Panel," composed of experts commissioned by the FDA but operating independently of it, released an exhaustive report on the safety and efficacy of the active ingredients in oral health care products placed on the market before 1962. Their report found that the active ingredients in Listerine were not *conclusively proven* to be germicidal and therefore should not be advertised as such. If the FDA were ultimately to accept these findings, Warner-Lambert might not be allowed to represent Listerine as anything more than a simple mouthwash. Without its germicidal capacity, its status would be the same as that of its competitor, Scope, and similar to Warner-Lambert's other mouthwash, Listermint.

Warner-Lambert contends that Listerine does indeed possess germicidal properties, and therefore is not simply a medicinally flavored version of the allegedly more pleasant-tasting Listermint. They are confident that their research will be conclusive enough to convince the FDA that Listerine kills germs. Moreover, the company holds that the FTC's present regulatory posture would not alter advertising of the product in any event.

[19] *Ibid.*, p. 1473.

[20] UPI, "Study Says Ads by Listerine had Limited Support," *Washington Post,* October 28, 1981.

Procter & Gamble's Rely Tampons

On September 22, 1980, Procter & Gamble voluntarily withdrew their Rely tampons from sale. The events surrounding that unusual corporate action were widely reported by the media under headlines about TSS or toxic shock syndrome. TSS was unknown by the medical profession until 1978. It was not until May of 1980 that the Center for Disease Control (CDC), a division of the U.S. Public Health Service charged with monitoring the incidence of disease in the United States, alerted physicians to the problem. They reported a disease characterized by a sudden onset of high fever, usually over 104 degrees, vomiting and diarrhea, a rapid drop in blood pressure (usually below 90 systolic in adults), and a sunburn-like rash that later peels off in scales with an acute phase of four to five days. About 10 percent of reported cases were fatal. The disease appears to occur most in women under age thirty during their menstrual periods, although early studies of the disease dealt with cases of TSS in young girls and boys. The CDC supported research on the growing number of reported cases and, in June 1980, announced the preliminary findings of a study linking tampon use to toxic shock syndrome.[1]

Rely tampons became widely identified with toxic shock syndrome when the CDC released a follow-up report on TSS on September 19, 1980. The report indicated that 71 percent of the women in the study (totalling fifty-two) had been users of Rely.[2] The research also indicated that cases of TSS occurred with tampons produced by all five of the major U.S. tampon manufacturers.

---

[1] U.S. Public Health Service, "Toxic Shock Syndrome," *Morbidity and Mortality Weekly Report* (June 26, 1980). The CDC first learned of a threat from TSS in January 1980.

[2] U.S. Public Health Service, "Follow Up on Toxic Shock Syndrome," *Morbidity and Mortality Weekly Report* 29, no. 37 (September 19, 1980), pp. 443–444.

Procter & Gamble had developed the Rely tampon to serve as its entry in the financially secure arena of feminine hygiene products. Introduced to the marketplace in 1974, Rely had reportedly garnered about 25 percent of the tampon market by September 1980.[3] Rely's design was innovative in the "superabsorbent" category, consisting in part of superabsorbent cellulose and polyurethane. It was test marketed in 1974 in Ft. Wayne, Indiana, and in 1975 in Rochester, New York.[4]

Consumers resisted the new product due to its use of polyurethane as an absorbent material. Women who were interviewed reported fears of cancer and other health risks. The Center for Health Services at the University of Tennessee concluded that polyurethane was not carcinogenic and, thus, that these fears were unfounded. Aware of consumer concerns, however, Procter & Gamble reformulated Rely. The revised tampon consisted of polyester foam and superabsorbent cellulose sponges encased in a polyester sack.[5] The Food and Drug Administration (FDA) had known for several years about unconfirmed claims of certain injuries related to such tampons, including Rely, before the toxic shock syndrome studies were made public. Although difficulty with the tampon removal and vaginal ulcerations and lacerations were the usual reports giving rise to consumer and physician complaints, two pages of the FDA's Device Experience Network computer printout were devoted to citations about other problems related to Rely.[6]

The FDA's regulatory role was unclear when the TSS problem arose because no research had demonstrated that tampons caused TSS. On the other hand, the FDA had a Congressional mandate to test all medical drugs and devices prior to marketing to the public. Prior to 1974–76, tampons were regulated under the drug section of the FDA, although they were not technically classified as drugs. In a reorganization process begun in 1974, tampons and other feminine hygiene products were reclassified as medical devices. Because tampons had a "history of safe use," they were placed in Class II, which bases safety on past performance rather than on specific pre-market testing,[7] as required for Class III medical devices. In Class II devices, small changes are permitted without review or testing by the FDA. Therefore, critics have argued, by spacing

---

[3] Carol J. Loomis, "P&G Up against a Wall," *Fortune* 103, no. 4 (February 23, 1981), p. 53. Some sources gave Rely only a 20% market share.

[4] From a series on Rely by the *Chicago Tribune,* called to the case writers' attention by Tampax.

[5] Nancy Friedman, "The Truth about Tampons," *New West* 5, no. 21 (October 21, 1980), pp. 35–36.

[6] *Ibid.,* pp. 38, 40.

[7] More precisely, Class II devices are those devices which for safety and efficacy can be guaranteed by performance standards. As an "old" device, tampons are assigned to Class II, as devices were classified after the Medical Device Amendments of 1976.

minor changes over time, manufacturers have been able to change tampons without regulatory challenge.[8] That there *have* been such changes is denied by Tampax, and no doubt by others.[9]

When presented with the findings of the CDC study, Procter & Gamble executives were faced with a crisis. They could continue to market Rely tampons despite the publicity linking it to TSS; they could wait until the FDA took action attempting to restrict sale of the product; or they could voluntarily withdraw the product. At first, when scientific research indicated that the material in the tampons did not encourage bacterial growth, Edward G. Harness, Chairman of the Board and Chief Executive of Procter & Gamble, said he was "determined to fight for the brand, to keep an important brand from being hurt by insufficient data in the hands of a bureaucracy."[10]

At the time the FDA did not have enough data to order a legal recall. However, by September 18, 1980, Procter & Gamble stopped production of the Rely tampon, probably because of negative publicity and the first report from the Center for Disease Control that linked Rely statistically to TSS—a report Procter & Gamble's own physicians, microbiologists, and epidemiologists were unable to refute. "That was the turning point," Mr. Harness said. The company subsequently pledged their research expertise to the Center for Disease Control to investigate toxic shock syndrome and agreed to finance and direct a large educational program about the disease. In addition, the company agreed to issue a warning to women not to use Rely. Referring to the Rely case, Mr. Harness later made the following public announcement:

> Company management must consistently demonstrate a superior talent for keeping profit and growth objectives as first priorities. However, it also must have enough breadth to recognize that enlightened self-interest requires the company to fill any reasonable expectation placed upon it by the community and the various concerned publics. Keeping priorities straight and maintaining the sense of civic responsibility will achieve important secondary objectives of the firm. Profitability and growth go hand in hand with fair treatment of employees, of direct customers, of consumers, and of the community.[11]

[8] Charlotte Oram and Judith Beck, "Tampons: Looking beyond Toxic Shock," *Science of the People* 13, no. 5 (September/October 1981), p. 16.

[9] Private correspondence from Executive Vice President of Tampax, Thomas J. Moore (June 1, 1982).

[10] Dean Rotbard and John A. Prestbo, "Killing a Product," *Wall Street Journal,* November 3, 1980, p. 21.

[11] Edward G. Harness, "Views on Corporate Responsibility," *Corporate Ethics Digest* 1 (September/October 1980). This citation and other points in this paragraph are indebted to Elizabeth Gatewood and Archie B. Carroll, "Anatomy of a Corporate Social Response: The Procter & Gamble Rely Case," *Business Horizons* (September 1981).

Although there were strong objections inside Procter & Gamble to the methodology and scope of the CDC studies, the company clearly believed it could not risk its reputation on a product that had received so much adverse publicity. A prominent question in the deliberations of corporate executives had been whether a profit-making company could continue to market a product that had been associated (even if a causal relationship was not confirmed) with the sudden death of young women and the illness and disfigurement of others. Harness said the withdrawal was intended to remove Rely from the controversy "despite evidence that the withdrawal of Rely will not eliminate the occurrence of TSS even if Rely's use is completely discontinued."[12]

There are "medical problems" with the issue over the causes of TSS. First, no pathological mechanism has been demonstrated that shows the causal relationship between tampons and TSS. (By contrast, the USDA supports the tobacco industry even though there is direct evidence showing the harmful effects of by-products of tobacco smoke on the smoker and indirect evidence showing its effect on others.) Second, *staph aureus* (the implicated organism) is well known for changing patterns of presentation (*e.g.,* neonatal staph epidemics in the 1950s and 1960s) and severity. It may be that the TSS "epidemic" was secondary to the emergence of a strain or strains of *staph aureus*. This hypothesis is supported by the simultaneous emergence of other unusual *staphylococcal* disease (bacterial *tracheitis*).

FDA officials met with Procter & Gamble executives, with representatives of other tampon manufacturers, and with consumer groups to determine how women should be warned about the relationship of TSS and all tampons, lest the public think that removal of Rely ended the problem. On October 20, 1980, the FDA proposed a voluntary warning label for packages and shelves directed to the population at risk including new younger users of tampon products. Most tampon manufacturers volunteered to place the warning label on the outside of packages. Tampax did not, and it has been reported that this company increased its advertising budget while printing only part of the FDA's advice—omitting the FDA recommendation that women could reduce or eliminate the risk of TSS by not using tampons at all. In its package inserts, Tampax did mention TSS, but asserted that TSS is a "very rare illness" and that "tampons do not cause TSS," because "it is caused by a type of bacteria present in some women." Tampax's strategy apparently was financially successful, because in the month following Rely's withdrawal, Tampax's share of the market grew from 43 percent to 56 per-

---

[12] Richard Severo, "Sharp Decrease in U.S. Reported in Toxic Shock Syndrome Cases," *New York Times,* January 30, 1981, sec. D, p. 15.

cent.[13] Tampax Executive Vice-President Thomas J. Moore explains the company's view as follows:

> Research has not demonstrated *any* causal connection between tampons and TSS. . . . Tampax omitted from its warning a statement that TSS could be almost entirely avoided by not using tampons because that statement could not be proved true. It is now known that TSS affects non-menstruating women and girls and also men.
>
> The implication that Tampax increased its sales by the use of misleading advertising cannot be supported. Its advertising was complete and correct. In the eleven weeks following the withdrawal of Rely, the total U.S. tampon market shrank by nearly 20 percent. It should not be surprising that Tampax's share of the market increased following the withdrawal of a competitor that had accounted for 20–25 percent of the market.[14]

It is to be remembered that all warning labels on these products were *voluntary,* not required by federal regulations. The FDA had only a *proposed* rule to require warnings.

Procter & Gamble undertook a four-week advertising campaign announcing the association between TSS and Rely. The extensive media campaign, including TV and radio commercials as well as half-page newspaper ads in 1,200 papers, was unprecedented. Procter & Gamble also took a $75 million after-tax writeoff on Rely in fiscal 1981 to account for both its unrecovered investment in Rely and costs associated with the growing number of legal cases arising out of damages or death allegedly caused by Rely.[15] These lawsuits against Procter & Gamble were filed quickly after the first public announcement of the link between tampons and TSS. Within a year, Rely was named as cause of death or disfigurement from TSS in about 200 cases.[16] Some plaintiffs also named the Department of Health and Human Services and Food and Drug Administration officials in their suits, claiming that federal negligence permitted Rely to be marketed.

Procter & Gamble's decision to remove the product from sale may not have enhanced their position in these product liability suits, but it improved their tarnished image in the eyes of the general public.

Procter & Gamble executives continued to believe that the evidence linking Rely to TSS was unconvincing. They have subsequently undertaken further research of their own. By July 1981, Procter & Gamble

---

[13] Pamela Sherrid, "Tampons after the Shock Wave," *Fortune* 104 (August 10, 1981), p. 116.

[14] Private correspondence from Executive Vice President of Tampax, Thomas J. Moore.

[15] Loomis, "P&G Up against a Wall," p. 53.

[16] Dean Rotbart, "Rely Counterattack: P&G Is Going All-Out to Track Toxic Shock and Exonerate Itself," *Wall Street Journal,* June 26, 1981, p. 1.

had begun research projects into TSS at a cost of around $2 million.[17] This financial commitment enabled researchers to better understand the origins and effects of toxic shock syndrome. They are candid, however, about their hopes to clear consumer suspicion. Should the results of the research prove Rely does have a specific relationship with TSS, then the company will have paid for results that are at least satisfactory in its own eyes. It also would tend to justify the earlier decision to withdraw the product from the market. That judgment will become more circumspect in comparison to the judgments of others in the industry.

On the other hand, if the research does indicate that Rely is safe to use, Procter & Gamble could remarket the tampon or some other menstrual product. Rely tampons were first kept in storage at considerable expense, but they were all eventually destroyed, beginning in June 1981 (used as fuel in one of their plants).

Following the release of information linking toxic shock syndrome and all high-absorbency tampons in January 1981, consumer tampon buying patterns changed. Kimberly-Clark Corporation began replacing its superabsorbent brands with regular tampons late in 1980. As a company representative explained to the *Wall Street Journal*, "consumers no longer show a preference for the superabsorbent" product.[18] Tampax's president also noted that, "There isn't any question that many women have an objection to them."[19] Whether the changes in purchasing and use patterns have affected the incidence of TSS is a question still under debate. The CDC noted that since withdrawal of Rely, TSS cases have dropped. But this could be attributed to changes in reporting patterns and the general decline in tampon use following the publicity surrounding TSS. Further, the media coverage also may have caused increased reporting by physicians and consumers during the time between the first CDC announcements in May–June 1980, and withdrawal of Rely in late September 1980. TSS cases were reported throughout 1981–82, and by late December 1981, CDC had 1,400 cases on file, almost all involving menstruating women who wore tampons.[20]

For several months after TSS came to public attention the FDA considered a total ban on tampon products. After extensive consideration it was concluded that the benefits to the public of tampon use outweighed

[17] "Jury Still Out on Toxic Shock," *Globe and Mail* (Toronto, Canada), July 6, 1981, p. 13.

[18] Dean Rotbart, "State of Alarm: Tampon Industry Is in Throes of Change after Toxic Shock," *Wall Street Journal,* February 26, 1981, p. 1.

[19] *Ibid.*

[20] "Toxic Shock Linked to Diaphragms," *Washington Post,* December 24, 1981, sec. A, p. 2.

the risks, but that more consumer information on the risks of TSS must be made available. The FDA does not maintain that tampon use *causes* TSS. However, the agency does believe there is a statistically significant association between tampon use and increased risk of TSS. Although the FDA instituted a voluntary warning program, officials were dissatisfied with it for two reasons: (1) There was a noticeable lack of consistency among the manufacturers, and (2) there was not enough information disseminated to the public. For these reasons, in June 1982 the FDA promulgated a mandatory use–labelling program.

The rule instituted both a warning label for the outside of the package and guidelines for information to be enclosed in each package. The mandated warning was "ATTENTION: Tampons are associated with Toxic Shock Syndrome (TSS). TSS is a rare but serious disease that may cause death. Read and save the enclosed information." The manufacturer had flexibility with the content and setup of the insert as long as it covered certain topics. These topics included: warning symptoms, what to do if these symptoms occur and how to avoid the risks of TSS (*viz.*, by not using tampons). Today there is far more uniformity in the information provided by the manufacturers.[21]

Debate continues in the research community on the causal or catalytic role, if any, of tampons in toxic shock syndrome. Both diaphragms and sea sponges have been implicated in cases of TSS, although in numbers too small to be studied. The exact relationship of Rely to TSS is also still unresolved. The association between Rely and TSS is not understood beyond the fact that it is a high-absorbency tampon.[22] A study with a sample size larger than that used in the CDC research (fifty-two women), or perhaps Procter & Gamble's own TSS research team, may provide more information. It may be that marketing and purchasing patterns account for the increased statistical association of Rely with TSS. It is clear, however, that removal of Rely from the marketplace did not *eradicate* TSS, though there has been a marked *decrease* in tampon use and in reported cases of TSS since September 1980.[23] The disease continues in the United States, and is being reported in Sweden, Canada, West Germany, and other countries where Rely was never marketed. However, both CDC and the FDA continue to maintain that Rely posed a risk *significantly above* other tampon brands.

The research still continues. Procter & Gamble continues to fund

---

[21] 21 *Federal Register,* 26,982-26,990 (1982) [21 C.F.R. § 801 (1982)].

[22] Jerry Bishop, "New Study Links Toxic-Shock Syndrome to the Use of High-Absorbency Tampons," *Wall Street Journal,* February 19, 1981, sec. D, p. 16.

[23] Charles E. Irwin and Susan G. Millstein, "Emerging Patterns of Tampon Use in the Adolescent Female: The Impact of Toxic Shock Syndrome," *American Journal of Public Health* 72 (May 1982), pp. 464–467.

TSS research groups. From 1981 to 1986 they spent over $4 million in assistance to twenty-four outside university-based TSS research groups. The FDA, CDC, and the National Institutes of Health are administering a joint project of active surveillance. They are trying to catch cases of TSS not usually reported in order to obtain a better idea of the number of cases that occur. In 1987, the project averaged thirteen cases per month, as opposed to nine cases per month when no active surveillance was used.

Commissions on Sales at Brock Mason Brokerage

James Tithe is Manager of a large branch office of a major midwestern brokerage firm, Brock Mason Farre Titmouse. He now manages forty brokers in his office. Mr. Tithe used to work for E.F. Hutton as a broker and assistant manager, but when that firm merged with Shearson-Lehman/American Express, he disliked his new manager and left for Brock Mason. He knew the new firm to be aggressive and interested primarily in limited partnerships and fully margined common stock. He liked the new challenge. At Hutton his clients had been predominantly interested in unit investment trusts and municipal bonds, which he found boring and routine forms of investment. He also knew that commissions are higher on the array of products he was hired to sell at Brock Mason.

Although bored at Hutton, James had been comfortable with the complete discretion the firm gave him to recommend a range of investments to his clients. He had been free to consult at length with his clients, and then free to sell what seemed most appropriate in light of their objectives. Hutton of course skillfully taught its brokers to be salespersons, to avoid lengthy phone calls, and to flatter clients who prided themselves on making their own decisions; but the firm also did not discourage the broker from recommending a wide variety of products including U.S. government bills, notes, and bonds, which averaged only a $75 commission on a $10,000 investment.

This same array of conventional investment possibilities with small commissions is still available to him and to his brokers at Brock Mason, but the firm has an explicit strategy of trying to sell limited partnerships first and fully margined common stock second. The reason for this strategy at the brokerage house is that commissions on a $10,000 investment in a limited partnership run from $600 to $1000, and commissions on a $10,000 investment in fully margined common stock average $450.

James has been bothered for some time by two facts: The first fact is that in the brokerage industry the largest commissions are paid on the riskiest and most complicated forms of investment. In theory, the reason is that these investments are the most difficult to sell to clients. Real estate and oil and gas drilling partnerships, for example, typically return between 4 percent and 8 percent to sellers—although lately most have been arranged to return the full 8 percent. Some partnerships actually return more than 8 percent because they rebate management fees to any securities firm that acts as a participant in the partnership. The second fact is that James trains brokers to make recommendations to clients based on the level of commission returned to the broker and the firm. He is therefore training his brokers to sell the riskiest and most complicated forms of investment. Although Brock Mason, like all brokerage firms, advertises a full range of products and free financial planning by experts, all salespersons dislike financial planning per se because it carries zero commission.

James has long appreciated that there is an inherent conflict of interest in the brokerage world: The broker is presumed to have a fiduciary responsibility to make recommendations based on the best financial interest of the client; but the broker is also a salesperson who makes a living by selling securities and who is obligated to attempt to maximize profits for the brokerage house. The more trades made, the better for the broker, although this rule seldom works to the advantage of the client. Commissions are thus an ever-present temptation in the way of presenting alternatives or making an entirely objective recommendation.

Brock Mason does have a house mutual fund that is a less risky form of investment—the Brock Mason Equity-Income Fund. But the return to brokers and to the firm is again substantial. The National Association of Securities Dealers (NASD) allows a firm to charge up to an 8.5 percent commission or "load" on a mutual fund, and Brock Mason charges the full 8.5 percent. As an extra incentive, an additional percentage of the commission on an initial investment is returned to a broker if he or she can convince the client to automatically reinvest the dividends rather than have them sent by mail. Brock Mason also offers a fully paid vacation in Hawaii for the five brokers who annually sell the largest number of shares.

The firm has devised the following "piggy-back" strategy: Brokers, as we have seen, are trained to sell limited partnerships first and fully margined stock accounts second. In the latter accounts an investor is allowed to purchase stock valued at up to twice the amount of money actually deposited in the account. The "extra" money is a loan from the brokerage firm. Twice the normal stock entails twice the normal commission on the amount of money in the account. In addition, salespersons are given a small percentage of the interest earned on the loan made to the client.

Brock Mason, like most brokerage firms, is now suffering because a stock market slump has caused business to fall off sharply. In the last six months, business has been off 24 percent, and Brock Mason is encountering difficulty paying for the sophisticated electronic equipment that sits on each broker's desk. James's superiors are pressuring him to place pressure on his brokers to aggressively market limited partnerships as a solid form of investment during a period of instability in stocks.

Last year the average annual commission brought into a firm by a broker in the U.S. brokerage industry was $249,500. Each broker personally takes home between 25 percent and 50 percent of this amount, depending on the person's contract and seniority. James's own take-home earnings last year amounted to $198,000—35 percent more than he had ever earned at Hutton. A friend of his began his own financial planning firm last year and now retains 100 percent of his commissions, making $275,000 last year. His friend rejected the idea that he charge a *flat fee* or a percentage of *profits* in lieu of commissions for his recommendations and services. In his judgment, flat fees would have cost him more than 30 percent of his earnings.

Securities firms are required by law to disclose all commissions to clients. However, James and his brokers are aware that limited partnerships are generally easier to sell than straight stock and bond purchases, because the statistics on fees are buried beneath an enormous pile of information in a prospectus that most clients do not read prior to a purchase. Most clients do not even obtain the prospectus until after the purchase, and there is no report of a dollar figure for the commission. Brokers are not required to disclose commissions orally to clients and rarely do; moreover, it is well known that clients virtually never ask what the commission is. James has been instructed to tell his brokers to avoid all mention of commissions unless the subject is explicitly raised by the client.

The Securities and Exchange Commission (SEC) does not set ceilings on commissions and does not require a broker to receive a written consent from a client prior to a purchase. The SEC does occasionally determine that a markup is so high at a brokerage house that the commission amounts to fraud. It is here that James has drawn his own personal "moral line," as he calls it: He has tentatively decided that he will market any product that has passed SEC and NASD requirements. Only if the SEC is considering a judgment that a markup is fraudulent will he discourage his brokers from marketing it.

But James wonders about the prudence and completeness of these personal guidelines. He has been around long enough to see some very unfortunate circumstances—they are *unfortunate* but not *unfair*, in his judgment—in which unwary clients bought unsuitable products from brokers and had to live with the consequences. Recently one of his brokers had steered a 55-year-old unemployed widow with a total account of $380,000 (inherited upon the death of her husband) into the following "diversification": 25 percent in limited partnerships, 25 percent in dividend-paying but margined stocks, 25 percent in bonds yielding 9.8 percent, and 25 percent in the mutual fund. But the woman had not appreciated at the time of purchase how low-paying the dividends are on the stocks and the mutual fund. She now has far less annual income than she needs. Because she cannot sell the limited partnerships, she must now sell the stock for a high dividend-paying instrument.

James and his broker have been modestly shaken by this client's vigorous protest and display of anger. James decided as a result to take the case to the weekly staff meeting held on Wednesday mornings, which all brokers attend. There was a lively discussion of the best form of diversification and return for the widow. But James's attempt to introduce and discuss the problem of conflict of interest during this session fell completely flat. His brokers were not interested and could not see the problem. They argued that the brokerage industry is a free-market arrangement between a broker and a client, who always knows that fees are charged. Disclosure rules, they maintained, are well established, even if particular percentages or fees are sometimes hidden in the fine print. They viewed themselves as honest salespersons making a living through a forthright and fair system.

James walked away from this meeting thinking that neither the widow nor the broker had been prudent in making decisions, but again he viewed the outcome as unfortunate rather than unfair. He had to agree with his brokers. No client, after all, is forced to make any purchase.

Small-Time Insider Trading

Donald Davidson is a young accountant who only recently went into practice for himself. He literally placed a CPA shingle on a mantel post outside a basement office that he rented in a reconstructed part of downtown Frederick, Maryland. He chose this location because of its extremely low overhead, which was about all he could afford as he got his practice underway. He had only two clients in Frederick, but Washington, D.C., with its inexhaustible need for accountants, was only forty miles away. Donald had made a number of contacts in Washington during a brief previous job with an accounting firm. Donald's father was a lawyer/accountant with his own solid practice in Washington and was positioned to send some business Donald's way.

In fact his father had already sent him one important client, Warner Wolff, the President of a medium-sized bank in the Maryland suburbs of Washington, First National Bank of Beltsville. Donald had been doing the president's personal accounts—his income taxes and two Keogh pension accounts the president had amassed for himself and his wife through a consulting business managed by his wife. Donald often talked with Mr. Wolff about the bank's plans and programs, and he hoped that there would be some contract work to be done for the bank in the future.

One day while going over the books of the pension accounts, Donald noticed that Mr. Wolff had sold the entire diversified portfolio of stocks in his wife's pension account, which traded for a value of $249,000. Mr. Wolff had then bought $248,982 of stock in the First National Bank of Beltsville for his wife's pension account. Upon seeing these trades, Donald jokingly commented to Mr. Wolff that he must have supreme confidence in his managerial abilities to put all of his wife's pension money in the stock of his own bank.

A sober and forthright person, Mr. Wolff took Donald's comment as

This case was prepared by Tom L. Beauchamp. **Not to be duplicated without permission of the holder of the copyright,** © 1989 Tom L. Beauchamp.

a serious inquiry into the reason for the trades and gave a serious answer. "Although it won't be announced for three months and is top secret," he said, "we have signed a merger agreement with the largest bank in Maryland, and our stock price should rise dramatically on the date of announcement." Donald was surprised at being let in on the secret, but he presumed that Mr. Wolff took the disclosure to be protected by normal accountant/client confidentiality. He thought nothing more of it and concluded his work on the records with Mr. Wolff.

However, on the drive home he began to mull over his client's timely purchase and quickly saw that the same opportunity presented itself to him. He had no cash and had only an IRA (individual retirement account) worth $10,000 at this stage of his young career, but the bank certificate of deposit in which he had invested his IRA was coming due in three weeks, and thus he needed to reinvest this money anyway. Why not, he thought, put all $10,000 in the stock of the First National Bank of Beltsville?

As a student at the Wharton School, Donald had studied insider trading and the regulations governing it issued by the Securities and Exchange Commission. He vaguely remembered that the principle behind the SEC regulations is that it is illegal to trade on nonpublic, financially useful information that has been misappropriated or secured by a breach of fiduciary duty. Donald felt a need to bone up on his rusty understanding. He took off the shelves a textbook he had studied as a graduate student and read the following description:

> The practice of insider trading has long been banned in the United States. The Securities and Exchange Commission (SEC) has actively sought rules against such trading since the enactment of the Securities Exchange Act of 1934. Under the terms of this law, a trader is forbidden to use information obtained on the inside to buy or sell securities or to pass the information on to others so that they may benefit. In the important precedent case of *S.E.C.* v. *Texas Gulf Sulphur,* a court held, "Anyone in possession of material inside information must either disclose it to the investing public, or, if he is disabled from disclosing it in order to protect a corporate confidence, or [if] he chooses not to, must abstain from trading in or recommending the securities concerned while such inside information remains undisclosed."
>
> Insider trading has proven difficult to define. An inside trader is someone who trades in the stock of a corporation based upon material nonpublic information he has obtained by virtue of his relationship with the corporation. Some believe that the information should be relevant to the price and to the purchase of the stock. For example, one might have confidential information that could not be disclosed and yet would not likely affect the stock's price even if it were known. The SEC has said that the nonpublic information must be misappropriated by the trader, but a definition of the term "misappropriate" has likewise proven difficult.
>
> There is considerable moral ambiguity surrounding insider trading.

The SEC believes that the insider trading laws serve a moral purpose: preserving the fairness and integrity of the nation's securities market. Investors who have nonpublic inside information are thought to be unfairly advantaged. The underlying principles of these laws are that all investors in a free market should have equal access to relevant information, that securities markets must operate on faith and trust, and that insider trading undermines public confidence in the marketplace. The United States Supreme Court has stressed a different moral purpose. The court has held that an inside trader is one who violates a fiduciary duty to retain confidential information; insider trading is, therefore, like stealing from an employer. Insider trading is also believed to obstruct the market in capital formation.

Other authorities do not consider insider trading unfair. Several scholars have argued that permitting insider trades would make the securities market more efficient. The activity of the traders would be spotted and the market would respond more quickly to essential information. Ben R. Murphy, a partner in a merchant banking firm in Dallas, argues as follows: "My theory is that if we didn't have [insider trading laws] the market would eventually discount all the leaks and rumors and become more efficient. People would have to take a risk on believing the rumors or not." It is noteworthy that over $50 billion of securities trades daily on American exchanges, and no one is prepared to argue that even as much as 1 percent involves insider trading or any form of illegal transactions.

Jonathan Macey, Professor of Law at Emory University, has argued that a person who locates undervalued shares in a company through inside information can provide a valuable service to the market by the discovery, whether insider trading occurs or not. But in order to encourage such discovery the person or institution must be allowed to profit. This is basically what stock analysts do; they all try to get information not yet public before their rivals do in order to reward clients who pay for their activities. The amateur investing public has no chance against such professional knowledge and can only hope that the market price already reflects insider information. Macey concludes that "a complete ban on trading by those with confidential information about a company would be disastrous to the efficiency of the capital markets. If such a rule were enforced, nobody would have an incentive to engage in a search for undervalued firms, stock prices would not accurately reflect company values, and, perhaps worst of all, investment capital would not flow to its most highly valued users. Thus, we would all be better off if the SEC would de-escalate its war on insider trading."

Donald realized that the laws regulating insider trading were often inconsistent, and that there were no federal securities laws explicitly prohibiting insider trading as such. The laws had developed gradually from SEC and judicial decisions. Donald could see that the term "misappropriated" was too vague to be meaningful except in a highly subjective way from case to case. He did not think that he would be engaging in a breach of fiduciary duty by trading in the bank stock, because he had no relevant fiduciary duty. As he saw it, he had a fiduciary duty not to disclose the secret revealed by his client, but he did not intend to disclose anything. In his judgment, he no more obtained the information in a breach of fiduciary duty than does a bartender who overhears information at the bar about a merger of two companies. Donald asked himself, what fiduciary duty could I possibly have not to buy this stock?

Moreover, Donald knew that the Justice Department had traditionally construed insider trading to apply exclusively to *an insider* with a fiduciary duty *to a corporation* not to use confidential information obtained in their relationship. These insiders were almost always Wall Street professionals. He also knew that in one of the few cases to reach the U.S. Supreme Court, the court had dismissed charges of insider trading against a printer who had traded stocks based on the reading of confidential information he had been given to print. The court held that the printer had no legal obligation not to use the confidential information. Donald saw himself as in much the same situation as the printer.

Donald had read about the insider trading cases that had made the headlines in late 1985 and mid-1986. In fact, his current copy of *Business Week* magazine had a cover story dealing with the recent history of insider trading. He reached for his copy and began reading about the two most notorious insider trading "scandals." The first case involved a reporter, R. Foster Winans of the *Wall Street Journal,* who had taken advantage of his position as a reporter for personal financial gain (not very effectively), and had also helped his friends and associates gain financially (very effectively). The Winans case was not easy for Wall Street to dismiss, but Winans was an outsider looking in. The excesses of a juvenile journalist did not directly attack the staid atmosphere of the Wall Street investment firms on which Winans reported.

However, in the spring of 1986 a more consequential case erupted. Dennis Levine, a Managing Director who specialized in mergers and acquisitions at Drexel Burnham Lambert, was arrested for allegedly trading the securities of fifty-four companies (including major companies such as Nabisco and McGraw-Edison) on insider information to earn over $12.6 million. Levine was one of Wall Street's most successful figures and had taken home $3 million in salary and bonuses during the previous year. He had also just pulled off a major deal in his advising of Pantry Pride in its takeover of Revlon.

Levine's walk on the wrong side of the Street evidently began on a trip to the Bahamas in 1980, where he deposited $170,000 at secret branches of a Swiss bank. Using code names, he ultimately set up two dummy Panamanian corporations that traded through the Bahamian bank. On or about March 22, 1984, Levine bought 75,000 shares of Jewell Companies. He sold them on June 5, 1984. In 1985, he bought 145,000 shares of American Natural Resources Company on February 14 and sold them March 4. The continuous pattern of such trading netted Levine the $12.6 million in a short period of time. The SEC launched its investigation after noting the pattern of suspiciously well-timed stock trading at the Swiss bank's U.S. trading accounts.

The Levine conviction reinforced a view that is strongly held at the SEC: Insider trading is rampant on Wall Street. Repeatedly the stock of a takeover target will jump in price immediately before a takeover offer is announced to the public. For example, just before Levine's arrest, General Electric acquired RCA. Immediately prior to the announcement the stock had jumped a dramatic sixteen points. When the SEC immediately began a massive investigation, it became clear that the SEC has dedicated itself to major policing efforts in the attempt to contain insider trading. Since Levine's arrest, several other prominent Wall Street figures have been arrested.

The SEC discovered that insider trading was not confined to corporate insiders, but that many Wall Street outsiders were actively involved. In reporting on the Winans case, *Business Week* pointed out, "Executives do it. Bankers do it. Accountants, secretaries, and messengers do it. And so do printers, cabdrivers, waiters, housewives, hairdressers—and mistresses. Some do it on their own. Others work in rings with connections as far away as Switzerland and Hong Kong. But they all work the shadowy side of Wall Street by trading on inside information to make money in the stock market."

The SEC and the Congress have been working together to crack down on insider trading. Ambiguities and inconsistencies in the laws regulating insider trading have often prevented effective enforcement. Prosecutors have often had difficulty in convicting offenders. Donald read in the *Wall Street Journal* that government prosecutions for insider trading could be delayed for as much as a year, pending a Supreme Court decision in *United States* v. *Carpenter,* which would set a precedent for insider cases.

Responding to this urgent need, both the SEC and the Congress have been considering statutory definitions of insider trading. The Congressional legislation introduced by senators from Michigan and New York and the SEC proposal would both toughen penalties on insider trading. The proposals would define it as the "possession of material, nonpublic information concerning the subject security if such information has been used or obtained wrongfully, whether knowingly or recklessly." The information is obtained wrongfully "only if it has been obtained by, or its use would constitute, directly or indirectly, theft, conversion, misappropriation or a breach of any fiduciary, contractual, employment, personal or other relationship of trust and confidence." The prohibition would apply, according to the SEC proposal, to anyone with a "regular nexus to the operation of the nation's securities markets."

Donald could see that he had obtained his information in confidence, but, again, he could not see that he was violating that confidence or that he had either directly or indirectly stolen information. Although the new Congressional definition was disquieting, Donald was buoyed to read a quotation taken from the leading investment journal *Barron's,* which maintained that the SEC is "riding roughshod over due process of law," drying up the free flow of information, and harming the interest of those it is sworn to protect. In discussing the Winans case, the *Barron's* article adamantly insisted that Winans had done no legal wrong and that the SEC had twisted the idea of "misappropriation" of information to the breaking point in getting a conviction of him. Winans's only wrong, said *Barron's,* was the moral wrong of violating the *Wall Street Journal's* rules of ethics. But this was clearly just a matter of journalism ethics, not business ethics, as far as Donald could see.

Donald had been around accounting long enough to know that government rules, especially Internal Revenue Service rules, always had multiple interpretations and borderline case situations. He recognized that he might be in a borderline situation morally, but he could not see that he would be violating any clear legal principle by purchasing the bank stock. After considerable thought, he decided that he would buy the stock in three weeks, unless he saw new reasons not to do so. However, he felt very uneasy with his decision. He was not worried about the law, although the proposed new laws would be more restrictive. Donald was more concerned with his integrity.

Seizure of the S.W. Parcel

The European Petroleum Consortium (EPC) is a major European oil company with several affiliates and subsidiaries in the United States. In November 1983 EPC leased three contiguous parcels of land near Chico, California—exactly 300 acres, subdivided into three distinct units of 100 acres—from a wealthy farmer, Mr. Buck Wheat, who owned the property. The parties signed three oil and gas leases, one for each of the three contiguous parcels, which were labelled N.W., S.W., and N.E. because of their geographical location.

Within a year a significant gas-producing well had been drilled on the S.W. property, and Mr. Wheat was earning royalties from the gas production. Through 1987 Mr. Wheat had earned in excess of $500,000 in royalties from this well. He was already a multimillionaire by virtue of other wells that had long been operated on his property by oil and gas companies.

Under the terms of the lease, EPC had the option of extending the lease under the original terms of royalty payments for as long as oil or gas was being produced on any parcel of the land that had been leased. If production ever ceased for a period of one year, the agreement would be invalid. If there were no producing wells on a parcel and EPC wished not to extend the lease on that parcel, EPC was required to file a quitclaim deed (a deed of conveyance that is a release of rights) to this effect.

In November 1988—five years after the initial agreement—the lease was scheduled to expire. EPC notified Mr. Wheat by a phone call ninety days prior to the expiration date of the lease of its intention to extend the lease on one parcel of land, the S.W. parcel, but not on the other two. Mr. Wheat responded that he naturally was pleased that royalty payments would continue. Under the terms of the lease, EPC had thirty days beyond the date of expiration to record the quitclaim deed with the county and to record the continuation of the lease arrangement.

Twenty-two days beyond the expiration date, EPC did file both the quitclaim and the extension, and twenty-nine days beyond the expiration date an EPC official had a copy delivered to Mr. Wheat by a messenger service. EPC was not required by the terms of the lease to deliver this copy, because Mr. Wheat had already been notified by phone of its intentions.

Thirty-one days beyond the expiration date, Mr. Wheat signed an oil and gas lease on the producing S.W. parcel—all 100 acres—with Oklasas Oil Company, a small independent headquartered in Anadarko, Oklahoma. That is, Wheat leased to Oklasas the whole S.W. parcel on which EPC believed it had an exclusive lease. Obviously two leases to competitors on the same property cannot be valid.

Mr. Wheat's new lease of the S.W. parcel and his rapid change in relations with EPC may be explained as the result of an inadvertent clerical error and the enterprising activities of the President of Oklasas Oil Company, Mr. B. Sly. He devised a method of acquiring land that is highly unconventional but that has thus far paid off handsomely. He hired a low-salaried clerk to go into several California counties known to have a large number of producing gas wells. The clerk checks all the leases that have been filed, looking for technical violations of the law or for lease loopholes. Whenever a technical violation or potential problem that shows the lease to be invalid is found in a lease on a producing property, Mr. Sly contacts the owner and makes a lease offer that exceeds the terms found in the original lease. Mr. Sly can afford to give the property owner a much larger percentage of the royalties than is conventional because he has no drilling costs and encounters no real speculative risk in an industry filled with drilling risk.

Only about 15 percent of the landowners are willing to meet and discuss the possibility of a lease with Mr. Sly because most believe they have a prior commitment to the company with whom they have signed an agreement. About 10 percent renegotiate with the company with whom they originally signed the lease—often using Mr. Sly's offer as a way of obtaining better terms in the new lease, although not terms as favorable as those offered by Mr. Sly. Instead of the standard one-sixth royalty share to the owner, Mr. Sly offers one-third, doubling the owners' royalties overnight.

Mr. Sly has been able to sign agreements with approximately one-third of the 15 percent willing to meet with him. Thus, about 5 percent of his contacts eventually come to terms with him. His clerk finds one promising legal problem or technical violation that suggests an invalid lease per nine days of full-time research. Mr. Sly is already bringing in over $3 million annually for Oklasas from the wells he has acquired on these properties, and his operating costs are extremely low because he always obtains properties with producing wells.

Very fortunately from Mr. Sly's perspective, his clerk was working in the county offices on the day EPC filed its quitclaim deeds and extension. The clerk's trained eye detected a serious error almost immediately: EPC had inadvertently quitclaimed the S.W. parcel and extended the lease on the nonproducing N.W. parcel. This error resulted from a slip of the pen; the clerk at EPC had penned in "N.W." rather than "S.W." Although the system at EPC was set up to avoid such "erroneous legal descriptions," the error passed through six checkpoints in six offices at EPC without detection.

Within two hours of the clerk's discovery of the misfilings in the county office, the relevant papers had been copied and sent by overnight mail to Mr. Sly. Two days later he was in California to pay a visit to Mr. Wheat. After a two-hour meeting they were joined by their lawyers for a lunch and afternoon meeting, and by 5:00 an agreement had been signed. Neither party had contacted EPC to ascertain whether a mistake had been made, as it was obvious that it had.

Mr. Wheat asked not only for a one-third royalty share but also that Mr. Sly lease for a sum of $7,500 per year the N.E. property that had been quitclaimed and drill on that property. (EPC had several times said it was not interested in drilling on this property after it had discovered gas on the S.W. property.) Mr. Wheat also asked for a full indemnification in the event of a lawsuit by EPC. That is, he asked to be fully secured against loss or damage in the event of a lawsuit over the leases—including any loss from the shutdown of operations at the well. Mr. Sly agreed that he would pay all legal costs and reimburse for any loss that Mr. Wheat might incur.

This was not a difficult decision for Mr. Sly. In oil and gas leases, the written record is everything, so far as the law is concerned. One simply cannot tell the legal status of the property unless there is a written legal record. Unrecorded statements of intention and verbal promises count for nothing. Mr. Sly's lawyer was certain that no suit by EPC would stand a chance of success.

The next day EPC was notified of the new arrangement, and told that it must abandon the property immediately. Within twenty-four hours EPC replied that it considered the negotiations over this property to have been in bad faith. EPC said it considered any entry upon the land and any drilling to constitute a trespass and also to be in bad faith. EPC added, however, that it was willing to negotiate and settle out of court. Oklasas replied immediately that it was not interested in negotiation.

CHAPTER 3

The Environment

INTRODUCTION   Much discussion about the environmental responsibilities of corporations has emerged in the past two decades. The public has become increasingly concerned about the environmental impact of chemical dumping, airborne emissions, nuclear power, oil pipelines and shipping, and the like. There is now a widespread consensus that environmental problems, whether caused by business or not, are critical. However, no comparable consensus has emerged regarding the proper lines of responsibility or the seriousness of the threat to the environment and to human and animal health.

It is often said that these contemporary environmental problems are novel and without historical precedent. In fact, however, environmental problems have a long history. In the eighteenth century in English courts of common law and equity, numerous cases were brought by individuals who sought to be compensated for the costs of pollution caused by various businesses. Indeed, as early as 1273, the burning of coal was legally prohibited in certain English jurisdictions on grounds of harm to the public health—precisely the issue in the acid rain case in this chapter.

Of course, early cases are only precedent models, and recent cases before courts involving industrial discharge, the use of asbestos, hazardous waste disposal, and the like are largely unprecedented. Millions of dollars are now at stake in the courts (in the effort to secure compensation for harms), and society is confronted with anticipated and sometimes tragic tradeoffs—including choices between the health of workers and the economic health of corporations. The Reserve Mining and Love Canal cases in this chapter are clear instances of such tradeoffs.

Classic conflicts between public and private interests have emerged in these environmental debates. For example, in recent years industrial disposals of hazardous wastes that include mercury, benzene, and dioxin have been faulted for the contamination of public groundwater, landfills, and even waste recovery plants. In one of the most famous law cases in the history of United States courts, *U.S.A.* v. *Allied Chemical,* Judge

Robert R. Merhige stringently penalized the Allied Chemical Corporation in 1976 for the environmental pollution of a river. This case is somewhat one-sided and therefore is not included among the cases in this chapter. Nonetheless, the case has become symbolic of the struggle between environmentalists and business interests, and so deserves at least brief mention.

In the case, Allied and five of its employees were indicted on 153 charges of conspiracy to defraud the Environmental Protection Agency and the Army Corps of Engineers in their efforts to enforce water pollution control laws. Allied denied all charges, saying the indictments displayed an "extreme reaction" by public officials. However, Allied pleaded *nolo contendere* (no contest) to the charges. Judge Merhige fined Allied $13.2 million, but later reduced the fine to $5 million because Allied put $8 million into a fund set up to relieve suffering that resulted from its pollution. This fine was the largest ever imposed in an environmental case, but the indictments were also the most ever returned in a single such case.

In his ruling Judge Merhige argues the utilitarian thesis that corporations will "think several times before anything such as this happens again." But he also argues what would be construed by many in the business community as an unacceptable non-utilitarian thesis: "I don't think that commercial products or the making of profits are as important as the God-given resources of our country." He then advances the striking claim that we are all collectively responsible for what happened in this case because we tolerate too much environmental pollution. This important judicial ruling, as we might expect, has been severely criticized by representatives of the business community.

The quality of air, water, soil, food, and health are of course at the center of all discussions about the environment, the public interest, and the interest of businesses. Since 1960 the U.S. Congress has repeatedly enacted major pieces of legislation dealing with these problems. But legislative documents are vague, broadly worded pronouncements that direct federal agencies to act "in the public interest" or "to protect the public health." The agencies are chartered to regulate business by deciding which chemicals should be regulated and what the standards of discharge and dose levels should be. Many value judgments must be made as to "reasonable" levels of discharge and "dangers" to human health.

Environmental problems do not always involve the public interest in conflict with the interest of business. Sometimes environmental problems involve the interests of one business in conflict with another. Thus, a fishing industry may be crippled by the airborne or waterborne discharges of chemical industries or factories—as the acid rain case illustrates. Naturalists' interests in species or wilderness preservation may also conflict

with the ambitions of business. These conflicts call for balancing considerations that fairly take into account the different interests of disputing
parties. They also call for difficult judgments about the extent to which
business or government can be trusted in taking the most reasonable
course of action. The Reserve Mining case reflects problems of both
balancing interests and making discretionary judgments.

Another range of issues about the environment concerns whether
businesses and other responsible parties have obligations to natural ob-
jects, especially to certain forms of animal life, which are understood
as parts of the living environment. Some argue that various forms of
nonhuman life deserve the same general moral protections afforded
humans. For example, various forms of poisoning, slaughtering, and
trapping animals without utilizing "humane methods" and without formal penalty have been denounced by animal protection leagues as bar-
baric. Animals are often more convenient and profitable for businesses
than any alternative as a source for research, labor, and food. Research
involving the use of animals and various techniques of raising animals
for food have gone largely unchallenged in the past. However, critics
are now arguing that animal life deserves new protections against various
methods of research, production, and slaughter. They ask, "What justifies
the food and research industries in treating animals in ways they would
never treat humans?" The challenge presented by this question is to
find some morally relevant property of human beings that will justify
restricting the protections afforded by principles of the "sanctity of life"
to *human* life.

To take this problem one step further, many argue that animals deserve
protection not simply because it is in the interest of humans to protect
them, but because animals *inherently* deserve and have a *right* to protection.
This is a debate over whose interests are to count, and how heavily
they are to count, but it is also a debate over the worth of nonhuman
life. Two cases in this chapter bluntly bring these questions forward.
The case of pâté at Iroquois Brands raises the issue of the force-feeding
of geese and ducks for a commercial market, and the cosmetics industry
case involves the testing of cosmetics by dropping irritants into the eyes
of rabbits. The pâté industry has thus far been unreceptive to its critics,
whereas the cosmetics industry has been forthrightly concerned about
the issue for years. Companies like Avon, Revlon, and Procter & Gamble,
for example, have reduced the volume of irritants to one-tenth the
amount they used in the past and also have funded research into alternatives to the use of animals. However, the industry continues to use the
irritant tests and to defend the research based on its protection of human
consumers. The number of animals used still is not small by anyone's
standards. For example, in the year before this book went to press,
Procter & Gamble alone used 174 dogs, 392 hamsters, 1,486 rabbits,
4,740 pigs, and approximately 45,000 mice and rats.

In addition to considerations of whose interests are to count, important problems have arisen as to where the burden of proof rests in environmental matters. Most major controversies involve considerable uncertainty about the extent to which a chemical discharge, storage procedure, and the like present a threat to humans or nonhuman life. Is the burden of proof on industry or on the regulatory agencies of government to prove that a product or practice is safe or harmful? If this determination can be made, who should be responsible for taking steps to remove the problems—especially when these problems are new? How is possible future harm to the environment to be weighed against the economic harms of tighter regulation of business? These issues are especially prominent in the Reserve Mining, Love Canal, and acid rain cases.

Almost everyone now believes that there will be further loss of liberty for corporations to use the environment. The major ethical issue in environmental problems is how to balance the liberties of those who want to use the environment for business purposes against the rights of those who desire safe workplaces and an environment free of contamination.

Reserve Mining's Silver Bay Facility

Since 1950, the Reserve Mining Company has been a jointly owned subsidiary of large steel corporations. Reserve Mining was formed in 1939, on behalf of four steel firms, for the purpose of mining and crushing taconite (low-grade iron ore). It was called "Reserve" because the iron ore was considered in 1939 a long-term investment in need of new technology to be processed efficiently. In an expensive and innovative move, the Reserve Mining Company decided in 1944 to locate its prospective plant on Lake Superior, and so began to acquire the land in 1945. This great body of water was considered essential because large amounts of water are needed for the processing. The taconite must be crushed into fine granules and collected into "pellets" before the residue is flushed back into the water.

After nine hearings in Duluth, St. Paul, and Silver Bay, the state of Minnesota issued the necessary environmental permits in 1947. In 1948 the U.S. Army Corps of Engineers granted Reserve a permit to construct harbor facilities that called for the deposit of tailings (the residue waste product) in Lake Superior. The taconite was to be mined near Babbitt, Minnesota, and then shipped by rail approximately 45 miles to the plant on the northwest shore of Lake Superior. Both the tax laws in Minnesota and mining technology had improved dramatically by then to the point that efficient mining and crushing were possible. Work began on the Lake Superior facility in 1951, and full operations commenced at the plant in 1955.

The town of Silver Bay was built especially for these mining operations. Soon thereafter 80 percent of the 3,000 adult inhabitants of Silver Bay were employed by Reserve, and the total taconite work force in the state grew to 9,000. So successful was the operation that between 1956 and 1960 Reserve sought and received permission for substantially in-

This case was prepared by Tom L. Beauchamp and revised by Joanne L. Jurmu. **Not to be duplicated without permission of the holder of the copyright,** © 1989 Tom L. Beauchamp.

creased production and correspondingly increased discharges into Lake Superior. A final modest increase in production was achieved in 1965. This increase brought Reserve's annual production capacity to 10.7 million tons of pellets. To achieve this level of production, Reserve dumped 67,000 tons of waste material into Lake Superior each day. The state had approved such discharges under the assumption they would sink and remain forever at the bottom of the lake.[1]

The basic technology at the facility has been summarized as follows by Professor Presson S. Shane of the George Washington University School of Business:

> Taconite is a hard, gray rock in which are found particles of magnetite, a black oxide of iron which is magnetic and has the approximate oxygen content designated as Fe_3O_4. The deposits of taconite near Babbitt, Minnesota are sufficiently near the surface to permit their being taken from open pits. The taconite is crushed to a nominal 4-inch size and hauled along the Reserve railroad line to Silver Bay at a rate of about 90,000 tons per day.
>
> At Silver Bay the crushing operation is continued in order to free the particles of iron oxide for recovery and molding into pellets. A series of crushers, rod mills, ball mills, and magnetic separators are operated in processing the water slurry of ore. Two million tons of water are taken from Lake Superior each day (and returned) in the processing. The low-iron tailings are discharged back into the lake in the direction of a trough about 500 feet deep a few miles offshore. The discharge stream comprises the tailings, and the finest fraction, about 1½ percent solids, forms a dense current which flows toward the bottom of the lake. The magnetically recovered particles are the concentrate which is compressed to a cake with 10 percent moisture. It is then mixed with bentonite, which is a cohesive agent, and rolled into green pellets about ⅜ inch in diameter. The pellets are hardened by heating to 2350°F and are then ready for loading into ore boats at Silver Bay for the trip to the blast furnaces in Cleveland, Youngstown, Ashland, etc.[2]

ENVIRONMENTAL LITIGATION BEGINS

Environmental questions about Reserve's discharges were publicized in 1963, when U.S. Senator Gaylord Nelson of Wisconsin investigated the possibility of water pollution violations. Various forms of new environmental legislation were passed in the next few years, and by 1968 concerns

---

[1] Points of early history mentioned in this case rely on E. W. Davis, *Pioneering with Taconite* (St. Paul: Minnesota Historical Society, 1964). Points of later history often depend upon Robert V. Bartlett, *The Reserve Mining Controversy* (Bloomington: Indiana University Press, 1980), and on a telephone conversation with Professor Bartlett in April 1982.

[2] Presson S. Shane, "Silver Bay: Reserve Mining Company" (1973). Reprinted by permission of Professor Shane.

were being expressed about Lake Superior by Senator Nelson, by a Taconite Study Group, and by Secretary of the Interior Stewart Udall. A "Save Lake Superior Association" was founded in 1969. In 1971–72 the Environmental Protection Agency, the U.S. Justice Department, and the Minnesota Pollution Control Board all charged Reserve with violations of the Federal Pollution Control Act. The argument was that the plant discharges mineral fibers into the air and that the water can be hazardous to health and can endanger drinking water supplies. Similar fibers were known to cause asbestosis, mesothelioma, and various cancers. Concerns in the past had been predominantly about water pollution—including effects on fish life and the water supply—but as the issues entered the courts, the focus of the case quickly shifted to threats to human health.

In 1973 a U.S. District Court in Minnesota entered an order closing Reserve's Silver Bay facility on grounds that it was discharging dustlike asbestiform (asbestos-like) particles into both the air and the water at great threat to human health. Asbestos workers had been shown to be vulnerable to cancer when they inhaled the product. Some 200,000 persons drank the water from Lake Superior, and many more might potentially be affected by airborne fibers. Reserve appealed this decision to the Eighth Circuit Court of Appeals, where Judge Myron H. Bright summarized the situation as follows in an extremely influential opinion delivered on June 4, 1974 (139 days had been spent in the courtroom, and over 100 witnesses and 1,620 exhibits had been considered):

> Although there is no dispute that significant amounts of waste tailings are discharged into the water and dust is discharged into the air by Reserve, the parties vigorously contest the precise nature of the discharge, its biological effects, and particularly with respect to the waters of Lake Superior, its ultimate destination. . . .
>
> The suggestion that particles of the cummingtonite-grunerite in Reserve's discharges are the equivalent of amosite asbestos raised an immediate health issue, since the inhalation of amosite asbestos at occupational levels of exposure is a demonstrated health hazard resulting in asbestosis and various forms of cancer. However, the proof of a health hazard requires more than the mere fact of discharge; the discharge of an agent hazardous in one circumstance must be linked to some present or future likelihood of disease under the prevailing circumstances. An extraordinary amount of testimony was received on these issues. . . .
>
> The theory by which plaintiffs argue that the discharges present a substantial danger is founded largely upon epidemiological studies of asbestos workers occupationally exposed to and inhaling high levels of asbestos dust. A study by Dr. Selikoff of workers at a New Jersey asbestos manufacturing plant demonstrated that occupational exposure to amosite asbestos poses a hazard of increased incidence of asbestosis and various forms of cancer. Similar studies in other occupational contexts leave no doubt that asbestos, at sufficiently high dosages, is injurious to health. However, in

order to draw the conclusion that environmental exposure to Reserve's discharges presents a health threat in the instant case, it must be shown either that the circumstances of exposure are at least comparable to those in occupational settings or, alternatively, that the occupational studies establish certain principles of asbestos-disease pathology which may be applied to predicting the occurrence of such disease in altered circumstances.

Initially, it must be observed that environmental exposure from Reserve's discharges into air and water is simply not comparable to that typical of occupational settings. The occupational studies involve direct exposure to and inhalation of asbestos dust in high concentrations and in confined spaces. This pattern of exposure cannot be equated with the discharge into the outside air of relatively low levels of asbestos fibers. . . . In order to make a prediction, based on the occupational studies, as to the likelihood of disease at lower levels of exposure at least two key findings must be made. First, an attempt must be made to determine, with some precision, what the lower level of exposure is. Second, that lower level of exposure must be applied to the known pathology of asbestos-induced disease, i.e., it must be determined whether the level of exposure is safe or unsafe.

Unfortunately, the testimony of Dr. Arnold Brown indicates that neither of these key determinations can be made. Dr. Brown testified that, with respect to both air and water, the level of fibers is not readily susceptible of measurement. This results from the relatively imprecise state of counting techniques and the wide margins of error which necessarily result, and is reflected in the widely divergent sample counts received by the court. . . . In commenting on the statement, "This suggests that there are levels of asbestos exposure that will not be associated with any detectable risk," Dr. Brown stated: "As a generalization, yes, I agree to that. But I must reiterate my view that I do not know what that level is. . . ."

A fair review of this impartial testimony by the court's own witnesses— to which we necessarily must give great weight at this interim stage of review—clearly suggests that the discharges by Reserve can be characterized only as presenting an unquantifiable risk, i.e., a health risk which either may be negligible or may be significant, but with any significance as yet based on unknowns. . . .[3]

The Court's reluctance to pronounce or even attempt to quantify an actual health hazard was a victory for Reserve, although the court went on to suggest that better air control and the "termination of Reserve's discharges into Lake Superior" should take place as quickly as possible. Judge Bright, speaking for the Court, then granted Reserve a 70-day stay of Judge Lord's order on the condition that Reserve submit an adequate pollution-control plan. During this 70-day period Reserve jostled still further with Judge Lord, who, in August 1974, declared a new Reserve disposal plan environmentally inadequate. Reserve then asked the Eighth Circuit Court of Appeals for an extended stay, which was granted; but the judges who heard the application for a stay warned Reserve that they must continue work underway on development of alternate disposal sites.

[3] 498 F.2d 1073 (1974).

DISPOSAL PLANS PROPOSED

Reserve quickly announced plans for an on-land disposal facility to be called "Mile Post 7." Reserve applied to the state of Minnesota to construct this new facility; however, the state was displeased with these plans, and negotiations were undertaken. On April 8, 1975, the Eighth Circuit Court of Appeals handed down its much-anticipated "final" decision on the merits of Judge Lord's order and on Reserve's responsibilities. The key parts of this decision, which to many were surprising, read as follows:

> As will be evident from the discussion that follows, we adhere to our preliminary assessment that the evidence is insufficient to support the kind of demonstrable danger to the public health that would justify the immediate closing of Reserve's operations. We now address the basic question of whether the discharges pose any risk to public health and, if so, whether the risk is one which is legally cognizable. . . .
>
> Plaintiffs' hypothesis that Reserve's air emissions represent a significant threat to the public health touches numerous scientific disciplines, and an overall evaluation demands broad scientific understanding. We think it significant that Dr. Brown, an impartial witness, whose court-appointed task was to address the health issue in its entirety, joined with plaintiff's witnesses in viewing as reasonable the hypothesis that Reserve's discharges present a threat to public health. Although, as we noted in our stay opinion, Dr. Brown found the evidence insufficient to make a scientific probability statement as to whether adverse health consequences would in fact ensue, he expressed a public health concern over the continued long-term emission of fiber into the air. . . .
>
> The . . . discussion of the evidence demonstrates that the medical and scientific conclusions here in dispute clearly lie "on the frontiers of scientific knowledge." . . .
>
> As we have demonstrated, Reserve's air and water discharges pose a danger to the public health and justify judicial action of a preventive nature.
>
> In fashioning relief in a case such as this involving a possibility of future harm, a court should strike a proper balance between the benefits conferred and the hazards created by Reserve's facility.
>
> Reserve must be given a reasonable opportunity and a reasonable time to construct facilities to accomplish an abatement of its pollution of air and water and the health risk created thereby. In this way, hardship to employees and great economic loss incident to an immediate plant closing may be avoided. . . .
>
> We cannot ignore, however, the potential for harm in Reserve's discharges. This potential imparts a degree of urgency to this case that would otherwise be absent from an environmental suit in which ecological pollution alone were proved. Thus, any authorization of Reserve to continue operations during conversion of its facilities to abate the pollution must be circumscribed by realistic time limitations. . . .[4]

[4] 514 F.2d, 492 (1975).

In all essentials, Judge Bright and his colleagues on the Court of Appeals had reversed their earlier views, now holding that Reserve's water and air discharges did create a major public health threat and that the courts need not shy away from decisions in the face of scientific uncertainties. (The judges shrouded their apparent reversal in some legal technicalities.)[5]

For several years after this decision, various courts witnessed arguments to show whether, as the Court of Appeals put it, "the probability of harm is more likely than not." Neither side succeeded in providing definitive scientific evidence, and the focus of the controversy shifted to the problem of finding a satisfactory on-land disposal site. A major battle erupted over Mile Post 7. Reserve was given heart when Judge Lord was removed from the case by the Eighth Circuit, which cited Lord's bias against Reserve. Lord's replacement, however, quickly fined Reserve almost $1 million for past violations, and the search for a proper on-land site continued in and out of the courtroom. The state preferred an alternative to Mile Post 7, known as Mile Post 20. Reserve complained bitterly about the costs that would be involved in constructing on this site, and disputed with the state as to whether financing would be possible. (Their separate cost estimates varied by $50 to $60 million.)

ON-LAND DISPOSAL
FACILITY BUILT

Every health issue mentioned above, and new ones as well, remained in dispute, and each side won several major victories in the courts. Reserve repeatedly threatened to close its Silver Bay facility permanently in the face of costs imposed by courts and the state. Finally, a bargain was struck: On July 7, 1978, Reserve agreed both to build the new facility at Mile Post 7 and to satisfy stringent conditions the state insisted upon for approval of the permits. The total investment in the new facility was set at $370 million. The facility would contain one of the largest and most expensive pollution control programs in the world. The company agreed to stop all discharges into Lake Superior by April 15, 1980. It faithfully carried out this promise, and the new facility began operations in August 1980.

Several scientific studies of health hazards had been completed by July 1978 and other studies followed. These studies, several of which were sponsored by Reserve, did not show any significant increase in

[5] A useful analysis of this second decision is found in William A. Thomas, "Judicial Treatment of Scientific Uncertainty in the *Reserve Mining* Case," *Proceedings of the Fourth Symposium on Statistics and the Environment* (Washington, D.C.: American Statistical Association, 1977), pp. 1–13.

disease related to asbestos in the region or in workers at the plant. Studies have not even shown a buildup of asbestiform bodies in the lung tissue (of sufficient size to be detected), or in the bloodstream, among persons drinking the water from Lake Superior. Reserve's work force has not shown a significant outbreak of asbestosis or any similar disease. Reserve claims that it has yet to see a single dust-related disease in one of its employees.[6] Nevertheless, Reserve's claim depends in part on the lack of clear-cut evidence. Just as government officials have never been able to show any increased incidence of disease as a result of the Silver Bay facility, so Reserve has no way of showing that there will not be latent and serious long-term effects in 15 to 20 years—as is commonly the case with asbestos-caused diseases.

RESERVE CEASES OPERATIONS

With the decline of the steel industry in the early 1980s Reserve's economic usefulness also declined. High-grade Brazilian ore became available to steel-makers for a price well under that of taconite.[7] Contributing to the steel industry's problems has been the decline in the auto industry. Auto sales are down, and recent technological advances have allowed auto-makers to reduce by hundreds of pounds the amount of steel in their cars.

After 1982 Reserve also experienced a number of temporary shut-downs and employee layoffs. While operating at 40 percent of capacity, Reserve had 1,200 of its 2,600 employees laid off between 1982 and 1986.[8] Shut-downs were long, with Reserve losing six and a half months in 1982 and nine months in 1983.[9]

After using the on-land settling pond for four years, Reserve requested permission to build a filtration plant to allow the company to resume the dumping of waste water into Lake Superior. The filtration plant was necessary, according to Reserve, because their settling ponds were filling up more quickly than expected. This was due to the fact that Reserve's facilities were operating well under capacity. Water was collecting quicker because less of it was being recirculated through the plant.[10]

---

[6] Bartlett, *The Reserve Mining Controversy*, p. 209.

[7] Bill Richards, "Minnesota Iron Range Is Hurt and Despairing as More Plants Close," *Wall Street Journal*, November 26, 1984, p. 1.

[8] "Reserve Mining Schedules Another Operations Suspension," *Skillings Mining Review* (March 26, 1983), p. 5.

[9] *Ibid.;* also "Reserve Will Cut Taconite Output in Half," *Minneapolis Star and Tribune*, September 19, 1984.

[10] Bill Sternberg, "Reserve Mining Waste Plan Draws Fire from Activist Mize," *Marquette Mining Journal* (May 26, 1984).

Reserve believed that the filtration plant was the only viable alternative. Management stated that the filtration process would remove more than 99 percent of the pollutants and make the water "safe to drink."[11] Discharge from the plant would be between 2,500 and 3,500 gallons per minute. Cost estimates were approximately $2 million to complete the plant. Reserve hoped to have it operational within six months. The Minnesota Pollution Control Board received the request and after three board meetings filled with controversy, the permit was approved, under the assumption that the proposed filtration plant was the best available technology.[12]

This permit allowed Reserve to dump water into Lake Superior as long as the fiber content was at or below one million fibers per liter. On those days when the fiber content exceeded that limit the water was to be dumped on land and recycled until it met standards. The filtration plant was built and became operational late in 1984. Reserve monitored the fiber content using samples sent to the Minnesota Health Department Laboratory for analysis.

The final blow to Reserve's viability came on July 17, 1986, when LTV Steel, which owned 50 percent of Reserve, declared Chapter 11 bankruptcy. Problems included smaller than expected steel shipments in the second quarter and lower pricing levels. LTV abandoned all responsibilities for Reserve. Reserve's facilities temporarily closed while Armco surveyed the situation. Armco considered operating Reserve on its own or finding another partner for the operations, but neither option was deemed financially feasible. On August 7 Reserve was placed into Chapter 11 bankruptcy by Armco. The move was linked to industry conditions; no connection was made between the installment of the on-land disposal site and the bankruptcy.

In August 1986 unemployment for the state of Minnesota was between 5 and 6 percent, while Lake County (including Silver Bay) experienced rates of approximately 40 percent. Some families of laid-off workers had remained, but many others elected to leave the area in search of other employment. All of the 2,200 laid off or retired Reserve employees were without health-care and pension benefits until mid-1987. At that time a trust was established by using three sources: (1) a portion of tax overpayments owed to Reserve by the state of Minnesota; (2) funds from the sale of pellets stockpiled before the shut-down; and (3) 10 percent of revenues from the sale of Reserve assets. Reserve has sold off all equipment that was not necessary to process four million tons

---

[11] *Ibid.*

[12] The following information on the filtration plant is the result of a telephone conversation with Robert Criswell of the Minnesota Pollution Control Agency on April 1, 1987.

of taconite per year. They had originally a capacity of nine million tons per year.[13]

Although the plant is not in operation, Reserve continues to recycle water into Lake Superior that collects in the on-land facility. Since the shut-down the water quality has improved significantly, well below the one million fibers per liter limit. Should Reserve reopen and not be able to meet the one million per liter limit, the Minnesota Pollution Control Board might now be willing to modify the permit. In January 1987 the Governor of Minnesota decided to undertake a study of the feasibility of reopening Reserve under new management. With market conditions as they exist, most industry analysts are skeptical that Reserve will reopen in the near future.

[13] Telephone conversation, Gene Skraba, Staff Representative, United Steelworkers of America, Hibbing, Minnesota, April 6, 1987.

Hooker Chemical and Love Canal

Today the Love Canal area of Niagara Falls looks like a war zone. The 235 houses nearest the landfill are boarded up and empty, surrounded by an 8-foot-high cyclone fence that keeps tourists and looters away. Still other houses outside the fenced area are also boarded up and deserted, their owners having fled the unknown. Here and there throughout the neighborhood, newly erected green signs mark the pickup points for emergency evacuation in case there is a sudden release of toxins. An ambulance and a fire truck stand by in the area as workers struggle to seal off the flow of chemicals and render the area once again safe—if not exactly habitable.[1]

THE HISTORY OF LOVE CANAL

Love Canal is named for William T. Love, a businessman and visionary who in the late nineteenth century attempted to create a model industrial city near Niagara Falls. Love proposed to build a canal that would figure in the generation and transmission of hydroelectric power from the falls to the city's industries. The combination of an economic recession that made financing difficult and the development of cheaper methods of transmitting electricity dampened Love's vision, and the partially dug canal in what is now the southeast corner in the city of Niagara Falls is the sole tangible legacy of the project.

However, industry was still drawn to the area, which provided easy access to transportation, cheap electricity, and abundant water for industrial processes. Several chemical companies were among those who took advantage of the region's natural resources. The Hooker Electrochemical Company, now Hooker Chemical & Plastics Corporation and a major

---

[1] Thomas H. Maugh, II, "Toxic Waste Disposal a Gnawing Problem," *Science* 204 (May 1979), p. 820.

This case was prepared by Martha W. Elliott and Tom L. Beauchamp and revised by Joanne L. Jurmu and Anna Pinedo. **Not to be duplicated without the permission of the holder of the copyright,** © 1989 Tom L. Beauchamp.

figure in the later events at Love Canal, built its first plant in the area in 1905. Presently a subsidiary of Occidental Petroleum Corporation, Hooker manufactures plastics, pesticides, chlorine, caustic soda, fertilizers, and a variety of other chemical products. With over 3,000 employees, Hooker is still one of the largest employers and an economic force in the Niagara Falls area.[2]

In the early 1940s the abandoned section of Love Canal—for many years a summer swimming hole—became a dump for barrels of waste materials produced by the various chemical companies. Hooker received permission in 1942 to use the site for chemical dumping. It is estimated, although no accurate records were kept, that between the early dumping period and 1953, when this tract of land was sold, approximately 21,000 tons of different kinds of chemical wastes, some extremely toxic, were deposited in the old canal. The chemicals were in drums, and the site was considered ideal for chemical dumping. It was in an undeveloped, largely unpopulated area and had highly impermeable clay walls that retained liquid chemical materials with virtually no penetration. Research indicated that the canal's walls permitted water penetration at the rate of a third of an inch over a 25-year period.

In 1947 Hooker purchased the Love Canal site from Niagara Power and Development Company. In 1953 the dump was closed and covered with an impermeable clay top. The land encompassing and surrounding the dump was then acquired by the Niagara Falls School Board. This acquisition was against the advice of Hooker, which had warned of the toxic wastes. However, the board persisted and started condemnation proceedings to acquire land in the area. Subsequently an elementary school and a tract of houses were built adjacent to the site. Thousands of cubic yards of soil were removed from the top of the canal in the process. The construction apparently damaged the integrity of the clay covering. Water from rain and heavy snows then seeped through the covering and entered the chemical-filled, clay-lined basin. Eventually the basin overflowed on the unfortunate residents, who were treated to the noxious smell and unwholesome sight of chemicals seeping into their basements and surfacing to the ground.

In April of 1978 evidence of toxic chemicals was found in the living area of several homes, and the state health commissioner ordered an investigation. A number of health hazards came to light. Several adults examined showed incipient liver damage; young women in certain areas

[2] John F. Steiner, "Love Can Be Dangerous to Your Health," in George A. Steiner and John F. Steiner, *Casebook for Business, Government and Society*, 2d ed. (New York: Random House, 1980), pp. 108–109.

experienced three times the normal incidence of miscarriages; and the area had three and a half times the normal incidence of birth defects. Epilepsy, suicide, rectal bleeding, hyperactivity, and a variety of other ills were also reported.

Upon review of these findings, the health commissioner recommended that the elementary school be temporarily closed and that pregnant women and children under the age of two be temporarily evacuated. Shortly thereafter the Governor of New York announced that the state would purchase the 235 houses nearest the canal and would assist in the relocation of dispossessed families. President Carter declared Love Canal a disaster area, qualifying the affected families for federal assistance.[3] However, families in the adjacent ring of houses were not able to move—although they firmly believed that their health was endangered. Early studies tended to confirm this view, but in mid-July 1982, the EPA released a study that concluded there was "no evidence that Love Canal has contributed to environmental contamination" in the outer ring of 400 homes. This report focused on "health hazards" and did not address symptoms of stress that had been noted: For example, the divorce rate among remaining families increased as wives and children fled, while husbands tried to hold onto their houses and jobs.[4]

Since the investigation first began more than 100 different chemicals, some of them mutagens, teratogens, and carcinogens, have been identified. A number of unanswered questions are still being probed. One question concerns the long-range effects of chemical exposure. Cancer, for instance, often does not develop for 20 to 25 years after exposure to the cancer-producing agent. Chromosomal damage may appear only in subsequent generations. Other unanswered questions involve determining how to clean up the "mess" and who should be held responsible for it.

CRITICISMS OF THE HOOKER CHEMICAL COMPANY

The Hooker Chemical company figures in both of these questions. In 1977 the city of Niagara Falls employed an engineering consulting firm to study Love Canal and make recommendations. Hooker supplied technical assistance, information, and personnel. The cost of a second

---

[3] Maugh, "Toxic Waste Disposal."

[4] Constance Holden, "Love Canal Residents under Stress," *Science* 208 (June 13, 1980), pp. 1242–1244, and "Some Love Canal Areas Safe, a New EPA Study Concludes," *Washington Post*, July 15, 1982, Sec. A, pp. 1, 9 (Byline: Sandra Sugawara). See also Beverly Paigen in note 16 on the earlier data.

study was shared equally by Hooker, the city, and the school board that had originally purchased the land from Hooker. Hooker also offered to pay one-third of the estimated $850,000 cost of cleanup.[5]

In 1980 Hooker was faced with over $2 billion in lawsuits stemming from its activities at Love Canal and other locations. Thirteen hundred private suits had been filed against Hooker by mid-1982. The additional complaints and suits stemmed from past and current activities in other states as well as from additional sites in New York. In addition, in 1976, suits totalling more than $100 million were filed by Virginia employees of Life Sciences who had been exposed to Kepone, a highly toxic chemical known to cause trembling and sterility in humans. Hooker was named in the suit as a supplier of some of the raw materials used in the Virginia manufacturing process. (The suit was ultimately settled out of court.) In 1977 Hooker was ordered to pay $176,000 for discharging HCCPD, a chemical used in the manufacture of Kepone and Mirex, which had caused cancer in laboratory animals, into White Lake in Michigan. In 1979 that state's officials sued Hooker for a $200 million cleanup due to air, water, and land pollution around its White Lake plant. Hooker in 1978 acknowledged that it had buried an estimated 3,700 tons of trichlorophenol waste—which includes some quantities of the potent chemical dioxin—at various sites around Niagara Falls from 1942 through 1972.[6]

While Hooker was defending its actions in Virginia and Michigan, the state of California was investigating the company and ultimately brought suit on charges that Hooker's Occidental Chemical plant at Lathrop, California, had for years violated state law by dumping toxic pesticides, thereby polluting nearby ground water. While Hooker officials denied the charges, a series of memos written by Robert Edson, Occidental's environmental engineer at Lathrop, suggests that the company knew of the hazard as early as 1975 but chose to ignore it until pressured by the state investigation. In April 1975 Edson wrote, "Our laboratory records indicate that we are slowly contaminating all wells in our area, and two of our own wells are contaminated to the point of being toxic to animals and humans. . . ." A year later he wrote, "To date, we have been discharging waste water . . . containing about five tons of pesticide per year to the ground. . . . I believe we have fooled around long enough and already over-pressed our luck." Another year later, Edson reiterated his charges and added that "if anyone should complain, we could be the party named in an action by the Water Quality Control

[5] Steiner, "Love Can Be Dangerous," p. 112.

[6] Michael H. Brown, "Love Canal, U.S.A.," *New York Times Magazine* (January 21, 1979), p. 23, *passim*, and Gary Whitney, "Hooker Chemical and Plastics" (HBS Case Services, Harvard Business School, 1979), p. 3.

Board. . . . Do we correct the situation before we have a problem or do we hold off until action is taken against us?"[7]

Other complaints about Hooker stemmed from the same general area of Love Canal. In 1976 the New York Department of Environmental Conservation banned consumption of seven species of fish taken from Lake Ontario, claiming that they were contaminated with chemicals, including Mirex. It was alleged that Mirex had been discharged from the Hooker Niagara Falls plant. A Hooker-sponsored study of Lake Ontario fish disputed this allegation of Mirex contamination. While this study has not been accepted by the state, the ban has, for the most part, been lifted.

Hooker's Hyde Park chemical waste dump, located in the Niagara Falls area, has also been a source of continuing concern and dispute to residents and government officials. In 1972 the manager of a plant adjacent to the dump complained to Hooker about "an extremely dangerous condition affecting our plant and employees . . . our midnight shift workers has [sic] complained of coughing and sore throats from the obnoxious and corrosive permeating fumes from the disposal site."[8] Apparently the "dangerous condition" was not adequately rectified, and in 1979 Hooker's Hyde Park landfill became the subject of a lawsuit seeking nearly $26 million filed by the town of Niagara Falls. New York State filed a suit for more than $200 million for alleged damages at the Hyde Park site. A remedial program agreement, signed by the state, entailed an estimated $16 million in proposed work at this site.

In 1980 Hooker was also faced with four additional suits by the Environmental Protection Agency for $124.5 million in remedial work. Barbara Blum, EPA Deputy Administrator, explains the EPA concern and strategy as follows:

> To help protect against toxic by-products, EPA has launched a major regulatory and enforcement drive, including suits using EPA's "imminent hazard" or "emergency" provisions to force the cleanup of the most dangerous hazardous waste problems. I anticipate that 50 such cases will be filed before the end of 1980.
>
> The most widely recognized symbol of the hazardous waste crisis is Love Canal in Niagara Falls, where an entire neighborhood has been abandoned. There are, however, hundreds of other graphic examples scattered across the country.
>
> The issue of how to deal with our legacy of dangerous waste disposal sites and to prevent the development of new "Love Canals" may be the

---

[7] "The Hooker Memos," in Robert J. Baum, ed., *Ethical Problems in Engineering*, 2d ed. (Troy, N.Y.: Center for the Study of the Human Dimensions of Science and Technology, Rensselaer Polytechnic Institute, 1980), Vol. 2, *Cases*, p. 38, and "An Occidental Unit Knowingly Polluted California Water, House Panel Charges," *Wall Street Journal*, June 20, 1979, p. 14.

[8] Whitney, "Hooker Chemical and Plastics."

most difficult environmental challenge of the 1980s. EPA has launched four interrelated efforts to bring this problem under control.[9]

⟶ Two of these efforts are relevant to the actions against Hooker: (1) litigation under "imminent hazard" provisions of existing EPA laws, and (2) the creation of programs, financed by government and industry, to clean up hazardous waste sites. The "imminent hazard" litigation is described as follows: "Primarily emphasizing injunctive relief, this program seeks to halt dangerous disposal practices and to force privately-funded cleanup. This approach gets results, of course, only where a responsible party can be identified and has adequate financial resources to carry some or all of the cleanup costs."[10]

Blum also describes the specific statutes the EPA is acting under and discusses the EPA's collaboration with the Justice Department in enforcing the statutes:

> Sections of the Resource Conservation and Recovery Act, Safe Drinking Water Act, Toxic Substances Control Act, Clean Water Act, and Clean Air Act all authorize EPA to ask the court for injunctive relief in situations which pose threats to public health or the environment. Section 309 of the Clean Water Act levies a penalty of up to $10,000 a day for unpermitted discharges to navigable waters (a leaking dump can be considered a discharge). The 1899 "Refuse Act" provides additional penalties for unauthorized discharges or dumping. Available common law remedies include the common law of nuisance and trespass, restitution, and "strict liability" for damages caused by those who engaged in ultra-hazardous activities. We are aggressively using each of these legal tools to address the hazardous waste disposal problem.
>
> The Agency—working with the Department of Justice—has launched a top-priority effort to pursue imminent hazard cases. . . .
>
> People are frightened by Love Canal and by the emergence of threatening hazardous waste sites in their local communities. They are demanding action—and they are getting it.[11]

The EPA has estimated that only 10 percent of all hazardous wastes are disposed of in strict compliance with federal regulations. According to Thomas H. Maugh, II, "nearly 50 percent is disposed of by lagooning in unlined surface impoundments, 30 percent in nonsecure landfills, and about 10 percent by dumping into sewers, spreading on roads, injection into deep wells, and incineration under uncontrolled conditions."[12] Maugh argues that "legal dump sites gone awry" are actu-

[9] Barbara Blum, "Hazardous Waste Action," *EPA Journal* (June 1980), p. 2.

[10] *Ibid.*

[11] *Ibid.,* p. 8.

[12] Maugh, "Toxic Waste Disposal," pp. 819–821.

ally a lesser problem than the growing problem of illegally dumped wastes in unsecured dump sites, often in the middle of cities.[13] In October 1981 the EPA announced that "there are at least twenty-nine toxic waste disposal sites around the country as dangerous or more so than Love Canal. . . ."[14]

HOOKER'S DEFENSE AGAINST THE CHARGES

Hooker Chemical believes that its role and position have been misunderstood. While the company neither denies using the canal as a chemical dump nor denies that the dump has created a serious problem, company officials contend that (1) the company's efforts to prevent first the public and then the private development of the canal area are generally unrecognized; (2) the company has been an industry leader in safety; (3) Hooker is being unfairly blamed and singled out for waste disposal practices that were then almost universal throughout the chemical industry; and (4) a certain level of risk is an inevitable hazard in an industrial society.

Hooker has marshalled data to support its contentions. In the first place, Hooker believes that its efforts to warn the school board and city against interfering with the waste disposal area are unappreciated. When the Niagara Falls School Board expressed an interest in selling a portion of the Love Canal tract to a developer, Hooker representatives argued against the plan in a public meeting and later reiterated to the board its warnings of possible hazards. When the school board persisted in its plans and began to obtain adjacent parcels of land through condemnation proceedings, Hooker, in the deed to the school board, again referred to the past use of the property and stipulated that all future risks and liabilities be passed to the school board. One part of the deed stipulated:

> Prior to the delivery of this instrument of conveyance, the grantee herein has been advised by the grantor that the premises above described have been filled, in whole or in part, to the present grade level thereof with waste products resulting from the manufacturing of chemicals by the grantor at its plant in the City of Niagara Falls, New York, and the grantee assumes all risk and liability incident to the use thereof. It is, therefore, understood and agreed that, as a part of the consideration for this conveyance and as a condition thereof, no claim, suit, action or demand of any nature whatsoever shall ever be made by the grantee, its successors or assigns, against the grantor, its successors or assigns, for injury to a person

---

[13] Steiner, "Love Can Be Dangerous," p. 110.

[14] Joanne Omong, "EPA Names 115 Toxic Waste Dump Sites for Cleanup," *Washington Post*, October 24, 1981, p. 4.

or persons, including the death resulting therefrom, or loss of or damage to property caused by, in connection with or by reason of the presence of said industrial wastes.[15]

When the school board later sold part of the land to a private developer who planned to build houses, Hooker officials protested the sale both verbally and in writing. Executives believe that the company is being unjustly blamed for the improvidence of others. Hooker also claims that it has no legal responsibility for the problem at Love Canal and that it has more than met its social and moral obligations in time and money spent on the cleanup effort. Through its experiences at Love Canal, Hooker environmental health and safety specialists have developed knowledge and skills that have enabled the company to take a leadership role in problems of underground pollution.

Hooker officials also argue that their past practices more than met then-operative industry standards for waste disposal. During the period from 1942 to 1953 when Hooker was filling Love Canal with barrels of chemical wastes, the long-term environmental and personal hazards of these industrial "leftovers" were not adequately recognized either by the industries involved or by the health and regulatory professions. Putting the chemical wastes into a clay canal was actually an improvement on common methods of disposal in unlined and unsecured landfills.

The company's defense of its behavior in the Love Canal situation parallels in some respects the reaction of certain Love Canal residents. They directed the major thrust of their antagonism not toward Hooker Chemical, but toward the New York State Health Department, which had failed to provide open access to the results of state-conducted health studies and left unexplained delays in admitting that a health problem existed. The health department attempted to discourage and actively harassed independent researchers whose reports indicated more widespread risks to the health of the community than the Department was willing to admit—or prepared to pay to rectify. On these premises, it was the health department, not Hooker Chemical, which did not meet its obligations to the community.[16]

Hooker supports the common industry position that society will have to learn to accept a certain level of risk in order to enjoy the products of industrial society. Environmental hazards are one form of industrial "tradeoff." Industrialists cite persons such as Margery W. Shaw, an independent scientist who reviewed a chromosomal study of Love Canal residents. She points out that the level of acceptable risk is a general societal problem merely instanced in this case.

[15] Steiner, "Love Can Be Dangerous," p. 110.

[16] Beverly Paigen, "Controversy at Love Canal," *Hastings Center Report* 12 (June 1982), pp. 29–37.

In our democratic society, perhaps we will decide that 500,000 deaths per year is an acceptable price for toxic chemicals in our environment, just as we have decided that 50,000 traffic deaths per year is an acceptable price for automobile travel. On the other hand, we may say that 5,000 deaths per year is an unacceptable price for toxic chemicals.[17]

THE CONTINUING CONTROVERSY OVER HOOKER AND THE CANAL CLEANUP

⟶ Over the years, Hooker has been among the most heavily criticized corporations for its environmental policies. Ralph Nader attacked Hooker as a "callous corporation" leaving toxic "cesspools." An ABC news documentary was highly critical of the company, focusing on the increased incidence of disease at Love Canal. On the other hand, Hooker has won a number of defenders. In a July 27, 1981, editorial in *Fortune* magazine, the corporation was defended for having explicitly conformed to government standards of waste disposal, for resisting the construction at the canal, and for being the victim of exaggerated and irresponsible reports about the incidence of disease in the region.[18] An April 1981 editorial in *Discover* magazine laid the blame for the Love Canal on the school board, but argued that Hooker did act irresponsibly in waste dumpage at a number of other sites.[19] The 1982 study released by the EPA had the effect of blunting some federal efforts and some lawsuits.

In 1983 the U.S. Center for Disease Control (CDC) conducted a study of Love Canal residents. Forty-four residents were examined and compared to a control group chosen from Niagara Falls residents living at least one mile from the evacuated area. The CDC concluded that residents of Love Canal do not show increased incidence of cancer or reproductive abnormalities when compared to residents of other Niagara Falls neighborhoods.[20] The CDC did not draw any conclusions about the possibility of future illnesses developing in the region.

Critics of the CDC study claim it proved very little. They believe that the study group was too small to be conclusive. In addition, chemicals had seeped from Love Canal into the Niagara Falls drinking water, which placed all Niagara Falls residents at risk. Using a control from Niagara Falls, though not from the Love Canal neighborhood, allegedly failed to make the findings valid. Health officials and state legislators called for more conclusive information.

---

[17] Margery W. Shaw, "Love Canal Chromosome Study," *Science* 209 (August 15, 1980), p. 752.

[18] *Fortune* (July 27, 1981), pp. 30–31.

[19] *Discover* 2, no. 4 (April 1981), p. 8.

[20] "CDC Finds No Excess Illness at Love Canal," *Science* 220 (June 17, 1983), p. 1254.

Amidst the controversy, Niagara Falls city officials had a list of over 100 families from the Love Canal neighborhood who were waiting for housing.[21] Many people were eager to have the final word on conditions at Love Canal. While the 1982 EPA study purported that adjacent neighborhoods were safe, New York State health officials reported that they found dioxin (one of the most toxic chemicals known to man) at levels eight times higher than the lethal dose.[22] The U.S. Office of Technology Assessment undertook an evaluation of all available evidence, but its report shed no additional light on the conditions at Love Canal. It stated that "with available information it is possible either that unsafe levels of toxic contamination exist or that they do not exist."[23]

Voles, field mice common to the Love Canal area, were the subject of a 1983 study. The mice were ideal for the study because they are sedentary, rarely moving appreciable distances. The number of voles found living in the canal area was less than in the control area. (The control area was located one mile from the canal area.) Liver damage was evident in the mice living near the canal. Life expectancies varied significantly. Any vole in the canal area that reached an age of 30 days could be expected to live an additional 54 days. A similar vole in the control area would be expected to live 100 days past the 30-day mark. The life expectancy was cut in half for those mice living near the canal. The researchers cautioned against direct extrapolation to humans, but their results indicate that further research on humans is warranted before a clean bill of health is issued to the Love Canal neighborhood.[24]

A case study of live birth weights of children born to Love Canal women has provided some cause for concern. Children born to women who lived near chemical swales were significantly lower in weight than the New York average. A swale is a natural low area along water drainage pathways where chemicals might collect. There are several drainage pathways that pass through the Love Canal region. The study covered the years 1940–1978. (The years 1953–1978 had no chemical dumping into the Love Canal.) Researchers found that 12.1 percent of the children born to women who had lived near one of the swales were born with lower than average birth weights as compared to a 6.9 percent average for the state of New York (excluding New York City).[25]

Citizens and health officials have mobilized in an attempt to force

[21] "Love Canal: Still a Battleground," *U.S. News and World Report* 93 (July 26, 1982), p. 6.

[22] *Ibid.*

[23] "Hazards in Love Canal Monitoring," *Science News* 124 (July 9, 1983), p. 29.

[24] John J. Christian, "Love Canal's Unhealthy Voles," *Natural History* 92 (October 1983), pp. 8–14.

[25] Nicholas J. Vianna and Adele K. Polan, "Incidence of Low Birth Weights among Love Canal Residents," *Science* 226 (December 7, 1983), pp. 1217–1219.

the cleanup of Love Canal and keep area inhabitants informed of new findings and projects. Local citizens have grown weary of the problems and they want the area cleaned up as soon as possible. Progress has been made, but efforts will continue late into the 1990s. The complex cleanup project began in the spring of 1987 with the dredging of three local creeks. In August 1987, the site, which had remained covered with plastic sheeting and earth, was uncovered; officials began to dredge dioxin-contaminated mud and tainted sediment from the creeks. The creeks were dewatered and waste removed. The EPA and the state Department of Environmental Conservation stored the wastes in a temporary landfill and storage facility near the site.

Citizens opposed the storage, fearing that it would delay possible rehabilitation of the area. They charged the EPA with negligence and undue delay in cleaning toxic waste sites, in accord with its Superfund Project. In October 1987 the EPA announced plans to complete the cleanup of the area. The EPA planned to incinerate the stored wastes at an expected cost of $26 to $31 million. The incineration process, while costly, is considered a permanent solution. Buried wastes or other disposal methods, such as deep well injection, are considered hazardous.[26]

The final phase of a long-term habitability study began in the spring of 1987. The Technical Review Committee (TRC) will oversee testing of the air and soil of Love Canal and will compare its findings to those from other neighborhoods around the state, including two from Niagara Falls. The TRC was formed in 1983 to develop criteria for making a final Love Canal resettlement decision. Should the area ever be deemed uninhabitable, Love Canal will be converted to a reforested park.[27] If a final decision is made to resettle inhabitants, the Love Canal Revitalization Agency will begin to build new or renovate existing houses near the area. At this writing, 338 homes stand abandoned and boarded up in the neighborhood. Earlier 175 houses were demolished because weather and lack of heat or maintenance caused irreversible deterioration of the abandoned homes.[28]

In February 1988, a new court decision altered the circumstance of legal liability for Love Canal. Federal Judge John Curtin of the U.S. District Court for the Western District of New York ruled that Occidental Petroleum Corporation's chemicals unit is responsible for the costs of cleaning up Love Canal—costs estimated at $250 million. Occidental

[26] "EPA Will Burn Sediment to Clean Love Canal Area," *Wall Street Journal,* October 27, 1987, p. 72.

[27] Carolyn Kuma, "Resampling Could Delay Canal Revitalization Effort," *Niagara Gazette,* November 8, 1986, p. 1.

[28] Arch Lowery, "Falls Council Opposes Storage of Dioxin Waste at Love Canal," *Buffalo Evening News,* February 3, 1987, p. B1, and Carolyn Kuma, "Maintenance of Canal Homes Delayed," *Niagara Gazette,* January 22, 1987, p. A3.

was found "at least partially responsible" for the initially inadequate storage and for leakage that has occurred over the years. Occidental argued in the case that the city of Niagara Falls was "solely responsible" for release of the toxic wastes because city officials ignored warnings about the site and then disrupted its hydrology. But Judge Curtin rejected this "third-party defense" because Hooker Chemical had brought the wastes to the site.[29] New York State Attorney General Robert Abrams said the judge's opinion constitutes "a tremendous victory for the state and federal governments and a resounding defeat for Occidental's strenuous and expensive public-relations campaign to shift the entire blame for Love Canal to the city of Niagara Falls, the board of education, the state of New York, and even the people who were forced to abandon their homes."[30]

---

[29] *U.S.A.* v. *Hooker Chemicals,* U.S. District Court, Western District of New York, CIV-79-990C (February 23, 1988).

[30] See Roy J. Harris, Jr., "Occidental Unit Is Ruled Liable in Waste Case," *Wall Street Journal,* February 24, 1988, p. 2, and Michael Weisskopf, "Company Ruled Liable for Love Canal Costs," *Washington Post,* February 24, 1988, p. A10.

The Cosmetics Industry and the Draize Test

In a survey conducted in the United Kingdom, the vast majority of respondents objected to cosmetic testing on animals.[1] More recently, *Glamour* magazine asked its readers whether we should do cosmetic tests on animals and 84 percent said no.[2] However, in a 1977 BBC television program on animal experimentation, the following question was put to a number of shoppers: Would you use a shampoo if it had not been safety-tested on animals? All answered that they would not. The difference in the responses to the two surveys illustrates the complex nature of the problem.

Some argue that society does not need cosmetics but offer few constructive suggestions as to how a $10 billion industry should be prevented from innovation in Western "free" market economies. Others argue that the products should not be tested on animals since humanity has no right to subject animals to pain and suffering for the sake of frivolous vanity products. However, many consumer organizations consider that cosmetics should be even more closely regulated and subjected to more intensive animal tests.[3]

Faced with the continuing threat of litigation as a result of adverse reactions, the cosmetics industry is unlikely to retreat from animal testing. It is known that tests do not necessarily protect consumers from all risk, but they reduce the extent of risk and also provide some protection for a company in the event of a large claim for damages.

[1] National Opinion Polls, *Report to Annual General Meeting of Royal Society for the Prevention of Cruelty to Animals* (June 28, 1974).

[2] *Glamour* (December 1981).

[3] R. Nader, on the regulation of the safety of cosmetics, in S. S. Epstein and R. D. Grundy, eds., *The Legislation of Product Safety: Consumer Health and Product Hazards—Cosmetics and Drugs, Pesticides, Food Additives,* vol. 2 (Boston, Mass.: MIT Press, 1974), pp. 73–141.

Nevertheless, in a case against Beacon Castile, in which a woman accidentally splashed concentrated shampoo in her eye, the verdict went against the FDA and in favor of the company.[4] The judge's ruling was based primarily on the contention that the concentrated shampoo would be unlikely to enter the eye under normal conditions. However, he also noted that "the rabbit studies, standing alone, do not warrant condemnation of this product." This indicated that this court, at least, was not impressed by the applicability of the rabbit data.

HISTORICAL BACKGROUND
ON EYE TESTING

The Draize eye test is a standard testing procedure for eye irritation. It is named after the principal author of a paper that outlined the main element of the test, together with a numerical scoring system to provide an idea of the irritancy of the tested substance.[5] Such irritancy testing primarily involves cosmetics, toiletries, agricultural chemicals, occupational and environmental hazards, and certain therapeutics, especially ophthalmological formulations. The development of the test followed the passage of the Federal Food, Drug, and Cosmetic Act of 1938 that required, *inter alia,* that cosmetics be free of poisonous or deleterious substances to the user.

In 1933, a woman suffered ulceration of both corneas as a result of having her eyelashes dyed with a coal-tar product called "Lash-lure." She was left blind and disfigured and the American Medical Association (AMA) documented seventeen similar cases, some resulting in death. "Lash-lure" remained on the market for five more years because the federal government did not have the authority to seize the product under the 1906 Food and Drug Act because the "Lash-lure" manufacturer made no medical claims.[6] However, the 1938 act did not prevent accidents resulting in eye damage. In a 1952 hearing in Congress, a case was presented of an anti-dandruff shampoo containing a new polyoxyethylene compound that caused semi-permanent injuries.[7] A recent study of 35,490 people, covering a three-month period, turned up 589 adverse reactions that were confirmed by dermatologists as most likely to have

[4] U.S. District Court of the Northern District of Ohio, Eastern Division, No. C71-53, January 7, 1974, pp. 164–166.

[5] J. H. Draize, G. Woodard, and H. O. Calvery, on methods for the study of irritation and toxicity of substances applied topically to the skin and mucous membranes, in *Journal of Pharmacology and Experimental Therapy* 82 (1944), pp. 377–390.

[6] R. D. Lamb, *American Chamber of Horrors* (New York: Farrar & Reinhart, 1936).

[7] T. Stabile, *Cosmetics: Trick or Treat* (New York: Houston Books, 1966).

been caused by cosmetics. Of the 589 reactions, 3 percent were classified as severe, 11 percent as moderate, and 86 percent as mild.[8] It is thus clear that there is a need to determine whether or not a new cosmetic product is likely to cause eye irritancy before it is released on the market. The question, therefore, concerns the method of determining a product's potential hazard, rather than whether or not testing is required.

Eye irritation usually has one or more of the following characteristics— ulceration or opacity of the cornea, iris inflammation, and conjunctival inflammation. The Draize test utilizes this fact and scores the extent of the injury to each part of the eye. The various scores are then combined to give a total, which is used to indicate the irritancy potential of the test substance.

The Draize test has undergone several modifications since 1944 and was adapted for use in enforcing the Hazardous Substances Labeling Act. In the modified version, 0.1 ml is instilled into the conjunctival sac of one eye of each of six rabbits, the other eye serving as a control. The lids are held together for one second and the animal is then released. The eyes are examined at 24, 48, and 72 hours.[9] The scoring system is heavily weighted towards corneal damage (80 out of 110) because corneal damage leads quickly to impairment of vision.

The Interagency Regulatory Liaison Group issued draft guidelines for acute eye irritation tests a few years ago.[10] They selected the albino rabbit as the preferred test animal and recommended the use of a single, large-volume dose (0.1 ml) despite the advantages (obtaining a dose-response effect) of using a range of volumes.[11] They also recommended that, in most cases, anesthetics should not be used. However, if the test substance were likely to cause extreme pain, the use of a local anesthetic (0.5 percent proparacaine or 2 percent butacaine) was recommended for humane reasons.[12] The eyes should not be washed. Observations should be made 1, 24, 72, and 168 hours after treatment. The

---

[8] M. Morrison, "Cosmetics: Some Statistics on Safety," *FDA Consumer* (March 1976), pp. 15–17.

[9] F. N. Marzulli and M. E. Simon, on eye irritation from topically applied drugs and cosmetics: preclinical studies, in *American Journal of Optometry, Archives of the American Academy of Optometry* 48 (1971), pp. 61–78.

[10] Interagency Regulatory Liaison Group, Testing Standards and Guidelines Workgroup, *Draft IRLG Guidelines for Selected Acute Toxicity Test* (Washington, D.C.: IRLG, 1979).

[11] J. F. Griffith, G. A. Nixon, R. D. Bruce, P. J. Reer, and E. A. Bannan, on dose-response studies with chemical irritants in the albino rabbit eye as a basis for selecting optimum testing conditions for predicting hazard to the human eye, in *Toxicology and Applied Pharmacology* 55 (1980), pp. 501–513.

[12] A. G. Ulsamer, P. L. Wright, and R. E. Osterbert, "A Comparison of the Effects of Model Irritants on Anesthetized and Nonanesthetized Rabbit Eyes," *Toxicology and Applied Pharmacology* 41 (1977), pp. 191–192 (abstract).

cut-off point for a nonirritant is set very low (*i.e.*, minimal reaction) in order to provide a large margin of safety in extrapolating the human response.

COMPARATIVE STUDIES

The parts of the eye that are most affected by topically applied substances are the cornea, the bulbar and palpebral conjunctivae, and the iris. The corneas of laboratory mammals are very similar in construction[13] and variations are, for the most part, minor. (The mean thickness of the cornea does vary: In man it is 0.51 mm; in the rabbit, 0.37 mm; and in the cat, 0.62 mm. The composition of the corneas of man and other species differs in the quantity and kind of enzymes.)[14]

The rabbit has historically been the animal of choice for the Draize eye test, but this seems to have occurred more by accident than by design. The use of the rabbit eye for predicting human ophthalmic response has been challenged from time to time. It has been suggested that the greater thickness of the human cornea and other anatomical differences may contribute to the rabbit's greater susceptibility to alkali burns of the cornea.[15] However, the rabbit is less sensitive than man to some other substances.[16] Tears are produced in smaller quantities in the rabbit than in man, but the rabbit nictitating membrane may supplement the cleansing effect of tears.

Procter & Gamble produced an extensive critique of the Draize test in their comments on the draft IRLG Guidelines for Acute Toxicity Tests.[17] They expressed disappointment at the fact that federal agencies have been singularly unresponsive to widespread criticism of the Draize test and have made little or no effort to encourage innovation. They commented on the differences between the human and rabbit eye[18] and the fact that the rabbit's response to the test material is greatly exaggerated when compared to human responses.[19] Procter & Gamble

[13] S. Duke-Elder, *System of Ophthalmology, Volume 1: The Eye in Evolution* (St. Louis, Mo.: C. V. Mosby Co., 1958), p. 452.

[14] R. Kuhlman, on species variation in the enzyme content of the corneal epithelium, in *Journal of Cell Composition Physiology* 53 (1959), pp. 313–326.

[15] C. P. Carpenter and H. F. Smyth, on chemical burns of the rabbit cornea, in *American Journal of Ophthalmology* 29 (1946), pp. 1363–1372.

[16] Marzulli and Simon, on eye irritation.

[17] Procter and Gamble Company, Comments on Draft IRLG Guidelines for Acute Toxicity Tests (Washington, D.C.: IRLG, 1979).

[18] J. H. Beckley, "Comparative Eye Testing: Man versus Animal," *Toxicology and Applied Pharmacology* 7 (1965), pp. 93–101, and E. V. Buehler, "Testing to Predict Potential Ocular Hazards of Household Chemicals," *Toxicology Annual*, ed. C. L. Winek (New York: Marcel Dekker, 1974).

[19] R. O. Carter and J. F. Griffith, on experimental bases for the realistic assessment of safety of topical agents, in *Toxicology and Applied Pharmacology* 7 (1965), pp. 60–73.

suggest that, when the rabbit result is equivocal, organizations should have the option of using monkeys.

The monkey has been proposed as a more suitable model because it is phylogenetically closer to man,[20] but there are still species differences.[21] In addition, use of monkeys for eye irritancy testing is inappropriate, in part because of their diminishing availability. Also, the expense does not warrant the purported fine-tuning involved in the use of monkeys. The rat has also been suggested as an alternative model but has not been investigated in any depth. Studies at Avon indicate that it may be less sensitive than the rabbit.[22] If one must use an animal for eye irritancy testing, then the rabbit would appear to be as appropriate as any other species.

TECHNICAL

It has already been stressed that the Draize eye irritancy test cannot be *routinely* used to grade substances according to their potential irritancy for human beings but only as a "pass-fail" test. In 1971, Weil and Scala[23] reported the results of a survey of intra- and inter-laboratory variability of the Draize eye and skin test. Twenty-four laboratories cooperated on the eye irritancy testing, including the Food and Drug Directorate (Canada), Hazleton Laboratories (USA), Huntingdom Research Centre (UK), Avon Products (USA), Colgate-Palmolive (USA), General Foods (USA), and American Cyanamid (USA). Twelve chemicals were selected for ophthalmic irritancy testing and distributed as unknowns to the various companies for testing according to a standard reference procedure employing the original grading scale.[24] Three of the substances were recorded as nonirritants by all the laboratories but there was considerable variation in the results for the other nine. For example, cream peroxide was recorded as a nonirritant by certain laboratories but as an irritant by others.

As a result of this study, Weil and Scala[25] concluded that "the rabbit eye and skin procedures currently recommended by the federal agencies

---

[20] J. H. Beckley, T. J. Russell, and L. F. Rubin, on the use of rhesus monkey for predicting human responses to eye irritants, in *Toxicology and Applied Pharmacology* 15 (1969), pp. 1–9.

[21] W. R. Green, J. B. Sullivan, R. M. Hehir, L. G. Scharpf, and A. W. Dickinson, *A Systematic Comparison of Chemically Induced Eye Injury in the Albino Rabbit and Rhesus Monkey* (New York: Soap and Detergent Association, 1978).

[22] G. Foster, 1980, personal communication.

[23] C. S. Weil and R. A. Scala, on the study of intra- and inter-laboratory variability in the results of rabbit eye and skin irritation test, in *Toxicology and Applied Pharmacology* 19 (1971), pp. 276–360.

[24] Draize, et al., on methods for the study of irritation and toxicity.

[25] Weil and Scala, on the study of intra- and inter-laboratory variability.

for use in the delineation of irritancy of materials should not be recommended as standard procedures in any new regulations. Without careful re-education these tests result in unreliable results." It is pertinent to note that Scala considers that the Draize test can be used to grade irritants, but only by experienced and careful researchers.[26]

RECENT PROPOSALS AND
POLITICAL ACTIVITY

Development of the Coalition to Abolish the Draize Test. During the last decade, the humane movement has increasingly called into question the testing of cosmetics on laboratory animals. With one or two minor exceptions, the campaigns that have been launched against such cosmetic testing have been poorly planned and their effectiveness has been undercut by inadequately researched position papers and a dissipation of energy in different directions. All this changed with the development of a coalition of over 400 humane societies aimed specifically at the use of the Draize eye irritancy test by cosmetic companies. This coalition was the brainchild of a New York English teacher, Henry Spira, and the Draize test was selected as the target for the following reasons. First, the test has been criticized in scientific literature as being inappropriate and, in routine use, the data produced are unreliable for regulatory purposes.[27] Second, the Draize test can cause trauma to rabbit eyes that is readily visible and that produces a strong reaction among the general public as well as scientists. As Henry Spira states, "it is the type of test that people can identify with—people know what it feels like to get a little bit of soap in their eyes."[28] Third, the test has remained essentially unchanged for over thirty years despite the fact that the prospects for humane modifications are good. Also, relatively little research has been undertaken in a search for an *in vitro* alternative and even fewer results have been made available in the scientific literature.

The cosmetics industry was selected as the target because it is vulnerable to the image problem raised by the use of the Draize eye test. The picture of the sultry model advertising a new beauty product does not juxtapose readily with an inflamed and swollen rabbit eye. It has been argued that the selection of the cosmetics industry is unfair since their products are, by and large, the least irritant. However, the coalition took the view that the cosmetics industry is not a discrete group, totally separate from other manufacturing companies. In many instances, a

---

[26] R. A. Scala, 1980, personal communication.

[27] Weil and Scala, on the study of intra- and inter-laboratory variability.

[28] L. Harriton, "Conversation with Henry Spira: Draize Test Activist," *Lab Animal* 10 (1) (1981), pp. 16–22.

single company will make a range of products including household cleaners, toiletries, cosmetics, and drugs. From the coalition's point of view, it is important that the activities of all the members be narrowly focused in order to create the maximum impact and ultimately persuade policy makers that it is worth their while to change their priorities on the Draize test. The campaign's success may be measured by the following actions taken after it started in March 1980.

Government Responses. The Consumer Product Safety Commission started, on May 8, 1980, a temporary (6-month) moratorium on all in-house Draize testing until the effects of using local anesthetics to reduce pain could be elucidated. They have now identified tetracaine (a double dose) as an effective local anesthetic. The Office of Pesticides and Toxic Substances of the Environmental Protection Agency established a similar moratorium on October 1, 1980. Furthermore, they proposed to "establish the search for alternative test methods to the Draize as a research priority for the coming year." The FDA committed funds in 1981 to study a new *in vitro* technique.[29] In Congress, Senator D. Durenberger (R-Minn) and Congressman A. Jacobs (D-Ind) introduced resolutions that it was the sense of Congress that funds should be allocated to the development of a non-animal alternative to the Draize. The National Toxicology Program has yet to make a serious commitment to look for an alternative.

Public pressure on government agencies regarding the Draize test in particular has abated since 1981. Until a feasible alternative (a battery of non-animal tests) becomes available, little more will be expected of the regulatory bodies than that they exhibit sensitivity to the issue. Recently, however, there has been some suggestion that the agencies could be more responsive. Scientists at Procter and Gamble have produced evidence indicating that use of a smaller test volume (0.01 ml instead of 0.1 ml) improves the predictive accuracy of the Draize test.[30] Nevertheless, the Environmental Protection Agency has not yet shown any inclination to change its testing requirements.

Industry Actions. The Cosmetics, Toiletries and Fragrances Association (CTFA) established a special task force to review alternative test systems. They sponsored a closed workshop of scientists to investigate the potential for modifying the Draize test and to develop an alternative.

A major breakthrough in the controversy occurred on December 23, 1980, when Revlon announced that it was giving Rockefeller University a grant of $750,000 to fund a three-year research effort aimed at finding

[29] *Congressional Record* E2953, June 15, 1981.

[30] F. E. Freebert, J. F. Griffith, R. D. Bruce, and F. H. S. Bay, "Correlation of Animal Test Methods with Human Experience of Household Products," *Journal of Toxicology— Cut. Ocular. Toxicology* 1 (1984), pp. 53–64.

an alternative to the Draize test. Revlon executives commented that while it would be naive to deny that the campaign, including an effort focused specifically on Revlon, did not have any effect, the grant was part of an ongoing program to research and develop possible alternatives. According to Donald Davis, editor of *Drug and Cosmetic Industry,* Revlon's plight engendered a great deal of sympathy from other leaders in the industry but there was a distinct lack of volunteers to help take the heat off Revlon. Revlon also called upon other cosmetic companies, including Avon, Bristol-Myers, Gillette, Johnson and Johnson, Max Factor, and Procter and Gamble, to join them as full partners in supporting this research effort.

The other cosmetic companies were taken by surprise by Revlon's action, but they moved rapidly. Early in 1981, the CTFA announced the formation of a special research fund or trust to support research into alternatives. Avon committed $750,000, Estee-Lauder $350,000, and Bristol-Myers $200,000. Chanel, Mary Kay, and Max Factor also contributed undisclosed amounts. These funds have now been passed on to the Johns Hopkins School of Hygiene and Public Health to establish a Center for Alternatives Research. In the meantime, a number of proposed modifications were suggested that would answer some of the humane concerns.

Possible Modifications to the Draize Test. Since there is no satisfactory non-animal alternative currently available for eye irritancy testing, any modifications that can be incorporated now to make the test more "humane" would be welcomed by humane groups. Such modifications range from not doing the test at all to the use of smaller volumes or local anesthetics. These proposals include the following:

(i) *Do not test substances with physical properties known to produce severe irritation* such as alkalis (above pH 12) and acids (below pH 3).[31] (Adopted by the IRLG, 1981)

(ii) Screen out irritants using *in vitro* or less stressful tests. The *in vitro* eye preparations described above could be used to screen unknown substances and irritant substances either labeled as such or discarded. One could also utilize results from skin irritancy studies and human patch testing to avoid testing substances that produce trauma since the skin is likely to be less sensitive than the delicate tissues of the eye.[32]

(iii) When the test is conducted in the living animal, smaller volumes should be used. It has been argued that the use of 10 μl, rather than the standard 100 μl, would be a far more realistic test in terms of assessing possible human hazard. The use of smaller volumes

[31] Interagency Regulatory Liaison Group, *Recommended Guidelines for Acute Eye Irritation Testing* (Washington, D.C.: IRLG, 1981).

[32] *Ibid.*

would produce less trauma and one could also do some superficial dose-response studies to ensure that a nonirritant has a sufficient margin of safety.

(iv) Where it is necessary to test substances that cause pain and irritation in the rabbit, then local anesthetics should be used. This is recommended by the IRLG.[33]

Recent Developments

Since 1981, over $5 million has been provided by industry to support research in America into alternatives to the Draize test. Additional funds have been provided to scientists in Europe, not to mention the costs of intramural industry programs. A number of meetings have been organized to explore the issue. In 1986, as a result of an initiative by Henry Spira, Bausch and Lomb contracted with the Johns Hopkins Center for Alternatives to Animal Testing to produce a critical evaluation of the research to date and to identify the most promising tests. The resulting monograph reviewed thirty-five different test methods that have been developed but stopped short of naming the five or six with the most promise on the grounds of insufficient data.[34] However, the volume does provide ample evidence of the thought and effort that has gone into the search for an alternative to the Draize since 1980.

Industry has also re-evaluated its safety testing program. Procter and Gamble took the opportunity to review and revamp its toxicology group and has made a serious commitment to reduce animal use. Avon has opened its own cell culture laboratory to validate *in vitro* assays and has reduced its use of rodents and rabbits from 14,500 in 1981 to 4,715 in 1986. Avon has asserted that it intends to be a leader in the industry in switching to *in vitro* assays. Bristol Myers, Noxell, Colgate, and others have also pursued aggressive programs to promote alternatives and the Soap and Detergent Association organized a validation study for eight *in vitro* tests. Ironically, the study was not made public because there was so much difficulty in obtaining sound, quantified animal data to compare with the *in vitro* results.

CONCLUSION

The results of the campaign indicate that before 1980, the companies and government agencies affected could have made more effort to seek an alternative to the Draize test or to modify the procedure to make it more humane. However, until the public raised the stakes on the issue,

---

[33] *Ibid.*

[34] J. M. Frazier, S. C. Gad, A. M. Goldberg, and J. P. McCulley, *A Critical Evaluation of Alternatives to Acute Ocular Irritation Testing* (New York: Mary Ann Liebert Inc., 1987).

there was little motivation for action. Revlon ended up spending $1.25 million instead of the $17,000 suggested at the beginning by the coalition, and all the companies had to deal with large numbers of consumer complaints. Seven years later, some companies have made considerable strides in addressing the concerns raised by the animal movement but others have been less progressive. Nonetheless, it is clear that there is a trend to reduce animal use in testing.

Pâté at Iroquois Brands

On April 6, 1985, proxy materials mailed by Iroquois Brands of Green-wich, Connecticut, to its shareholders contained a controversial proposal about its importation of goose liver pâté from French suppliers. The question put to shareholders was whether they wished the corporation to investigate charges made concerning cruelty to animals in France in the force-feeding of the geese used to make the pâté.

The officers of Iroquois Brands did not voluntarily place this proposal on the proxy agenda for shareholders. The issue had come to prominence through the persistent efforts of a single shareholder, Peter C. Loven-heim, who believed the charges of inhumane treatment had substance and relevance for shareholders. Lovenheim, who held 200 shares of stock, was initially attracted to the company because of its health-food orientation and its broad range of specialty products. When he received proxy materials detailing a new product, Edouard Artzner Pâté de Foie Gras, he was distressed. A proponent of animal welfare, he objected to what he understood as cruelty to geese.

He brought his concerns to a stockholders' meeting and obtained just over the 5 percent necessary support from other stockholders in the attempt to introduce the issue to management. The vote was 52,248 shares voting in favor and 953,094 shares voting opposed. Lovenheim wished to have mailed to the shareholders proxy materials advocating the formation of a committee to investigate the methods used to fatten the geese. However, Lovenheim met with stern resistance from manage-ment. Officers refused to include his proxy materials in the shareholders' report on grounds of an absence of economic significance to the company, the only condition management believed relevant for shareholder consid-eration.

Lovenheim rejected this argument. He maintained that ethical and social issues should not be excluded from proxy materials merely because

This case was prepared by Kelley MacDougall and Tom L. Beauchamp. **Not to be duplicated without permission of the holder of the copyright,** © 1989 Tom L. Beauchamp.

these issues failed to be of economic interest. He and other like-minded shareholders saw the proper treatment of animals as a perennial problem of Western morality that any sensitive person should consider, and therefore as relevant to the operations of a business. These shareholders wanted the other members to be aware of the cruelty to animals that was involved in the production of the "specialty food." In a "supporting statement," Lovenheim provided a description that can be paraphrased as follows:

> Commercial production involves the enlargement of an animal's liver by means of mechanical force-feeding. The prevailing practice is to restrain the animal's body in a metal brace and mechanically pump [corn] mash [up to 400 grams each feeding] through a funnel [inserted 10–12 inches] down its throat. An elastic band around the throat prevents regurgitation. Feeding is repeated 2–4 times a day for 28 days until the liver has been enlarged six times.

Some ducks die from intestinal malfunctions produced by the force-feeding, but most do not.

Lovenheim maintained that if undue stress, pain, or suffering are inflicted upon the geese, it was questionable whether further distribution of this product should continue unless a more humane production method was developed. Lovenheim was able to enlist the support of several animal welfare agencies. For example, the American Society for the Prevention of Cruelty to Animals (ASPCA) said about force-feeding, "This is not just raising animals for food. This is an aberrant and unethical practice."[1] John F. Kullberg, the Executive Director of the organization, explained the ASPCA's position on the force-feeding of geese:

> We consider the force-feeding of geese an act of cruelty and remain committed to having this practice stopped. . . .
> Hundreds of thousands of geese are subjected to force-feeding yearly. The pain and stress they endure are very real. The fact that all of this is justified solely on the basis of producing a luxury food item not only promotes the unethical stand that the end justifies the means, but makes the matter even more objectionable because of such a meaningless end.
> We are distressed that the results of this inhumane feeding practice are promoted for sale in the United States. It is further the opinion of our legal counsel that force-feeding violates several state anti-cruelty laws.[2]

The Humane Society of the United States also condemned this process as unnecessary cruelty to animals.

---

[1] American Society for the Prevention of Cruelty to Animals, Supporting Statement to Shareholders' Proposal. Included in Appendix 3 in the case cited in footnote 4.

[2] From a letter written January 13, 1984, by ASPCA Executive Director John F. Kullberg. Included in Appendix 5 in the case cited in note 4 below.

In his proposal, Lovenheim requested that a committee be formed to study the methods by which the French supplier produced pâté and report to shareholders its findings, together with an opinion whether this process caused undue distress, pain, and suffering to animals. Management at Iroquois Brands denied a need for such a committee. They cited figures that discounted the financial importance of the pâté, claiming the company suffered a net loss on the product. Their figures may be summarized as follows:

Iroquois's annual revenue:	$141 million
Iroquois's annual profit:	$6 million
Iroquois's sales from pâté:	$79,000
Iroquois's net loss on pâté:	$3,121

Management did acknowledge the importance of moral problems of cruelty to animals. However, the company contended that the real issue was whether a reseller of the end-product should be responsible for the means of production. The board claimed to "deplore cruelty to animals in any form"[3] and commended the Humane Society for its work to alleviate problems of animals in the United States. But they did not view themselves as responsible for the practices of the French over which they had no control. They maintained that upon importing the pâté, it was tested and approved by the federal Food and Drug Administration, which thereby lifted all responsibility from the company.

Iroquois also argued that it was illogical to form a panel to study an issue the company could not control, especially inasmuch as the costs of obtaining "expert consultation" would exceed any reasonably anticipated profit from the product. Furthermore, they contended that even if a committee were formed, it would have little if any impact on Iroquois's actual business and even less impact on the world pâté market or the feeding practices in France.

Lovenheim objected to this entire line of argument. He claimed that although Iroquois Brands might not actually force-feed the geese themselves, they did import, advertise, and sell the end-product. If the French supplier was using the process described, the Iroquois company was indirectly supporting animal mistreatment and must be held responsible. The very availability of a market for products obtained in this manner, he maintained, must contribute to the continuation of such treatment.

This struggle between company and shareholder was presented to a U.S. District Court, where the issues turned on legal technicalities rather

---

[3] Notice of 1983 Annual Meeting of Shareholders and Proxy Statement, Tuesday, May 10, 1983.

than on the substantive ethical question. At issue in the courtroom was whether a 1983 rule of the Securities and Exchange Commission (SEC) would determine the outcome of the dispute. This rule allows a company to omit proxy materials proposed by shareholders if the relevant operation of the firm—in this case imported pâté—accounts for less than 5 percent of the firm's total assets and is not "otherwise significantly related to the issuer's business." Because importing and selling pâté did not account for the required 5 percent, Iroquois management did not feel compelled to issue the proxy materials.

Judge Oliver Gasch, admitting the case involved a close call, sided with Lovenheim.[4] Judge Gasch held that the history of the rule in question showed no decision by the SEC that allowed a company to base its judgments solely on the economic considerations relied on by Iroquois. Upon learning of Judge Gasch's order that the proxy material must be sent to shareholders, Lovenheim said that he hoped his effort "reasserts the rights of shareholders in all companies to bring moral issues to the attention of management."[5]

The unit that imported the pâté was sold by Iroquois Brands in 1986, and the company officially considers the matter "a moot issue."[6]

---

[4] *Peter C. Lovenheim* v. *Iroquois Brands Ltd.* U.S. District Court, Washington, D.C., Civil Case No. 85-0734 (May 24, 1985). We have drawn from the data and arguments presented before this court in developing the basic facts in this case.

[5] This statement was quoted by Philip Smith, "Shareholders to Be Given Pâté Question," *Washington Post,* Thursday, March 28, 1985, p. E3.

[6] Personal correspondence (April 13, 1988) from Attorney Ralph L. Halpern of Jaeckle, Fleischmann & Mugel, Buffalo, New York.

Acid Rain and the Uses of Coal

Acid rain, which is created by burning coal and other fossil fuels, has been cited in some scientific studies as the leading cause of lake acidification and fish kills in the northeastern United States and southeastern Canada. It may also be adversely affecting forest ecosystems, farmlands, and groundwater. The coal industry and its power-generating and industrial consumers have been prime targets of this environmental concern.

The chemical process creating acid rain and its impact on the environment are not well understood. However, it is known that gaseous sulfur dioxide is released into the air when coal with a high sulfur content is burned (primarily in utility power plants and some industrial plants). The sulfur dioxide and nitrogen oxides from transportation vehicles and unregulated oil burner emissions combine with water vapor to produce sulfuric and nitric acids. Carried by prevailing winds perhaps far from the emission source, these acids infiltrate precipitation and lower the pH levels. "Pure rain" is naturally somewhat acidic, with a pH level of 5.6. The degree of acidity increases exponentially as the pH level decreases. Rainfall with pH levels of 3 or 4 is now common in the eastern United States and Canada, and thus is anywhere from ten to over a hundred times more acidic than a normal 5.6. Levels as low as 1.5—roughly the acidity of battery acid—have been reported in Wheeling, West Virginia.[1]

Ecological systems have natural alkaline properties that can neutralize moderately acidic rain, but continued precipitation of low pH levels is difficult to overcome. Large fish kills often occur in the early spring because, as environmentalist Anne LaBastille has graphically depicted,

---

[1] Lois R. Ember, "Acid Pollutants: Hitchhikers Ride the Wind," *Chemical and Engineering News* (September 14, 1981), p. 29.

all winter, the pollutant load from storms accumulates in the snowpack as if in a great white sponge. When mild weather gives the sponge a "squeeze," acids concentrated on the surface of the snow are released with the first melt. . . . This acid shock . . . produces drastic changes in water chemistry that destroy fish life."[2]

Those areas in the northeastern United States and southeastern Canada that show particularly high levels of acidification are naturally low in alkaline buffers, which neutralize the acids. As a by-product of acidification, toxic metals such as aluminum are leached from the earth's surface. The aluminum can be lethal to fish and other forms of life, and even fish that survive may become poisonous to predators who eat them—including, in some cases, humans.[3]

In the Adirondack region, which receives some acid rain, residents have noticed a steady decrease in the number of fish and other forms of wildlife. A forest ranger and lifelong resident of the area has noted that "the snowshoe rabbit is down, the fox is way down, deer are down, way down, the bobcat is down, the raccoon is down. Even the porcupine is disappearing. . . . Frogs and crayfish are way down. The loon has disappeared. . . . You don't see fish jump anymore. There are no fish to jump, and even if there were, there'd be no insects to make them jump."[4] Some lakes have become crystal clear and devoid of life.

Another example of the concern over acid rain is found in Scandinavia, where scientists have been studying the effects of acid precipitation in response to alarming changes in their rivers and lakes. Folke Andersson, coordinator of the Swedish acid rain research on soils, forests, and waters, has found that " '75% of nitrogen needed by forests comes from the work of soil organisms.' Laboratory studies show that increased acidity kills these microorganisms. 'Over the long term we ought to see a decrease in forest productivity due to the decrease in organisms releasing nitrogen to the soil. We can't see this yet.' "[5] Swedish researchers have found that soils store pollution. Even if all sulfur emissions were stopped today, it would be decades before the sulfur would stop flowing from the soil. It has been estimated that 80 percent of the sulfur in acid rain is retained in the soil and slowly bleeds out.[6] This effect is compounded by the fact that normal use of fertilizers contributes to soil acidity.[7]

---

[2] Anne LaBastille, "Acid Rain: How Great a Menace?" *National Geographic* 160 (November 1981), p. 672.

[3] Robert H. Boyle, "An American Tragedy," *Sports Illustrated* (September 21, 1981), p. 75.

[4] *Ibid.*, p. 74.

[5] From Ember, "Acid Pollutants," p. 24.

[6] Fred Pierce, "Unravelling a Century of Acid Pollution," *New Scientist* 111 (September 25, 1986), p. 24.

[7] "Acid Rain Briefing Reviews Recent Research," *Journal of the Air Pollution Control Association* 33 (August 1983), p. 782.

In the United States, many of those who wish to prevent acid rain and its possibly devastating consequences focus their attention on the coal mines of Ohio. Coal mining is a major industry in southern Ohio and the West Virginia panhandle, employing 15,000 miners. Ohio coal, which has a particularly high sulfur content, is used throughout the region and is thought by environmentalists to be one of the primary sources of the acid rain falling in the northeastern United States and southeastern Canada. However, existing environmental regulations controlling the use of high-sulfur coal have already taken their toll on the region's economy. The state of Michigan has cut back orders for Ohio coal, and some power plants in the area have switched to a low-sulfur coal. Miners are concerned about their jobs, and unemployment in the region is increasing.

However, the National Coal Association reports that because of greater use of low-sulfur coal and "scrubbers" in power plants, there is little more sulfur dioxide in the air than there was in the late 1940s. The Environmental Protection Agency (EPA) found a 28 percent decrease in sulfate levels from 1973 to 1983. This decrease has been linked to stronger Clean Air Act measures for coal burning utilities. From 1980 to 1985 there was a 2.7 percent decrease in sulfur dioxide emissions, while coal usage increased by 23 percent. Furthermore, ambient levels of sulfur dioxide fell by 36 percent from 1975 to 1984.[8] As of 1986, 98 percent of all U.S. counties were in compliance with the national standard for sulfur dioxide and nitrogen oxide.[9] Such figures have led some to question the necessity of imposing harsher standards.

Some regions such as the lower Mississippi Valley and the state of Colorado seem not to be affected by relevant prevailing winds, and yet both report highly acidic rain. Furthermore, fish sometimes thrive in lakes directly affected by acid rain. Other factors such as seepage from surrounding soils, the lake-bed composition, and fertilizer reactions may be contributory causal sources. Because of these many unknowns about acid rain, the *Wall Street Journal* cautioned as follows in mid-1980:

> At least five more years of study is required to identify correctly the causes and effects of acidic rainfall. Precipitous regulatory action by EPA could cost utilities and other industries billions of dollars. Until more is genuinely known about acid rain, these expenditures may end up only going down the drain.[10]

[8] Carl E. Bagge, "A Tale of UFO's and Other Random Anxieties," *Vital Speeches of the Day* 52 (September 1, 1986), p. 702.

[9] Richard E. Benedick, "U.S. Policy on Acid Rain," *Department of State Bulletin* 86 (September 1986), p. 56.

[10] "Review and Outlook: Acid Rain," *Wall Street Journal,* June 20, 1980.

Despite such warnings, EPA proceeded with regulatory efforts (by targeting coal- and oil-fired power plants) until the Reagan administration ordered the advice of the *Wall Street Journal* to become official policy. Anne Gorsuch, once an EPA administrator, adopted precisely the *Journal*'s position. In late 1981, however, critics of these "lax" regulatory efforts were supported by a panel report of the National Research Council. It pointed out that nitrogen oxide levels have tripled in the last 25 years, and the panel placed the burden of responsibility for environmental deterioration on coal-burning industries. The "circumstantial evidence" of a causal connection between coal-burning and environmental damage, it argued, is "overwhelming." It recommended stringent control measures.[11]

"Scrubbers," which remove sulfur dioxide from coal, are generally regarded as the most effective control technology, although decreased reliance on fossil fuel may be the most promising policy. To modify other plants with scrubbers would be very costly, but it has proven effective in Japan, where sulfur emissions have been reduced by 50 percent, while energy consumption increased by 120 percent. A cheaper though less efficient alternative is to "wash" coal prior to combustion. Many small industrial users of Ohio coal would find it difficult to survive if they were forced to comply with more stringent regulations. They contend that the cost of additional emission control equipment or out-of-state coal would be prohibitive.

Cost estimates vary, but whatever the method of calculation, the cost of effectively controlling sulfur dioxide emissions would be substantial:

> According to DOE's [Department of Energy's] Jim Bartis, an internal study estimates that to reduce emissions permanently 3 percent or 1 million tons per year in the utility sector alone would cost about $2 billion in 1981 dollars. Beyond that incremental reduction, the cost rises rapidly, he says. To reduce emissions a significant amount—5 million to 10 million tons per year—would cost $5 billion to $7 billion.
>
> EPA [the Environmental Protection Agency] estimated that a 10 to 30 percent reduction in sulfur dioxide emissions in the utility sector would cost $1 billion, and raise utility customer bills 2 to 3 percent per year on a national average. Customers in the Ohio River Valley, however, would be socked with rate hikes of 10 to 15 percent per year.[12]

It is also difficult to determine with precision who is responsible for the situation. Tracking the atmosphere routes of acid rain from sources to destinations is a complex problem that some believe must be solved

---

[11] Committee on the Atmosphere and the Biosphere, *Atmosphere-Biosphere Interactions* (Washington, D.C.: National Academy Press, 1981).

[12] Ember, "Acid Pollutants," p. 31.

if emissions are to be controlled effectively. Sulfur dioxide over the Adirondacks may vary only 10 percent through a given period while rainfall acid concentration may change 100 percent.[13] A DOE report has cast doubt altogether on the major role of acid rain that once was assigned to "imported" coal-produced pollutants, focusing instead on local automobile and oil-burner emissions as the source.[14] (This report was filed approximately nine months *before* the report of the panel of the National Research Council mentioned earlier. The studies ran concurrently, however.)

Uncertainties in the source/receiver relationship have prompted industry to claim that costly control techniques may prove ineffective if enacted without more adequate data. Raymond Robinson, Canadian Assistant Minister of the Environment, considers these demands for precise data on the source/receiver relationship a "dead herring" and has called for corrective measures as soon as possible.[15] On the other hand, the Canadian government has not closed perhaps the largest emitter of sulfur dioxide on the North American continent—the International Nickel copper smelter in Sudbury, Ontario. Even "goals" set for reducing these emissions have thus far not been met.[16]

Early in 1985, federal Judge Johnson ordered the EPA to require major cuts in sulfur dioxide emissions. The ruling was based on section 115 of the Clean Air Act, which requires the U.S. to take action when the pollution affects a foreign country. However, in April 1986, a federal Court of Appeals reversed Judge Johnson's decision, holding that the EPA has the discretion to wait for more definitive evidence on the receiving end of acid rain before it tightens sulfur dioxide emission standards.[17]

The issue of acid precipitation across the U.S.-Canadian border has received extensive attention. In March 1985 the U.S. and Canada appointed special envoys to study the issue and make recommendations for its resolution. One major recommendation in their January 1986 report was a 5-year, $5-billion program to develop innovative technology for new and existing sources of discharge. (This is not to imply that the United States has not been actively funding acid rain research. Between 1982 and 1987 the National Acid Precipitation Assessment Program appropriated over $315 million for such research.[18])

[13] "Review and Outlook," *Wall Street Journal.*

[14] Michael Woods, "Theory Blamed Midwest Utilities: Study Disputes Cause of Acid Rain," *Toledo Blade,* January 28, 1981.

[15] *Ibid.*

[16] *Acid Rain Fact Sheet, Canada's Campaign for Economic/Energy Supremacy,* Coalition for Environmental-Energy Balance, Columbus, Ohio.

[17] Robert Taylor, "Appeal of Ruling over Acid Rain Is Won by EPA," *Wall Street Journal,* September 9, 1986, p. 11.

[18] Benedick, "U.S. Policy on Acid Rain," p. 57.

Representatives of the coal industry generally contend that there are too few definite answers to warrant further emission regulations, and should they be instituted too quickly, there may be needless expenditures. The Electric Power Research Institute has therefore developed an extensive international research plan to look into the causes and effects of acid rain. The Tennessee Valley Authority, the U.S. Geological Survey, and the other government agencies mentioned above are also pursuing further research.[19] Industry spokespersons believe that further research is all that can and should be done until the phenomenon of acid rain is better understood. For example, Al Courtney, the designated spokesperson for the nation's investor-owned electric utilities, offers the following as that industry's preferred policy:

> A careful examination of the available facts leads to four conclusions: first, the only adverse effect which has been documented is the acidification of certain local water bodies; second, the causes of the acidification are not clear; third, the contribution of power plant emissions to this problem is not known, and as a result, it is not known whether emission reductions would retard or reverse this acidification; and further, requiring substantial additional emission reductions by the electric utility industry would impose great economic burdens on the financially troubled nation and on the already weak economy without assurance of commensurate benefits to the public. . . . It is clear that many of the critical chemical, meteorological, ecological, and economic questions related to acid rain remain unanswered. . . . Pending the completion of the research program established by the Acid Precipitation Act of 1980, claims regarding irreversible ecological impact should be investigated, and mitigating measures, such as liming, should be instituted where appropriate. . . . In enacting the Acid Precipitation Act of 1980, Congress recognized this essential prerequisite and in response, instituted a program designated to explore the acid deposition phenomenon in a deliberate, methodical manner. We should permit this rational, problem-solving approach to produce the information which we so badly need.[20]

The "receivers" of acid rain, on the other hand, have asked for international cooperation and quick responses to what they believe is a worsening environmental situation. In 1984 and again in 1986, Representative Henry Waxman of California introduced legislation to respond to the acid rain problem. His 1986 bill (HR 4567) was a two-phase plan to decrease sulfur dioxide and nitrogen oxide emissions by 1997. It allowed the states to develop their own methods for reduction. In addition, HR 4567 levied a nationwide fee on electricity to create a trust fund.

---

[19] "Acid Rain," *Energy Researcher*, Electric Power Research Institute, June 1981.

[20] Edison Electric Institute Information Service, Release of October 21, 1981, pp. 1–2.

The fund would be used to limit consumer utility fee increases to 10 percent or less. Most observers agree that the legislation would cause midwest consumers to pay increases of over 10 percent unless the fund existed. Costs to utilities for decreased sulfur and nitrogen emissions would have been in the range of $4.3 to $5.6 billion annually. Although the bill did not survive the 99th Congress, there is every indication that it or a similar bill will be proposed again in the future.[21]

Cost estimates vary, but whatever the method of calculation, the cost of effectively controlling sulfur dioxide emissions would be substantial. According to Sheldon Meyers of the EPA, the installation of one scrubber on an existing 300-megawatt utility boiler would cost between $60 and $90 million.[22] Because the scrubber creates a sludge, there are also new disposal methods to be concerned about. Also, levels of reduction vary in costs:

> There are annual dollar values usually assigned to the phased reductions: $2 billion would buy a reduction of four million tons annually in the thirty-one states east of the Mississippi; $4 billion would buy a reduction of eight million tons per year; and $8 to $10 billion would buy reductions of 12 million tons per year below the 1980 level.[23]

Even the basic facts about acid rain remain disputed, and the legislative and regulatory situation is cloudy. A report by the comptroller general of the United States on the debate over acid precipitation once summed up the situation as follows:[24]

> Summing up the evidence on the acid precipitation debate, even the most conciliatory representatives of the opposite sides arrive at different conclusions.
>
> Those most concerned with the additional costs and problems expected for further emissions controls argue for the point that there is no firm proof that reductions of emissions would result in lessening acid deposition. Therefore, they conclude, it is inappropriate to take any additional control actions at this time, because the controls would be certain to involve costs but would stand the risk of producing no benefits.
>
> On the other side, those most concerned with the present and anticipated damage due to acid precipitation start from the point that the oxide precursors of deposited acids, particularly SO_2, come predominantly from man-

---

[21] "Waxman Unveils Acid Rain Bill: Support is Strong," *Wall Street Journal*, April 11, 1986, p. 2.

[22] Sheldon Meyers, "Acid Deposition: A Search for Solutions," in Diane Suitt Gilland and James H. Swisher, eds., *Acid Rain Control: The Cost of Compliance* (Carbondale: South Illinois University Press, 1985), p. 7.

[23] *Ibid.*, p. 8.

[24] *The Debate over Acid Precipitation: Opposing Views; Status of Research*, Report by the Comptroller General of the United States (Washington, D.C.: General Accounting Office, September 11, 1981), pp. 7–8.

made emissions. From this they conclude that reducing oxide emissions upwind from threatened areas is most likely to prevent or reduce damage, so they urge that at least moderate steps in the direction should be started promptly. They view as inequitable the present situation, in which they see all costs and risks being borne by the regions suffering damage, contending that the emitting regions should also take some share of risks and costs.

Milton J. Socolar
Acting Comptroller General of the United States

CHAPTER 4

The Society

INTRODUCTION   The idea that a corporation should be "socially responsible" and should live up to the demands of "social justice" is at the
center of many controversies in this volume. However, some hold that
the corporation has no obligations to society. This means neither that
the corporation should *not* take actions that benefit others in society
nor that it is free to do whatever it determines to be its best course.
Rather, the view usually takes one of two mutually consistent forms:
Either it is held that the corporation is a legal fiction and so not a
moral or social agent, and therefore not responsible to others, or it is
held that the corporation's responsibility is chiefly to its stockholders
and others such as creditors to whom it is directly obligated. One version
of this thesis is the widely proclaimed maxim that "the business of business
is business"—meaning that the responsibilities of a business are exclusively the demands of the business world of contracts, stockholders,
profits, taxes, and the like.

This position strongly resists the encroachment of government and
rejects the proposition that a corporation has broad moral and social
responsibilities. Some who take this point of view even maintain that if
business were to set social goals for itself, it would be encroaching into
the region of government, because the latter is the social institution
properly equipped to set social goals and to protect the public interest.
The business community has no parallel role, and it has neither the
expertise, the motivation, nor the social charter to engage in such activities.

On the other hand, the legal system holds corporations responsible
in a variety of ways. Corporations are chartered, and this charter permits
a corporation to do business only within certain limits. These limits
are imposed by society under the assumption that the contract serves
the overall interests of society. In the cigarette advertising and Burroughs
Wellcome AZT cases in this chapter, issues are raised about whether
corporations should be held as responsible as governments for the public
health and possibly even for judgments of fairness in the distribution

of health care. However this may be, it is clear that corporate decisionmaking often involves complicated interactions and procedures, which may well involve moral deliberation about the welfare of the community and even about the welfare of persons beyond the corporation's home nation. Moreover, the welfare of the corporation and the welfare of society are intimately connected—indeed so closely bound that it would be artificial, under some conditions, to distinguish exclusive functions of government and business.

These problems of corporate responsibility have generally been raised if a corporation has a myopic focus on making a profit while excluding other factors about its actions. No one denies that corporations are entitled to profits, but it seems equally undeniable that not any means to a profit is acceptable. For example, as the previous chapter on the environment shows, corporate activities can cause various kinds of social harm. In this chapter, the cigarette advertising case grapples with the obligation not to cause harm (obligations of nonmaleficence), whereas the Lakewood Bank, Burroughs Wellcome AZT, and New York State Electric and Gas cases present problems of possible obligations business may have or may assume to contribute to the public welfare or the public interest. These cases turn on whether a corporation has social responsibilities, and if so, how to characterize them. This problem includes issues of whether corporations have affirmative obligations to contribute to the general good of society as well as obligations to avoid harmful practices.

Perhaps the most important of these issues is whether a business, like a government agency or a charitable organization, has some form of welfare responsibility to communities in which the business operates. If so, should a business assume the model of good citizenship or even of charitableness in fostering better health, education, and financial welfare for citizens? If so, how much of the corporation's resources may legitimately be devoted to these activities, and what is the justification of the activity if it is not a business justification, that is, if the activity is not directed at the economic welfare of the corporation and its shareholders? These issues are all present, in subtle ways, in the New York State Electric and Gas case.

These problems lead naturally to reflection on the proper objectives of the corporation, on what constitutes just and worthy business practices, and on what is generally referred to as social justice, meaning the proper or fair distribution in society of social benefits and burdens. The principles of social justice relied upon in law and morality say a great deal about the terms of cooperation in any given society, often specifying what one person or group may expect from another and what is fair in any social transaction. Such requirements of social justice are present in virtually all of society's major and pervasive institutions, including branches of government, laws of property ownership, lending institutions, and systems of allocating benefits. For example, in many socio-economic systems, government intervention beyond mere protection of individual rights is initiated specifically on grounds of social justice. Governments use progressive taxation scales and in effect redistribute wealth in order to satisfy the "welfare needs" of citizens.

On the other hand, law and government are rarely adequate to decide controversial matters of social justice of the sort raised in this chapter. For example, the "justice" of the present national distribution of wealth in which roughly 20 percent is owned by 5 percent of the population, while the poorest 20 percent of the population controls 5 percent of the wealth, is hardly decided by abstract principles of American law or morality. The Lakewood Bank case points directly to problems of businesses' responsibilities under such conditions of social imbalance. Such cases are often extremely difficult to resolve because different *theories* of justice may be at work in discussion of particular cases. Disputants will appeal to different *principles* of justice—some based on human needs, others on considerations of equality, and still others based on merit, performance, or effort. Utilitarian goals of efficiency conflict with egalitarian views about equal distribution and libertarian conceptions of a free market. This complexity of the demands of "justice" will be found in several cases in this chapter.

Among the most widely agreed upon theses about social justice is that programs, services, and opportunities in society must be available to *all* qualified members of the society. To provide some with access while denying access to others who are equally or more qualified is discriminatory and unfair. Social justice is often invoked in order to resolve such problems of social inequality as those generally involved in "unfair practices" of hiring, promotion, and firing.

Government policies intended to insure fairness in employment, promotions, and admissions for women and minority groups have sometimes eventuated in specific target goals and timetables established for corporations. These objectives have seemed to many persons in business to be unfair because these goals can work against the interest of the business and also discriminate against those not favored by the goals. More talented applicants who are excluded would be hired or accepted on their merits were it not for the preferential advancement of others. Government policies requiring preferential treatment are thus said to create a situation of "reverse discrimination" because white males and others not favored by the programs are discriminatorily excluded from consideration by the company, even though they may be the most qualified applicants or employees. Such practices therefore seem to violate rather than uphold basic principles of justice and equal opportunity.

This viewpoint has introduced sustained controversy, however, in that many hold that these practices simply reverse the flow of past discrimination and do *not* "reverse discriminate" in the present. They accept a different account of what constitutes justice in a society that has been characterized by a long history of discriminatory practices. In particular, they look to principles of "compensatory justice" requiring just compensation or reparation for injured parties when an injustice has been committed. Since discrimination from the past continues in the present (or at least its effects continue), the thought is that compensation is justified in the form of preferential programs for women, blacks, and other minorities or groups without power where there is a history of discrimination against them.

In this chapter government policies and corporate initiatives aimed at preferential treatment on grounds of social justice are encountered in the McAleer-AT&T case. A central issue is whether justice demands practices involving equal opportunity and merit alone, or also demands some form of preferential treatment.

In the American system of government, the free market economy and representative democracy function as final "procedures" or systems through which judgments about social and economic justice are made. Yet agreement that democratic procedures are just will not of itself resolve all problems of justice. Unjust results can emerge from the political process, and it often must be determined on the basis of reasons how a "representative" or "official" ought to vote on any given issue.

New York State Electric and Gas Corporate Responsibility Program

> We are responsible to the communities in which we live and work and to the world community as well. We must be good citizens and support good works and charities. . . . We must encourage civic improvements and better health and education.[1]

Many large companies have implemented "consumer responsibility" or "social responsibility" programs, which aim to return something to the consumer or to the community in which the company does business. New York State Electric and Gas (NYSEG) is one of the companies that has created a program to discharge what its officers regard as the company's responsibility to the public it serves.

NYSEG is a public utility that has approximately 83,000 shareholders and is traded on the New York stock exchange. It supplies gas and electricity in New York State. Of its revenues, 86 percent are from electricity while 14 percent are from gas. The company is generally ranked as having good but not excellent financial strength. Earnings per share have in recent years been modestly lowered because of the regulatory climate and because the company suffered a writeoff for its Nine Mile Point #2 nuclear unit. In order to finance this unit, the company at one point had to absorb delay costs of several million dollars per month. The dividend to shareholders had to be reduced for the first time in many years and is not as secure as in the past because of the lowered earnings per share and the increased plant costs. The corporate responsibility program discussed below has been in effect throughout this period of modest financial reversal.

NYSEG's corporate responsibility program has been designed to help customers who are unable to pay their utility bills for various reasons.

---

[1] "The Johnson and Johnson Way" (from the Johnson and Johnson Company credo), 1986, p. 26.

The point of the program is not merely to find a mechanism so that customers can pay their bills to the company. Rather, the objective is to find people in the community in unfortunate or desperate circumstances and alleviate their predicament. (Of course the two objectives to some extent coincide.) In pursuit of this objective, NYSEG has implemented a system of consumer representatives, social workers trained to deal with customers and their problems. Since the beginning of the program in 1976, NYSEG has maintained a staff of thirteen consumer representatives. They each handle an average of forty cases a month, over half of which result in successful financial assistance. The other cases are ultimately referred to organizations that can help them further.[2]

The process works as follows: When the credit department for the utility company believes a special investigation should be made into a customer's situation, the employee refers the case to the consumer representatives. Referrals also come from Human Service Agencies and from customers directly. Examples of appropriate referrals include unemployed heads of the household, paying customers who suffer serious injury, lengthy illness, or death, and low-income senior citizens or those on fixed incomes who are unable to deal with the rising costs of living. The only steadfast rule of the company is that these customers must have problems and must be suffering from hardships they are willing to work to resolve.

Consumer representatives are primarily concerned with preventing the shut-off of service to these customers, and employ an assortment of resources to get them back on their feet. These resources include programs offered by the New York State Department of Social Services and the Home Energy Assistance Program (HEAP), which awards grants of varying amounts once a year to qualified families. In addition, the consumer representatives provide budget and money management counselling and help customers with their medical bills and with planning for more education. They arrange assistance from churches and social services, provide food stamps, and help arrange VA benefits.

NYSEG also founded a program called Project Share, which enables its customers who are not in financial difficulty to make *charitable* donations through their bills. They are asked to voluntarily add to their bill each month one extra dollar, which is placed in a special fund overseen by the American Red Cross. This special Fuel Fund is aimed to help those sixty years and older on fixed incomes who have no other means

[2] Consumer representatives are viewed as liaisons between NYSEG and human services agencies. All of these representatives, therefore, have extensive training and experience in human services. Each employee must have 4–6 years of college with a degree in social work or social science. They must also have a minimum of 4 years of work experience in human services so that they are adequately qualified to deal with the problems facing customers.

of paying their bills. Help is also provided for the handicapped and blind who likewise have few sources of funds. Many who receive help from Project Share do not qualify for government-funded assistance programs but nonetheless face energy problems. So far NYSEG has raised over $1 million through Project Share and has successfully assisted more than 5,000 people.

The rationale or justification of this corporate responsibility program is rooted in the history of public utilities and rising energy costs in North America. Originally public utilities provided a relatively inexpensive product. NYSEG and the entire industry saw its public responsibility as limited to the business function of providing energy at the lowest possible costs and returning dividends to investors. Problems regarding unpaid bills were dealt with by either the customer or the social welfare system.

However, the explosive costs of energy in the 1970s gradually changed NYSEG's perspective. The energy crisis caused many long-term customers to encounter difficulty paying their bills and the possibility of power shut-offs. NYSEG then accepted its responsibility to make provisions for these valuable customers, and the consumer representative was born.

NYSEG believes its participation is especially important now because recent reductions in federal assistance programs have shifted the burden of addressing these problems to the private sector. Thus, Project Share is viewed as "a logical extension of the President's call for increased volunteerism at the local level."[3] NYSEG chose the American Red Cross to co-sponsor Project Share because of their experience in providing emergency assistance.

The costs of NYSEG's involvement in all phases of the program are regarded by the officers of the company as low. Other than the salaries and benefits of the consumer representatives, which total $462,625 annually and are treated as operating expenses, NYSEG has few additional costs. The company has also strongly supported Project Share by giving $290,000 over a five-year period. The company's annual revenues are in the range of $1.5 billion, and the company's total debt also runs to approximately $1.5 billion.

The company views some of the money expended for the corporate responsibility program as recovered because of customers retained and bills paid through the program. The assumption is that these funds would under normal circumstances have remained unpaid and would be eventually written off as a loss. NYSEG's bad-debt level is 20 percent lower than that of the average utility company in the United States. The company's view is that its corporate responsibility policy is both altruistic and good business, despite the costs encountered in maintaining the program.

---

[3] NYSEG, Project Share Procedures Manual, 1988, p. 2.

Lakewood Bank & Trust

INTRODUCTION

In 1973 Mr. George Elliot, President and Chief Executive Officer of Lakewood Bank & Trust, faced a critical decision about the bank's development. The older neighborhood in which the bank was located was beginning to deteriorate rapidly, a situation that could have an adverse impact on deposit growth and loan activity and risk. Elliot debated whether or not the bank should make a financial commitment to the neighborhood in the form of admittedly risky residential and commercial rehabilitation and purchase loans. If such a commitment were made, he had to decide also on its form and extent.

HISTORY

Lakewood Bank & Trust was one of the largest state-chartered banks in the Dallas metropolitan area in 1973. It ranked tenth among all city banks in total deposits ($63.4 million). Total ownership was held by some 400 individual stockholders. The bank was opened in 1942 near its present location some three miles east of Dallas's central business district. The East Dallas area at that time was stable and growing, providing substantial support for deposit growth and local lending opportunities. To the west of the bank were the older middle- to upper-income subdivisions of Munger Place and Junius Heights, with heavy concentrations of large prairie-style and smaller bungalow-style frame homes built in the first three decades of the twentieth century. Adjoining these subdivisions on the north was the Swiss Avenue district, a neighborhood of

This case was prepared by Kerry D. Vandell and Sydney C. Reagan of the School of Business Administration, Southern Methodist University. It is designed to be used as a basis for class discussion rather than to illustrate either effective or ineffective handling of an administrative situation. Presented at a Case Workshop. Reprinted with permission of the authors. **Not to be duplicated without permission of the author and publisher.**

distinction, traditionally the residence of Dallas's elite. To the north and east of the bank was the newer Lakewood upper-middle income subdivision. The Lakewood Country Club to the immediate east of the bank, opened in 1913, completed the area's prestigious image. The bank was located within Lakewood Shopping Center, which was designed to serve the surrounding affluent population.

Lakewood Bank prospered in the 1940s and 1950s, along with its neighborhood. However, in the 1960s several changes began taking place that threatened its position. The city in the 1950s rezoned most of the older East Dallas area to multifamily dwellings in the expectation that there would be considerable demand for close-in luxury-apartment living. This had the effect of reducing expectations of a single-family character for these neighborhoods. High rates of home-building on the suburban fringe and new expressways shifted upper-middle income housing demand away from the older, more established areas. The older prairie-style frame architecture was no longer in vogue, being replaced by the newer brick, ranch-style homes. Maintenance costs on the older structures were increasing. Finally, civil rights activity generated white flight through fears of racial transition to black or Mexican-American occupancy of the area. Large concentrations of black and Mexican-American households resided to the south of the East Dallas neighborhoods.

These factors created a generally perceived state of decline in the old East Dallas area by the early 1970s. Racial transition to largely Mexican-American occupancy was advancing from the southwest. Median incomes and property values in the area were dropping. Larger single-family homes were being partitioned into apartments and rooming houses. Physical conditions rapidly degenerated. By 1973, even property values in the more isolated Lakewood area were stabilizing or dropping, and considerable fears were expressed that decline there was imminent. To complement residential decline, Lakewood Shopping Center was being supplanted by the newer shopping malls in the suburbs; its design was considered outdated, accessibility was relatively difficult, and congestion was increasing. The older shops catering to an upper-middle income clientele were being replaced by thrift shops, liquor stores, record shops, bars, and other commercial establishments oriented more toward the incoming lower-income population.

BANK PROFILE

This change in conditions of the surrounding neighborhood had not as yet seriously affected the bank's profitability or growth by 1973. Profitability had consistently remained comparable to that of other banks of a similar size in Dallas. Deposits since 1960 had been rising at an average annual rate of 14.5 percent. The bank's growth in deposits was historically higher than average for the city of Dallas, although there were indications it might be falling below the average in the early 1970s. Elliot attributed this growth to aggressive loan and deposit development programs that actively sought loans and deposits beyond the bank's neighborhood. In the mid-1960s the bank began searching for additional lending opportunities in the real estate market. It had had some prior limited experience with financing the purchase of a few homes and commercial properties, largely as favors to regular customers, but no significant real estate investment effort had ever been made. A Real Estate Loan Department was established in 1967. In 1968 the bank expanded into construction financing in the profitable apartment and shopping center markets in Dallas. During the late 1960s and early 1970s the bank's real estate loan portfolio increased as a share of total assets, largely due to the higher yields available in real estate at that time.

CHANGES

Although the bank enjoyed continuing financial strength in the 1960s and early 1970s, Elliot observed certain changes in bank operating conditions that appeared to be related to the changes that were taking place in the surrounding neighborhood:

1. INABILITY TO GENERATE INSTALLMENT LOANS
    One type of loan that was very profitable but that Lakewood was increasingly unable to generate in large volumes was consumer installment loans. Elliot felt this lack of success was in part attributable to the bank's neighborhood, which was composed of mature households rather than young couples, many of whom did relatively little borrowing.

2. DECLINING DEPOSIT POTENTIAL
    The bank had for a number of years competed with four other banks in the area for deposits and lending opportunities. Elliot's aggressive development programs were successful at increasing the bank's size from fourth to first place in only a few years. In fact, one of the competing institutions moved out of the area entirely, relocating to a newer suburban market. Elliot regarded this as a victory of sorts but also as a warning of the declining potential of the area.

3. HEAVY FINANCIAL COMMITMENT TO NEW BUILDING
    In 1963 Elliot recommended, and the board of directors agreed to, the construction of a new $700,000 building that would replace the existing rented quarters. Although there was some talk of relocating, the decision was made with little debate to again locate in the same neighborhood in Lakewood Shopping Center, less than one block away from the old structure. Deterioration of the surrounding area had not advanced far enough at this time to arouse concern about the future of the bank in the East Dallas area. However, the decision of Elliot and the board to build in the same area meant to Elliot the bank had a substantial long-term financial stake in the community and was increasingly vulnerable to adverse change in the area. The

new structure was opened in 1965 and an addition was completed in 1971. It was the first new commercial construction in the area in 30 years.

4. DISPERSAL OF LOAN AND DEPOSIT SOURCES AND LOWERED LOCAL CREDITWORTHINESS
Most new lending and deposit sources were increasingly originating from outside the bank's area. Since Texas does not allow branch banking, the bank could not expand physically into surrounding areas. Elliot surmised that this geographical anchor would ultimately prevent the bank from penetrating more distant markets much more deeply than it already had through the development programs. In addition, those loan applications for commercial credit, installment credit, and construction and repair credit that did originate in the immediate area were increasingly of lower quality. Credit records of applicants were worse and loan security was generally less satisfactory.

The bank had established a goal in 1968 of $75 million in total resources by 1975. Elliot, with the support of long-term projections completed by the bank, by the early 1970s came to the conclusion that the growth trend the bank had enjoyed in the past could not continue, and this goal would not be met if current trends in migration, deterioration, and current bank attitudes and policies continued. At some point a decision would have to be made on a strategy designed to achieve this goal, with the most obvious strategies being a substantial redevelopment effort in the immediate area or relocation to a more profitable suburban location.

ARGUMENTS IN FAVOR OF REDEVELOPMENT

Several factors provided support to a redevelopment strategy. First, several officers, including Elliot, and several board members, including Conway Walker, a former Dallas mayor and very active board member, lived in the East Dallas or Lakewood areas and had a substantial personal commitment to the area. Walker was a long-time resident of the Swiss Avenue district that was being immediately threatened by change. Second, the bank already had some experience with community involvement. Elliot, as early as 1964, had emphasized community involvement by the bank, although more at the individual volunteer service level than at the institutional financial support level. Several officers and other employees had been active in organizations such as the local Chamber of Commerce, the Boy Scouts, and local business and professional associations. The bank had also been active in supporting enlargement and modernization of the shopping center, street widening programs, and the attraction of new business.

The most active involvement by Lakewood Bank in the redevelopment of the area had come recently, since 1972, in the form of over $800,000 worth of home improvement and home purchase loans on Swiss Avenue. Elliot had decided that default risks on such loans would not be excessive in view of the unique character of the area and the limited scope of lending activity. He was strongly supported in his decision by Walker and several other board members. The project was given impetus in the summer of 1973 with the creation of the Swiss Avenue Historic District by the city of Dallas, an act that re-established the future of the area as a prestigious single-family neighborhood and brought with it increased city services and development controls. The eleven loans made by Lakewood Bank on Swiss in 1972–73 acted as a catalyst for other lenders to return to the area. By late 1973 it was clear that Swiss Avenue would remain a stable upper and upper-middle income enclave.

Elliot enjoyed the success of the Swiss Avenue experience, and it encouraged him toward a redevelopment strategy. However, he realized several factors mitigated this success as a portent of future broader success in "revitalizing" East Dallas. First, the Swiss Avenue homes were large stately mansions—very unique and with a high degree of architectural quality. Such was not the case with all of East Dallas. Second, although some of the homes had been converted to rooming houses, the Swiss Avenue area had not declined to the extent that other neighborhoods, such as Munger Place and Junius Heights, had. Third, he had some doubt as to whether there would be sufficient demand for older homes in close-in deteriorated neighborhoods by middle and upper-middle income families to significantly impact the area.

ARGUMENTS OPPOSED TO
REDEVELOPMENT

There was also considerable skepticism from within and without the bank over expanding redevelopment lending activities in the East Dallas area. This skepticism originated from some lending officers and appraisers in the marketplace—individuals who should have expertise on market potential. None of them resided in the East Dallas–Lakewood area and thus were not influenced by personal commitments to the area. These individuals advanced several arguments against a further commitment, which Elliot seriously evaluated.

First, they said that physical and functional depreciation of the housing stock in older East Dallas (besides Swiss Avenue) was already far advanced and was irreversible. Any expectation of rising property values was pure speculation and not justified by appraisal practices. Only a limited number of younger households felt favorably toward older, deteriorated structures and even these households would move to the suburbs when their children reached school age, in view of the inferior reputation of Dallas public schools. There were few amenities in the area for such households.

City services were minimal in most areas, and the crime rate was increasing. Racial transition to Mexican-American and some black occupancy was now past the "tipping point" and extended to within a few blocks of Lakewood Shopping Center, further reducing middle-income white demand. Finally, many of the structures were of questionable architectural quality anyway, especially in the Heights area, lacking the "uniqueness" necessary to revitalize an area.

A second point of skepticism related to the expansiveness of the area and the limited resources of the bank. To turn an area around, they reasoned, would require substantial resources. Property values were in the $10,000–16,000 range for most of the run-down homes in the area. To bring most structures up to code would require roughly equivalent expenditures. Thus a combined home purchase–home repair loan would require an average commitment (and in some cases more) by bank and borrower of $20,000–32,000 or more. If the purchase and repair of 30 percent of the 22,000 units in East Dallas were assumed to provide a suitable critical mass for revitalization, to be successful the bank would have to commit itself to almost $150 million worth of such loan activity, an amount obviously far beyond its capability, especially since it was a commercial bank and not primarily in the business of long-term residential mortgage lending. The danger of making fewer than a critical number of loans in the area was that the loan program would have little impact and result in substantial losses in view of the low property values and high per-loan loss exposure. Reducing the area for lending to allow intensive lending would mean the neighborhood would be subject to adverse external forces hastening decay. Committing too large a portion of the bank's assets to such lending would unwisely expose the bank to high risks without compensating returns.

Rather than increasing commitment to the local area, these individuals advocated further loan and deposit development on a metropolitan-wide basis and gradual withdrawal from the area along with eventual relocation in more stable surroundings after finding a replacement tenant for the bank building.

[Postscript and editor's note: The Lakewood Bank case is developed from a single Dallas bank. Many banks in the United States have encountered parallel circumstances. A similar problem at the South Shore National Bank of Chicago was published in *Chicago* (February 1977). Since 1969 the Chemical Bank of New York has run social and economic development programs intended to alleviate problems of urban housing brought to the bank by local community leaders. In 1986 the city council of the District of Columbia passed a law requiring banks with charters in the District to invest in community development. Several banks, including Chemical Bank, said they could not comply with the stringent requirements of this law.—T.L.B.]

Banning Cigarette Advertising

Beginning in the late 1950s there was growing pressure from the health community for a governmental study on the health hazards of smoking. The hazards had been discussed for several years, but few definite conclusions had been drawn. In response to pressure from the medical community, President Kennedy asked the surgeon general in 1962 to study the risks of smoking.

THE SURGEON GENERAL'S REPORT

Surgeon General Luther Terry and his committee assumed the task of evaluating over 8,000 previous studies on the effects of smoking. No new research was undertaken. The goal of the committee was to decide, "Is smoking bad?" Besides the surgeon general, the committee consisted of nine persons selected to provide as much impartiality as possible. There were five smokers and five non-smokers, and none of the members had publicly taken a stand on the issue of smoking and its hazards. Surgeon General Terry hoped that this committee would allow fair assessment of the studies before it.

In January 1964 the committee presented its findings to the public. It found that smoking "contributes substantially to mortality from certain specific diseases and to the overall death rate." Among its other findings were: (1) risk increases in direct proportion to the number of cigarettes smoked; (2) the biggest health risk to smokers is contracting lung cancer, wherein smokers face a risk eleven times higher than non-smokers; (3) men and women are subject to the same risks; (4) smokers face high risks of contracting other diseases including emphysema, bronchitis, cancer of the larynx, coronary artery disease, and hypertensive heart disease; and (5) quitting appears to reduce risks of all types. The committee reached two broad conclusions: Smoking is a definite health hazard and the government should take "appropriate remedial action" to discourage smoking.[1]

Initial reactions to the report were predictable. Sales of all tobacco products declined, with cigarette sales dipping by 10 percent initially. Sales did begin to rise later in the year, and the end result was a decline of 3 percent for 1964.[2] However, when this decline is combined with the rapid population increases at the time, its significance becomes more evident.

Washington responded by considering the regulation of cigarette advertising. Critics of the tobacco industry claimed that advertisements (that showed healthy, happy, and appealing men and women smoking) were encouraging increased consumption, especially by American youth. Congressional examination resulted in the federal Cigarette Labeling and Advertising Act of 1965. The purposes of the act were to provide for uniform labeling of all cigarette packages and to inform the public of the health risks associated with smoking.[3] The act required a warning label which read "CAUTION: CIGARETTE SMOKING MAY BE HAZARDOUS TO YOUR HEALTH" to be included on every package in a "conspicuous" location. The act went into effect on January 1, 1966, and expired on July 1, 1969.

The act pre-empted actions by other authorities to regulate cigarette advertising. No state or federal agency could require additional package labeling or warnings in advertisements for the life of the act. Originally, the Federal Trade Commission (FTC) had pushed to extend the act to require the warning label in advertisements.[4] The FTC was also critical of Congress for not taking other action.

For their part, members of the tobacco industry were reserved. They agreed that the findings of the committee were significant, but they urged further medical research into the risks of smoking. Most of the studies evaluated by the congressional committee were statistical studies. The industry believed that other forms of evidence based on biomedical research of the risks should be undertaken before definite conclusions were drawn. Tobacco producers also adopted a voluntary advertising code. They vowed that smoking would not be associated with manliness, sex appeal, or social charm in any of their ads.[5]

Cigarette consumption in 1968 was approximately 530 billion, which translates into over 4,200 cigarettes annually per capita. This was the

[1] "Smoking: The Government Report," *Time* 85 (January 17, 1964), p. 42.

[2] *Ibid.*

[3] "Controversy Over Cigarette Advertising," *Congressional Digest* 48 (June/July 1969), p. 168.

[4] *Ibid.*

[5] "Smoking: One Year Later," *Time* 87 (January 22, 1965), p. 58.

first year during which cigarette consumption had declined since the surgeon general's 1966 report was released. The federal government hoped to further this decline through the adoption of educational programs. For fiscal year 1968 the U.S. Public Health Service expended $4.4 million on tobacco-related education and research. While most educational programs tried to address all Americans, PHS focused on youths. Health officials believed the best way to decrease smoking was to reach people before they started to smoke.[6]

Medical professionals emphasized the health risks linked to smoking, including an increased risk of cancer, emphysema, bronchitis, cancers of the larynx and esophagus, and pulmonary disease. The National Tuberculosis and Respiratory Disease Association found that emphysema and chronic bronchitis had become the second most frequent cause of disability retirements. The Social Security Administration paid out over $90 million annually in benefits to these retirees.[7]

Advertising for cigarettes is a large expenditure. In 1967 the industry spent $312 million on ads, or 11 percent of the year's total advertising revenues.[8] Of this figure, 73 percent or $226.9 million was spent on television advertising.[9] Combative advertising—that is, ads that try to influence brand choice—is the focus of industry attention. Some economists predicted that an ad ban could actually help existing tobacco firms by allowing them to decrease combative advertising and preventing other firms from entering the industry.

The FTC conducted a new study based on industry figures and found that the average American was exposed to 67 cigarette commercials per month.[10] The agency concluded that such a high exposure rate was encouraging youth to begin the habit. In 1967, the FTC invoked the Fairness Doctrine with regard to cigarette commercials. The Fairness Doctrine, implemented in the 1950s, requires that broadcasters present both sides of a controversial issue. [See the case on the Fairness Doctrine, pp. 191–196.] The FTC declared smoking a controversial issue and required that broadcasters make significant time available to anti-smoking messages. Anti-smoking interest groups were unable to afford advertising time in proportion to cigarette advertising, so broadcasters had to give them free air time. By 1970, the broadcast media had given anti-smoking messages roughly one third of cigarette-related advertising time, at a cost of $75 million.[11]

[6] Ibid., pp. 164–165.

[7] "Controversy," Congressional Digest, p. 180.

[8] "Rising Battle Over Cigarette Advertising," Time 93 (February 14, 1969), p. 85.

[9] "Controversy," Congressional Digest, p. 169.

[10] "Smoking: One Year Later," Time, p. 168.

[11] James Hamilton, "The Demand for Cigarettes: Advertising, the Health Scare, and the Cigarette Advertising Ban," Review of Economics and Statistics 54 (November 1972), p. 408.

BAN PROPOSED

Two factors led to a proposal to ban cigarette ads for all broadcast media. First, the surgeon general and the U.S. Public Health Service issued a follow-up report to the 1964 study entitled "The Health Consequences of Smoking, A PHS Review." This 1967 report supported or strengthened the 1964 conclusions. Second, in 1968 the Federal Communications Commission (FCC) announced a proposed rule to ban all broadcast ads. The Commission voted six to one in favor of such action to be implemented if Congress decided not to renew the Labeling and Advertising Act.[12]

Congress was encouraged to look closely at the soon-to-expire 1965 act. Some supporters argued that it was effective and should be extended as it stood. A second group called for a stronger warning label that cited specific health risks. Another group argued that warnings were not enough and that tar and nicotine content should be included on all packaging. Others favored a full ban on cigarette ads in broadcast media. The debate finally narrowed to those in favor of warnings only and those in favor of a ban on all ads. Each side was able to present a strong case in support of its viewpoint.

ARGUMENTS IN SUPPORT OF
THE AD BAN

Advocates of the ban acknowledged that adult smokers would not stop smoking even if all ads disappeared, but their hope was to prevent youths from starting to smoke. Teenagers presumably saw smoking glamorized in ads and tried to duplicate the conduct in the ads. Ban supporters predicted that each successive generation would foster a smaller percentage of smokers and eventually smoking would be eliminated. Any risk to jobs and the industry would be minimized because those involved in the industry would have a chance to find other work and invest in other endeavors. Ban supporters maintained that tobacco was a dangerous substance, unworthy of promotion through federally regulated broadcast media.

The 1965 Cigarette Labeling and Advertising Act was only a beginning in the eyes of ban supporters. They argued that the act had no major impact on the smoking habits of Americans. The warning was weak, could not be extended to advertising, and was regarded by 82 percent of those questioned as not discouraging smoking or encouraging quitting.[13]

---

[12] "Rising Battle," *Time*, p. 85.

[13] "Controversy," *Congressional Digest*, p. 184 (citing an FTC survey).

ARGUMENTS IN OPPOSITION
TO THE BAN

Tobacco is a legal product in the United States, and the federal government helps to subsidize tobacco farmers. Both state governments and the federal government depend on revenues generated by taxing cigarettes. In 1968 the industry paid $4.1 billion in state and federal taxes.[14]

Opposition to the ban rested primarily, from the industry perspective, on questions of First Amendment rights. With obvious state and federal backing for the manufacture of cigarettes, tobacco product manufacturers seemed to have the right to advertise their products under the freedom of speech provision of the Constitution. Banning tobacco industry ads was viewed as arbitrary discrimination against a targeted industry. As one advertising executive put it, "[N]o matter how well-meaning the social scientist, the reduction of choice for 'his own good' is the first step towards totalitarianism."[15]

The primary question thus became not whether the product was a health risk, but how its use should be discouraged. Few people would deny that there are some risks involved with smoking. But opponents of a ban noted that there were many "risky" products—eggs and milk contain cholesterol, which has been linked to heart disease; candy can lead to tooth decay and obesity; driving high-performance cars can be fatal. Opponents of an ad ban feared that one "health-related" ban could open the flood gates for other bans.

There was also continuing controversy over the character and strength of the causal link between the decision to smoke and advertising. Industry marketers often maintained that ads only induce consumers to change the brands they smoke.[16] Some studies done in the 1950s and 1960s found little consumer sensitivity to cigarette ads. Researchers found that ads were necessary for increasing market share, but did very little to increase aggregate demand.[17] Armed with this information, ban adversaries claimed that banning ads, or any action short of changing the status of tobacco to that of a controlled substance, would not eliminate smoking.

The National Broadcasters Association viewed the eventual banning of advertisements for cigarettes as inevitable. The association believed that if Congress did not accomplish the ban, the FCC would lead broadcasters to adopt a voluntary ad ban in 1969. Their strategy was to begin

[14] "Rising Battle," *Time*, p. 85.

[15] "The Moral Minefield of Cigarette Advertising," *Business and Society Review* 51 (Fall 1984), p. 14.

[16] *Ibid.*, p. 13.

[17] Hamilton, "Demand for Cigarettes," p. 401.

phasing out ads in 1969, with final elimination set for September 1, 1973. The effects of the ban would be far-reaching because NBA membership included two thirds of all commercial networks and 40 percent of all radio stations. In 1969 broadcaster revenues from cigarette ads were over $230 million. The NBA hoped a gradual phase-out would ease the burden on both industries.[18]

The tobacco industry fought the ban. They defended the use of ads to increase market share, and cited their voluntary efforts to monitor the content of ads. The industry also pointed to other countries' failed efforts to ban cigarette advertising. Great Britain, France, Switzerland, and Italy had all banned ads before 1966; yet each country was experiencing a positive annual growth rate of cigarette consumption between 2.7 and 8 percent.[19]

ALL BROADCAST ADVERTISING BANNED

Congress amended the Cigarette Labeling and Advertising Act in 1970 in the Public Health Smoking Act. The 1970 act provided for the banning of all cigarette ads "on any medium of electronic communication subject to the jurisdiction of the Federal Communication Commission."[20] Congress allowed the industry one concession: The effective date was January 2, 1971, to allow the industry the opportunity to advertise during the heavily watched football games on New Year's Day.

To the dismay of cigarette producers, the anti-smoking ads continued even in the absence of cigarette ads. The industry petitioned the FCC to be permitted significant time under the Fairness Doctrine to present industry views on smoking. The FCC denied the request, stating that the dangers of smoking were now well-known and the issue was no longer controversial. Because the FCC deemed the issue noncontroversial, anti-smoking advertisements were no longer guaranteed equal time under the Fairness Doctrine. Anti-smoking messages would not be subsidized by broadcasters; the messages were given a share of the time allotted for public service announcements. Anti-smoking interest groups were expected to pay for additional advertisements.[21]

James Hamilton, writing in the *Review of Economics and Statistics*, studied the comparative effects of cigarette advertising and anti-smoking messages. Hamilton noted that "the health scare was a several-fold more

---

[18] "Cigarettes: Down in Ash," *Newsweek* 74 (July 21, 1969), p. 82.

[19] "Where the Cigarette Men Go after the TV Ban," *Business Week* (November 21, 1970), p. 69.

[20] 15 U.S.C., § 1335.

[21] "A Bright Spark for Cigarette Makers," *Business Week* (December 26, 1970), p. 64.

potent determinant of per capita consumption than was promotional cigarette advertising, and since anti-smoking advertising simply promulgated and intensified the health scare, finding that anti-smoking ads were more potent than promotional ads does not seem surprising." In fact, Hamilton cited statistics indicating that an advertising ban would be less effective than continuing or intensifying the anti-smoking campaign. Anti-smoking messages from 1968 through 1970 lowered per capita consumption by 530.7 cigarettes per year, while advertising increased it by 95.0.[22]

The ban had the desired effect to a limited degree. Per capita cigarette consumption decreased. In 1985 per-adult consumption was down to 3,384 per year from a high of 4,345 per year in 1963.[23] This decline, accompanied by an increase in population, shows a significant decline in smoking. However, the medical community, especially the American Medical Association (AMA), was not satisfied with the results. It was disappointed that the tobacco industry was still advertising heavily, generally by switching media—from electronic to print—and undertaking sponsorship of sporting events, such as the Virginia Slims Tennis Tournament and Marlboro Tours.

CIGARETTE ADS IN PRINT MEDIA

Still today, a major source of marketing cigarettes is newspaper advertising. Newspapers are also a major source, probably *the* major source, of information transmitted to the public about the dangers of smoking cigarettes. Newspapers thus have an interest both in revenue from cigarette advertising and in informing the public about the dangers of what they advertise. Most newspapers are businesses with two goals—making a profit and satisfying the consumer—that in the case of cigarette advertising can be at cross purposes.

The *New Republic* once commissioned reporter David Owen to write an article on cancer and the cigarette lobby. He wrote a piece so blunt in stating the issues and laying blame that the editors killed the story. According to *USA Today*, which investigated the incident, "In the candid (and no doubt regretted) words of Leon Wieseltier, the editor who assigned it, the threat of 'massive losses of advertising revenue' did it in."[24]

The editors of the *New Republic* had been willing to report on the

---

[22] Hamilton, "Demand for Cigarettes," p. 408.

[23] "Rx from AMA: Snuff Out Tobacco Ads," *U.S. News and World Report* 99 (December 23, 1985), p. 8.

[24] Charles Trueheart, "The Tobacco Industry's Advertising Smoke Screen," *USA Today*, March 15, 1985, p. 3D.

dangers of smoking and on the pressures brought by lobbyists, but were not willing to print the forcefulness with which Owen stated his case. Owen later published his piece in the *Washington Monthly,* where he wrote that "the transcendent achievement of the cigarette lobby has been to establish the cancer issue as a 'controversy' or a 'debate' rather than as the clear-cut scientific case that it is." He went on to portray an industry that, among other things, uses newspapers and magazines to enhance the appeal of smoking by portraying the young smoker as healthy and sexy.

According to research conducted by Kenneth E. Warner, this example of burying Owen's article is but one of many cases in which American news media have refused to cover the story of the dangers of smoking for fear of loss of advertising revenue.[25] The *Washington Post,* using statistics taken from the *New York State Journal of Medicine,* found that only 6 out of 1,700 daily American newspapers attempt wholeheartedly to report on the dangers of smoking.[26] However, the American Newspaper Publishers Association and the Magazine Publishers Association continue to appeal to First Amendment protections of the right to advertise and to present the facts as newspapers see fit in order to justify their view that this matter should be left up to each individual newspaper.

The AMA in 1985 set the goal of having a "smokeless society by the year 2000." In an effort to achieve this goal, the association proposed a total ban on all cigarette advertising. Included in the ban are (1) no distribution of samples or discount coupons; (2) no sponsorship of sporting events; (3) no advertising by skywriting; and (4) no portrayal of smoking in films.[27]

Most, if not all, advertising associations are opposed to the contemplated ban on print cigarette ads. Ad agencies maintain that the government cannot ban an industry's ads merely because they do not like that industry's product. They remind Congress that if cigarettes are legal to sell, they should be legal to advertise. Furthermore, agencies believe that banning cigarette ads will not accomplish the goal of reducing consumption by youth. Several studies have found that young smokers are most often influenced to start smoking by friends and parents, rather than by media ads.[28] Similar conclusions regarding the psychological

[25] Kenneth E. Warner, "Cigarette Advertising and Media Coverage of Smoking and Health," *New England Journal of Medicine* 312 (February 7, 1985), pp. 384–388.

[26] Sam Zagoria, "Smoking and the Media's Responsibility," *Washington Post,* December 18, 1985, p. A26.

[27] "Cigarette Ads: Round Two," *Newsweek* 106 (December 23, 1985), p. 55.

[28] Eugene E. Levitt and Judith A. Edwards, "A Multivariate Study of Correlative Factors in Youthful Cigarette Smoking," *Developmental Psychology* 2, no. 2 (1970), pp. 5–11; and E. E. Levitt, "Reasons for Smoking and Not Smoking Given by School Children," *Journal of Public Health* (February 1971), p. 101–104.

effects of advertising on consumption by youth were obtained by researchers studying alcohol advertising bans in other countries.[29]

Most major cigarette companies have already reduced their share of print advertisements. In 1985 tobacco companies purchased $375 million in advertising space, a 12 percent decline from 1984. The tobacco marketers have begun to focus on the use of discount ads, point of sale displays, and sponsorship of sports events to replace print advertisements. These techniques are directed to those who already smoke rather than potential smokers. Philip Morris, marketer of the nation's largest-selling Marlboro brand, has developed the "Philip Morris" magazine. The magazine, a voice for industry concerns, is distributed free of charge to 1.3 million smokers.[30]

Congressional consideration of the cigarette ad ban continues. Representative Mike Synar (D., Okla.) introduced a bill in August 1986 that would ban all tobacco advertisement. Public hearings continue to reconsider the issue. U.S. Surgeon General C. Everett Koop repeatedly expressed support for an industry ban in public hearings during the years of the Reagan administration. Hearings have also evaluated several alternatives to a ban. These options include limiting ads to "tombstone" messages containing only the product brand name and a health warning, or requiring the tobacco industry to finance a counteractive anti-smoking campaign, or eliminating the tax deductibility of tobacco ads and promotional expenditures.[31]

A final determination on the cigarette advertising issue will prove difficult because of the many conflicting interests involved. Any policy must balance public health concerns and First Amendment rights. Many state and local governments are beginning to restrict smoking in open areas, including restaurants, offices, and hospitals. The U.S. tobacco industry is fighting to hold on to its $15.1 billion market amidst declining domestic sales that have dropped 2 to 3 percent annually and renewed public attention to the health hazards of smoking.

[29] M. J. Waterson, *Advertising and Cigarette Consumption* (London: Advertising Association, 1981), pp. 19–20.

[30] "Goodbye to Marlboro Man," *Forbes* (June 2, 1986), p. 208.

[31] Steven W. Colford, "Something Less Than Ban Seen for Cigaret Ads," *Advertising Age* (August 11, 1986), p. 59.

AIDS and the Availability of AZT

The realization that AIDS will potentially affect millions of people world-wide has proved to be a terrifying prospect. The U.S. Department of Health and Human Services has, at this writing, received reports of 31,982 AIDS cases in the United States, with approximately 18,462 deaths so far. At least 1.5 million Americans are infected with the virus but have not yet shown symptoms of the disease.[1]

This crisis has prompted massive research on possible treatments and cures. In the United States, the effort and expense were exemplified by the National Cancer Institute's mass-screening process to find a drug that would kill or at least inactivate the virus that causes AIDS, the Human Immunodeficiency Virus (HIV). This process rapidly identified fifty candidate products whose effectiveness was then measured under laboratory conditions. After testing was completed in February 1985, a drug known as "compound S" was found to be a potent anti-viral agent *in vitro* (in the test tube). Compound S is azidothymidine, or AZT. In clinical trials, there was strong evidence that groups of AIDS patients receiving AZT were faring far better than comparison groups receiving a placebo. In all, only 1 of 145 patients receiving the drug died, while 19 of 137 patients receiving a placebo died. An independent board of experts advised the research group conducting the study that it would be unethical to continue the trials, arguing that it would deny some patients a life-prolonging drug. The trials were stopped and all participants were given AZT.

The drug AZT does not cure AIDS, but rather slows the progress of

---

[1] Robert E. Windom, M.D., Assistant Secretary for Health, Public Health Service, U.S. Department of Health and Human Services, in testimony before the Subcommittee on Health and the Environment of the House Committee on Energy and Commerce, March 10, 1987, p. 1.

the HIV by interfering with the virus's reproductive mechanism. The drug "fools" the HIV into incorporating AZT into its replicating DNA in place of the normal functional base thymine, and hence producing only non-functional new viruses, thereby stemming the course of infection. Unfortunately, this mechanism of action also causes severe side effects, especially in patients with poor underlying bone marrow function. The drug is incorporated into the DNA of HIV, but it may affect all body cells in which DNA is replicated. For instance, AZT may inhibit the bone marrow, hampering red blood cell production and causing severe anemia (low red blood cell count) in one third to one half of the patients treated, requiring transfusions, dose reduction, or a discontinuation of the drug regimen.

AZT is marketed by Burroughs Wellcome Company of Research Triangle Park, North Carolina, under the name Retrovir. On March 20, 1987, the FDA approved the drug for sale. Burroughs Wellcome was awarded a use patent on February 9, 1988. As is the case with all patents, exclusive proprietary rights are given for seventeen years. The drug was at the time of the award of the patent the only approved treatment for AIDS. The pharmaceutical company is the only producer and is free to set its own price for the drug. It is common practice for pharmaceutical companies to recover research and development expenditures by charging whatever the market will bear before competition and new drugs enter the market, even if the cost is too steep for some consumers. Thus, the potential for profit as well as abuse is significant. Burroughs Wellcome projected a price of $10,000 retail (the company's price was $8,300, wholesale) for a year's supply of the drug, which was projected to be used by an estimated 30,000 patients. The estimated (anticipated) annual revenue was therefore between $130 and $200 million.

The company quickly came under fire by critics who charged that the price was unreasonably high, creating a potential hardship for patients who lack any real treatment alternative. Within a year the price was reduced to $8,000 for a year's supply. Critics still complained about both the price and the firm's monopoly on the drug, and in January 1988, nineteen people were arrested in a show of civil disobedience at Burroughs Wellcome distribution center in Burlingame, California. Many physicians and consumer advocates are still demanding that the pharmaceutical firm justify what appears to be an exorbitant price.

The federal government closely monitors the pricing of new drugs, especially with innovative therapies like AZT. The Subcommittee on Health and the Environment of the House Committee on Energy and Commerce conducted extensive hearings concerning the manufacture and marketing of AZT, during which Burroughs Wellcome representatives were called to testify. The company defended the price of AZT as fair and as necessitated by the costs it incurred,[2] contending that the process of manufacturing AZT was lengthy and expensive, and that labor and technology were and still are intensive and financially burdensome.

However, the company has consistently refused to give out precise figures on costs to Congress, holding these figures to be confidential. It does state that it made a commitment of $80 million to the research and development of the drug, including $10 million in free AZT administered to 4,500 patients who participated in the clinical trial.

Mr. T. E. Haigler, Jr., President and CEO of Burroughs Wellcome, testified that the company's calculation of the AZT product's cost included the following:

> [The] costs of developing, producing and marketing the drug, the high costs of research, and the need to generate revenues to cover these continuing costs . . . [including] the possible advent of new therapies, and profit margins customarily generated by significant new medicines. . . . We also examined factors that might be considered to be unique with respect to Retrovir. These included the very real high cost of producing this drug and the very real needs of the patients for whom this drug was developed.[3]

Burroughs Wellcome further defends its price, claiming that AZT will reduce the costs of treating each AIDS patient by 25 percent and each ARC patient by 60 percent. In addition, the prolongation of life and the reduced incidence of infections realized through the use of AZT will result in fewer hospitalizations for AIDS patients.[4]

Individuals with AIDS, many of whom are young, indigent, and uninsured, are often unable to pay the market price for AZT. Therefore, much of the financial burden for treatment falls to public programs such as Medicaid. Federal officials have estimated that in coming years as many as 40 percent of all AIDS patients will receive Medicaid benefits. Federal programs often do not pay for prescriptions or, if they do, place a dollar limit on drug benefits (for example, $22 per month in Florida and 80 percent of the dollar cost in many other states and the District of Columbia). In September 1987 the U.S. Congress allocated $30 million to fund AZT for *indigent* patients. Health officials have esti-

---

[2] David Barry, Vice President for Research at Burroughs Wellcome, spoke to this issue in Marilyn Chase, "AIDS Drug Comes to a Worried Market," *Wall Street Journal,* March 23, 1987, p. 6.

[3] T. E. Haigler, Jr., President and CEO, Burroughs Wellcome, in testimony before the Subcommittee on Health and the Environment of the House Committee on Energy and Commerce, March 10, 1987, p. 12.

[4] *Ibid.*, p. 13.

mated that given current trends, Medicaid may incur costs of $150 million per year for AZT alone, beginning in 1988. The obvious financial burden of obtaining AZT has prompted one physician to say, "Either it'll be on the taxpayer's back, or patients will be robbing pharmacies. . . . These are desperate, dying patients."[5]

The limited supply of AZT required Burroughs Wellcome to tightly control the distribution of the drug during the first six months of general sale, allocating it to only the sickest patients. To prescribe the drug, physicians were required to obtain a form from the pharmaceutical company by calling a toll-free number, provide a description of the patient's symptoms, and then wait for an independent group of physicians employed by the company to "approve" the patient for receipt of the drug. This procedure has angered the large number of AIDS sufferers denied access to the drug. However, supplies of new chemically synthesized thymidine, the raw material for AZT, and manufacturing expansions at Burroughs Wellcome plants have made increased supplies of AZT available for regular distribution to patients suffering in earlier stages of the disease.[6]

AIDS patients eagerly await the introduction of other potential treatments. Charges have been made that newer and better drugs exist but await the long process of testing and approval. Criticism of these delays has been directed at the FDA (which approves new drugs) and at the National Institutes of Health (which is conducting some of the drug trials). The FDA argues that while it usually takes eight years to test and approve a new drug, for AZT the process time was cut to only two years.

A new group of drugs that, like AZT, disrupt the replication of the HIV are now being developed. These new drugs are believed to be less toxic to human cells and may result in fewer and milder side effects. The first of this group, called dideoxycytidine, is presently in the testing phase, but has already manifested serious and painful side effects in the majority of those who receive it. To further speed up the testing process, Dr. Frank Young, chief of the FDA, proposed that physicians be permitted to prescribe drugs for patients with life-threatening diseases after initial safety and efficacy trials have been completed.[7] These measures were approved by the FDA and became law in June 1987.[8]

At present no U.S. federal policy addresses the complex issues sur-

[5] An anonymous physician, as quoted in Chase, "AIDS Drug Comes to a Worried Market."

[6] Marilyn Chase, "Wellcome Unit to Expand AZT Supply; More Treatment, and Profits, Expected," *Wall Street Journal*, September 11, 1987, p. 31.

[7] Matt Clark, "Uproar over AIDS Drugs," *Newsweek* (April 6, 1987), p. 24.

[8] Michel McQueen, "FDA Clears Use of Experimental Drugs; Reagan Is Likely to Favor AIDS Testing," *Wall Street Journal*, May 22, 1987, p. 22.

rounding the treatment costs of AIDS. There is no recognition of a social obligation to control the allocation of such commodities by fixing or lowering the market price. The prevailing view is that such controls are counterproductive because controls inhibit economic incentives for research and development, which are advantageous to society as a whole. Although it seems likely that competition in the market and availability of new drugs will eventually force down the cost of AIDS treatment, it may be several years before viable alternatives have been approved and marketed.

McAleer *v.* AT&T

Daniel McAleer was a $10,500-per-year service representative who handled orders for telephone service in AT&T's Washington, D.C., Long Lines Division. In 1974 he asked for a promotion that he did not receive. Instead, a staff assistant named Sharon Hulvey received the promotion. She was qualified for the job, but she was not as qualified as McAleer, had less seniority, and had scored slightly lower on the company's employee evaluation scale. The job was given to Hulvey because of an affirmative action program at AT&T. McAleer claimed that he had been discriminated against on the basis of sex. He then brought a lawsuit against AT&T asking for the promotion, differential back pay, and $100,000 damages (on grounds of lost opportunity for further promotion). Joined by his union (Communications Workers of America), he also claimed that AT&T had undermined the ability of the union to secure employment rights to jobs and fair promotions under the relevant collective bargaining agreement.

Some historical background is essential to understand how this situation arose, and why AT&T acted as it did.

This case was prepared by Tom L. Beauchamp and revised by Joanne L. Jurmu. Sources consulted include: *McAleer* v. *American Telephone and Telegraph Company*, 416 F.Supp. 435 (1976); Earl A. Molander, *Responsive Capitalism: Case Studies in Corporate Social Conduct* (New York: McGraw-Hill Book Co., 1980), pp. 56–70; Theodore Purcell, "Management Development: A Practical Ethical Method and a Case," unpublished; "A.T.&T. Denies Job Discrimination Charges, Claims Firm Is Equal Employment Leader," *Wall Street Journal,* December 14, 1970, p. 6; "A.T.&T. Makes Reparation," *Economist* 246 (January 27, 1973), p. 42; Byron Calame, "Liberating Ma Bell: Female Telephone Workers Hit Labor Pact, Says Men Still Get the Best Jobs, More Pay," *Wall Street Journal,* July 26, 1971, p. 22; "FCC Orders Hearing on Charge that A.T.&T. Discriminates in Hiring," *Wall Street Journal,* January 22, 1971, p. 10; "Federal Agency Says A.T.&T. Job Bias Keeps Rates from Declining," *Wall Street Journal,* December 2, 1971, p. 21; Richard M. Hodgetts, "A.T.&T. versus the Equal Employment Opportunity Commission," in *The Business Enterprise: Social Challenge, Social Response* (Philadelphia: W. B. Saunders Company, 1977), pp. 176–182. **Not to be duplicated without permission of the holder of the copyright,** © 1989 Tom L. Beauchamp.

HISTORICAL BACKGROUND

The U.S. Equal Employment Opportunity Commission (EEOC) had long been in pursuit of AT&T on grounds of discrimination. In 1970, the EEOC claimed that the firm engaged in "pervasive, system-wide, and blatantly unlawful discrimination in employment against women, blacks, Spanish-surnamed Americans, and other minorities."[1] The EEOC argued that the employment practices of AT&T violated several laws, including the Civil Rights Acts of 1964 and 1866, the Equal Pay Act of 1963, and the Fair Employment Practices Acts of numerous states and cities. In hearings the EEOC maintained that AT&T "suppressed" women workers and that for the past thirty years "women as a class have been excluded from every job classification except low paying clerical and telephone-operator jobs. . . ."[2] AT&T denied all charges brought against it, claiming that its record demonstrated equality of treatment for minorities and women. It produced supporting statistics about minorities in the work force, but these statistics were all vigorously challenged by the EEOC.

In the spring of 1972, the Department of Labor intervened and assumed jurisdiction in the matter. Negotiations reached a final agreement on December 29, 1972. An out-of-court settlement was proposed and a Consent Decree was entered in and accepted by a Philadelphia court (January 18, 1973). This agreement resulted in AT&T's paying $15 million in back wages to 13,000 women and 2,000 minority-group men and giving $23 million in raises to 36,000 employees who had presumably suffered because of previous policies.

Out of this settlement came an extensive, company-wide affirmative action recruitment and promotion program. AT&T set rigorous goals and intermediate targets in fifteen job categories to meet first-year objectives. The goals were determined by statistics regarding representative numbers of workers in the relevant labor market. Also as part of the agreement, if during this campaign its progress were to fall short of deadlines, AT&T would then have to depart from normal selection and promotion standards by more vigorously pursuing affirmative action goals.[3]

---

[1] U.S. Equal Employment Opportunity Commission, "Petition to Intervene," Federal Communications Commission Hearings on A.T.&T. Revised Tariff Schedule, December 10, 1970, p. 1.

[2] "Bias Charges in Hiring: A.T.&T. Fights Back," *U.S. News and World Report,* August 14, 1972, p. 67.

[3] The stipulations of the agreement were met by the company before an established 1979 deadline.

At the same time, AT&T had a union contract that established ability and merit as the primary qualifications for positions, but also required that seniority be given "full consideration." This contract stood in noticeable contrast to the Consent Decree, which called for "an affirmative action override" that would bypass union-contract promotion criteria if necessary to achieve the affirmative action goals. Therefore, the decree required that under conditions of a target failure, a *less* qualified (but *qualified*) person could take precedence over a more qualified person with greater seniority. This condition applied only to promotions, not to layoffs and rehiring, where seniority continued to prevail.

McALEER AND THE COURTS

The McAleer case came before Judge Gerhard A. Gesell, who held on June 9, 1976, that McAleer was a "faultless employee" who became an "innocent victim" through an unfortunate but justifiable use of the affirmative action process. More specifically, Gesell ruled that McAleer was entitled to monetary compensation (as damages), but was not entitled to the promotion because the discrimination the Consent Decree had been designed to eliminate might be perpetuated if Hulvey were not given the promotion. The main lines of Gesell's ruling are as follows:

> After the filing of the Philadelphia complaint and AT&T's contemporaneous answer, and following an immediate hearing, the Court received from the parties and approved a Consent Decree and accompanying Memorandum of Agreement which had been entered into by the governmental plaintiffs and AT&T after protracted negotiation. This settlement was characterized by Judge Higginbotham as "the largest and most impressive civil rights settlement in the history of this nation."
>
> . . . "Affirmative action override" requires AT&T to disregard this standard [seniority] and choose from among basically qualified female or minority applicants if necessary to meet the goals and timetables of the Consent Decree and if other affirmative efforts fail to provide sufficient female or minority candidates for promotion who are the best qualified or most senior. . . .
>
> This entire process occurred without the participation of Communication Workers of America (CWA), the certified collective bargaining representative of approximately 600,000 nonmanagement employees at AT&T and the parent union with which plaintiff Local #2350 is affiliated. Although it was consistently given notice in the Philadelphia case of the efforts to reach a settlement, and although it was "begged . . . to negotiate and litigate" in that proceeding, 365 F. Supp. at 1110, CWA persistently and repeatedly refused to become involved. . . .
>
> Judge Higginbotham presently has before him and has taken under advisement the question of modification of the Consent Decree because it conflicts with the collective bargaining agreement. . . .
>
> It is disputed that plaintiff McAleer would have been promoted but

for his gender. This is a classic case of sex discrimination within the meaning of the Act, 42 U.S.C. § 2000e-2(a)(2). That much is clear. What is more difficult is the issue of defenses or justifications available to AT&T and the question of appropriate relief under the circumstances revealed by this record. McAleer seeks both promotion and damages. The Court holds that he is entitled only to the latter.

General principles of law also support plaintiff McAleer's right to damages. It is true that AT&T was following the terms of the Consent Decree, and ordinarily one who acts pursuant to a judicial order or other lawful process is protected from liability arising from the act. . . . But such protection does not exist where the judicial order was necessitated by the wrongful conduct of the party sought to be held liable. . . .

Here, the Consent Decree on which the defendant relies *was necessary only because of AT&T's prior sex discrimination.* Under these circumstances the Decree provides *no defense against the claims of a faultless employee such as McAleer.* . . . [Italics added]

Since McAleer had no responsibility for AT&T's past sex discrimination, it is AT&T rather than McAleer who should bear the principal burden of rectifying the company's previous failure to comply with the Civil Rights Act of 1964. An affirmative award of some damages on a "rough justice" basis is therefore required and will constitute an added cost which the stockholders of AT&T must bear.

In the year that Judge Gesell's decision was reached, the same Judge (A. Leon) Higginbotham mentioned by Gesell rejected the new union petition to eliminate the affirmative action override from the Consent Decree—a petition that Gesell noted as pending. Higginbotham went out of his way to disagree with Gesell, saying Gesell's findings wrongly decided the case. He found AT&T to have immunity as an employer because of its history with and commitments to a valid affirmative action plan. However, because he was hearing a *union* case, Higginbotham's ruling did not directly overturn or otherwise affect Gesell's ruling. AT&T's lawyers—Mr. Robert Jeffrey, in particular—felt strongly that Judge Gesell's arguments were misguided and that Judge Higginbotham did the best that he could at the time to set matters right.

AT&T and McAleer settled out of court for $14,000; $6,500 of this amount went to legal fees for McAleer's attorney. Both McAleer and Hulvey continued their employment by AT&T. Mr. Jeffrey, AT&T's lawyer, maintained that this case was an aberration and that subsequent legal developments vindicated his point of view. From the moral point of view, Mr. Jeffrey believes that both Judge Gesell's ruling and the law being promulgated at the time in the White House deserve the most serious ethical scrutiny and criticism.[4]

---

[4] According to Mr. Jeffrey of the legal staff in AT&T's Washington, D.C., office, in a phone conversation on March 10, 1982.

REVERSE DISCRIMINATION
IN 1989

Numerous large firms have continued to adopt voluntary affirmative action plans for promoting and hiring women and minorities. Whenever such plans are adopted, questions inevitably arise about the practice of substituting one type of discrimination for another type. Decided by the U.S. Supreme Court in March of 1987 was a case involving reverse discrimination that many believe sets a strong precedent for the future of affirmative action plans. In this case, *Johnson* v. *Transportation Agency, Santa Clara County, California,*[5] the majority held affirmative action plans to be proper because the plan

(1) was intended to *attain,* not *maintain,* a balanced work force,

(2) did not unnecessarily trammel the rights of male employees or create an absolute bar to their advancement, and

(3) expressly directed that numerous factors be taken into account, including qualifications of female applicants for particular jobs.

Justice Brennan stated in the court's opinion that "[o]ur decision was grounded in the recognition that voluntary employer action can play a crucial role in furthering Title VII's purpose of eliminating the effects of discrimination in the workplace and that Title VII should not be read to thwart such efforts."[6] Many firms view the Supreme Court decision as encouraging affirmative action plans already in place, and adoption of new plans where they have not previously been in place. It is clear, however, that both corporate America and American courts continue to be divided over both the morality and legality of affirmative action plans such as the one that generated the McAleer case. Many firms continue to adopt plans almost identical to the one that led to the promotion of Hulvey rather than McAleer, whereas other firms insist that these policies involve immoral forms of discrimination.

In March 1988 AT&T's shareholders were in sharp disagreement over the company's employment history and affirmative action program. One set of shareholders fought for a stronger affirmative action program, whereas another set recommended phasing it out.

---

[5] Supreme Court of the United States, slip no. 85-1129.

[6] *Ibid.,* pp. 18–21.

CHAPTER 5

The Government

INTRODUCTION   Many industries have long been "self-regulated," that is, they have determined their responsibilities to society, to employees, and to others free from government regulation. Many of these industries have adopted formal codes of ethics that presumably serve to regulate the conduct of their members. The strategy has been to institutionalize moral behavior as a part of professional practice. However, almost everyone is suspicious when a professional or trade group providing public services is allowed to develop its own codes of conduct *independent of external warrant or scrutiny*. Moreover, enforcement of even good codes and corporate review procedures has proved lax in some cases and impossible in others.

The government has therefore intervened and regulated with the intent to provide a fair public policy. The policies of corporations, hospitals, trade groups, and professional societies may have a deep impact on their own conduct or even on the formation of public policy; but their policies are private rather than public. As government power has grown in the Western world, the identical complaint of "too much power" that used to haunt industry has come to haunt government.

The original idea of regulation had been to help the free enterprise system remain free, but now criticism is increasingly heard that regulation inhibits the free enterprise system; the system is shackled by other goals—such as nondiscriminatory hiring, a pollution-free environment, smut-free broadcasting, and the like. Consequently, regulation in the public interest has spawned two major controversies: First, what is the public interest, and how is the protection of a free market related to the public interest? Second, how can the public interest be protected without unduly harming the private interests at stake in free competition? This latter question is raised in a poignant way in the first four cases in this chapter, all involving controversial government mechanisms for regulating industries in the United States.

As social and political systems have become more complex, the problem of fair and adequate government regulation has compounded in difficulty and become mired in controversy—as the Laetrile, Fairness Doctrine, OSHA-benzene, and the automobile air bags cases in this chapter all indicate. Skepticism has emerged from various quarters that business has any capacity to regulate itself, and from other quarters that government has an adequate body of information and expertise to regulate business. The OSHA-benzene case, for example, examines some of the severe constraints presented by lack of information and expertise. State and local governments have complained almost as much about federal intervention and ownership as have corporate officials, who tend to view federal, state, and local requirements as jointly overwhelming. The compromise has been to regulate most heavily where the problems seem most acute, for example, in the regulation of fetus-deforming drugs and dangerous chemicals that produce nervous disorders. The OSHA-benzene case presents a clear example of the problem of changing and even vacillating regulatory efforts in circumstances of acute threats to health.

The result of government uncertainty and political influence is a hodge-podge of sometimes inconsistent government regulations directed at particular problems, rather than comprehensive or systematic programs of regulation and enforcement. A situation thus prevails where virtually no one is satisfied with the current government-business relationship—a situation rife for the conflicts of interest and uncertainties reflected in the cases in this chapter. In the case of consulting for Jones and Jones Pharmaceutical, for example, the problem of establishing consulting contracts with government representatives who regulate an industry's affairs is explored as a problem of conflict of interest.

Despite the patchwork character of the contemporary regulatory environment, it would be dubious to claim, as some critics have, that the United States has remained passively oblivious to problematic issues raised by regulatory activities. Since the inception of government requirements, the regulatory structure has undergone repeated modification and refinement in light of both internal and external scrutiny, even though special problems remain. The precise and changing implications of the developing regulations are therefore difficult to distinguish, and it is only fair to remember that regulation is an ongoing process often responsive to constructive criticism and legislative initiative.

Moreover, even in those domains of business activity that have been left free of government control, the initiatives of self-regulation discussed above have often proved less than satisfactory. Professional codes and mechanisms such as internal peer review are beneficial if they provide effective and defensible rules in the relationships they govern. But some of these formal mechanisms oversimplify moral requirements or boast more completeness and authority than they are entitled to claim. As a consequence the affected professionals may suppose that everything morally required has been done if the rules of the code have been obediently followed, just as many believe that all obligations have been discharged when *legal* requirements have been met. Professional codes and internal corporate mechanisms such as grievance procedures can be ambiguous, and some moral dilemmas are compounded rather than eased by these procedures. Codes and internal corporate guidelines have also traditionally been expressed in formulations so abstract that they either dispense only vague and nondirective moral advice or are subject to competing interpretations. Some of these problems in self-regulation are posed in this chapter in the case of peer review at Shamrock-Diamond Corporation.

The specter of government regulation raises a number of important ethical issues. One question is whether the government can legitimately play a paternalistic role. Can business activities be regulated to protect business against itself?—to protect customers against their own foolish decisions?—to protect clients against their own ignorant choices? The government often makes judgments about "consumer waste," "health foods" that are not nutritious, drugs that are inefficacious, and the like. Are the legitimate freedoms and rights of citizens and businesses unduly restricted by such judgments? These questions are raised in this chapter in the Laetrile case, which involves a decision by the Food and Drug Administration (FDA) to ban the manufacture and marketing of a product popular with cancer victims but declared ineffective by the FDA. These questions are also raised in more subtle forms in the air bags and Fairness Doctrine cases.

Another question is whether the government should support businesses that have sustained losses because of government intervention but that are not guilty of moral and legal violations. Sometimes a business or an entire industry is threatened by government-imposed standards. Is the government acting unfairly by regulating and not indemnifying small, under-capitalized industries that could fold or sustain serious losses because of regulatory intervention? (See, for example, the Reserve Mining case in Chapter 3.)

Many questions have also been raised about the use of cost/benefit judgments of efficiency as a way of establishing public policies. The basic idea behind cost/benefit judgments is to measure costs and benefits objectively, while identifying uncertainties and possible tradeoffs, in order to present policymakers with relevant information on which to base a decision. Many believe that such information can be used to make clear which tradeoffs are being made and why one alternative is more efficient than another. Yet this rational ideal has proved difficult to achieve, and in many cases we are faced with *moral* choices rather than *economic* choices. Considerations of justice, for example (as found in some of the cases in Chapter 4), might lead us to choose a *less efficient* but *more just* outcome. It can also be debatable as to what counts as a "cost," a "benefit," or a "valuable" outcome; and government regulatory activities often spark debates over these matters—as the OSHA-benzene, air bags, Laetrile, and Fairness Doctrine cases all illustrate.

Finally, one of the central problems in both business and government ethics is conflict of interest. These conflicts arise when an employee (or employer) has a personal interest that is at variance with the interests of the firm or of another party with whom the individual is associated. Generally, the conflict is found in contexts in which reasonable objectivity and impartiality are expected. Thus, for example, a manager who wants to promote his daughter instead of more experienced and more senior employees has two interests at least potentially in conflict: his interest in his family's welfare (including his own pride and satisfaction) and his company's welfare. Doctors who serve on boards of directors of health insurance companies can have a similar conflict of interest: They have an interest in their personal income and the income of hospitals in which they work, but they are also charged to keep payments low to protect those who take out company policies. Similar questions are probed in the case of the Jones and Jones consultant in this chapter.

As the whistle-blowing cases in Chapter 1 showed, many conflict of interest situations raise questions about an employee's loyalty to an employer or to another institution. Must an employee always put the employing firm's interest above his or her own personal, familial, or social interests? Although this question has traditionally been answered affirmatively in the courts (see Chapter 1), government agencies have tended to answer negatively in almost all difficult contexts of conflict of interest—especially if the employee and the firm involved are working on a government contract.

The FCC's Fairness Doctrine

Government intervention in the publication and dissemination of news is inconsistent with the notion of a free press in a democracy. However, the government also has a responsibility to ensure that the public is well-informed and exposed to a wide range of views on matters of community interest. These two obligations inevitably come into conflict. Until recently, there was a government mechanism of media accountability known as the Fairness Doctrine. The Doctrine was an attempt to mediate between the First Amendment rights of broadcasters and those of the public, and was designed to require broadcasters to provide balanced coverage of important public issues.

The origins of the Fairness Doctrine are traceable to both Congressional and Federal Communications Commission (FCC) legislation. The doctrine was clearly outlined in 1949 by the FCC in its "Report on Editorializing by Broadcasters," which stressed the importance of the development, through broadcasting, of an informed public opinion in a democracy. It affirmed the "right of the public in a free society to be informed and to have presented to it for acceptance or rejection the different attitudes and viewpoints concerning these vital and often controversial issues."[1] In 1959 Congress amended the Communications Act of 1934 to impose, in section 315(a), a statutory "obligation upon [broadcasters] to operate in the public interest and to afford reasonable opportunity for the discussion of conflicting views on issues of public importance."[2]

Broadcasters were not required by the Fairness Doctrine to give equal time to contrasting views; however, if "during the presentation of views on a controversial issue, an attack [was] made upon the honesty, character,

[1] "Report on Editorializing by Broadcasters," 13 F.C.C. 1246 (1949), p. 1249.
[2] Communications Act of 1934, 47 U.S.C. § 315(a).

integrity, or like personal qualities of an identified person or group,"[3] that person or group had to be given an opportunity to respond on the air. The broadcasting company had to bear the costs of all presentations.

The policy was traditionally confined to broadcast rather than print media because of the former's inaccessibility to the private citizen. There is a relative scarcity of the electronic spectrum usable as a means of communication, in that the number of people who want to broadcast exceeds the number of available broadcast licenses. This limited resource has been allocated through a government licensing system designed to protect the public interest through the enforcement of various regulations.

The U.S. Supreme Court held the Fairness Doctrine to be constitutional and consistent with the intent of the First Amendment in *Red Lion Broadcasting Co.* v. *Federal Communications Commission* (1969). The Court ruled that the scarcity of available radio frequencies justifies the imposition of a government regulatory system intended to ensure that broadcasters, as fiduciaries, act in the public interest. The First Amendment rights of the public to hear differing viewpoints was declared "paramount" to the rights of broadcasters. Justice Byron White expressed the opinion of the Court as follows:

> Where there are substantially more individuals who want to broadcast than there are frequencies to allocate, it is idle to posit an unabridgeable First Amendment right to broadcast comparable to the right of every individual to speak, write or publish. . . . A license permits broadcasting, but the licensee has no constitutional right to be the one who holds the license or to monopolize a radio frequency to the exclusion of his fellow citizens. There is nothing in the First Amendment which prevents the Government from requiring a licensee to share his frequency with others and to conduct himself as a proxy or fiduciary with obligations to present those views and voices which are representative of his community and which would otherwise, by necessity, be barred from the airwaves.[4]

The Court has reaffirmed the scarcity of the radio airwaves and the responsibility of broadcasters as public trustees in subsequent cases. Similar reasoning was used to justify the application of the Fairness Doctrine to cable programming.

The Fairness Doctrine was neither stringently enforced nor widely applied. It was invoked to restrict virulent racism and other use of the airwaves to intimidate and attack persons and institutions. The FCC also used the doctrine in 1967 to require broadcasters to give significant

---

[3] In *Red Lion Broadcasting Co.* v. *Federal Communications Commission* (1969), in Marc A. Franklin, ed., *Mass Media Law*, 2d ed. (Mineola, N.Y.: Foundation Press, 1982), p. 652.

[4] *Ibid.*, pp. 658–659.

time to anti-smoking messages. [See the case, "Banning Cigarette Advertising," pp. 168–176.] It was never used to enforce accountability for claims made in documentaries, no matter how hard-hitting or speculative.

The doctrine was most frequently applied to ensure that the presentation of candidates for public office would not be controlled by the preferences of licensed station owners. These regulations, however, were also loosened over the years. For example, the FCC held that any station endorsing or criticizing a candidate on the air had to give the opposing or criticized candidate air time to respond. In 1983 FCC Chairman Mark Fowler revised the commission's policy on televised political debates. He announced that broadcasters could schedule political debates with the candidates of their choice without being required to provide air time to excluded candidates.[5] Broadcasters could cover debates as "bona fide" news events without having to make time available to those who did not participate.

THE CURRENT LEGAL SITUATION

The Fairness Doctrine has come under fire from both sides of the political spectrum. Conservatives have opposed it as an expendable form of government intervention. Liberals have perceived it as a means of intimidating or even silencing journalists. In October 1981, the FCC recommended that the Fairness Doctrine be repealed. The commission issued in 1985 a detailed study of the doctrine. It concluded that the doctrine was "an unnecessary and detrimental regulatory mechanism . . . [that] disserves the public interest."[6] The FCC did not at this point repeal the doctrine because it believed that Congress had already codified it. However, a ruling by the U.S. Court of Appeals in September 1986 held that the Fairness Doctrine was *not* a statutory requirement. According to the ruling, Congress had merely ratified the doctrine in amending section 315(a) of the Communications Act of 1934. The FCC was left free by this decision to modify or to abolish the doctrine, and did abolish it in the summer of 1987, claiming that it violates First Amendment rights and stifles controversial programming.

The Court of Appeals ruling spurred controversy in Congress, where a majority has consistently voiced support for the Fairness Doctrine. There have been several proposals to codify the doctrine and make it an explicit requirement of the Communications Act. Representative John Dingell (D., Mich.) of the House Committee on Energy and Commerce

[5] "More Debates?," *Time* 122 (November 12, 1983), p. 59.

[6] "In re Inquiry into Section 73.1910 of the Commission's Rules and Regulations Concerning the General Fairness Doctrine Obligations of Broadcast Licenses," 102 F.C.C.2d 143 (1985).

introduced an amendment to the Communications Act that would "require expressly that licensees of broadcast stations present discussion of conflicting views on issues of public importance."[7] President Reagan vetoed the measure, and the Congress lacked the two thirds majority needed to override the veto. But in November 1987, Senator Ernest Hollings (D.–S.C.), Chairman of the Senate Commerce Committee, deftly steered a bill through this committee that would restore the Fairness Doctrine. Hollings has argued vigorously that fairness to political candidates can be assured only if this doctrine is reinstated. The votes in the Senate seem to be on Hollings' side.

THE CURRENT DEBATE

On August 4, 1987, the FCC voted unanimously to eliminate the Fairness Doctrine. There are still several cases contesting the constitutionality of the doctrine pending in court, and Congress is continuing its consideration of measures to codify the doctrine.

Doctrine opponents have challenged the Supreme Court decision in the *Red Lion* case, claiming that it is based on the mistaken premise of airwave scarcity and need for improved communication of information, which are no longer valid. According to this argument, technological advances since the *Red Lion* case have eliminated the scarcity. The 1985 FCC report noted a "dramatic" increase to more than 10,000 radio and television broadcasting stations, a 400 percent growth since 1949.[8] Commercial broadcasters opposed to the doctrine point out that in many cities listeners and viewers can pick up dozens of radio and television stations and have access to only one significant newspaper. The FCC also observed that the growth of cable television, satellite television, and new telecommunications services offer an almost unlimited number of broadcast options. From this perspective, the Fairness Doctrine is an unfair restraint on free market trade.

The 1985 FCC report noted that the "fairness doctrine in operation thwarts the laudatory purpose it is designed to promote. Instead of furthering the discussion of public issues, the fairness doctrine inhibits broadcasters from presenting controversial issues of public importance."[9] Broadcasters sometimes hesitate to air controversial materials for fear that they will be forced to use expensive air time to present another side of the issue. For some broadcasters, the loss of advertising

[7] Report together with additional and dissenting views submitted by Representative John Dingell from the House Committee on Energy and Commerce concerning the Fairness in Broadcasting Act of 1987 (HR 1934), p. 2.

[8] FCC 1985 Report as quoted in Report on Fairness in Broadcasting Act of 1987, pp. 38–39.

[9] "In re Inquiry into Section 73.1910," 102 F.C.C.2d 143 (1985).

time alone would prevent them from making room in their schedule for these materials. For example, there may be as many as fifteen candidates running in a presidential primary, which makes the provision of "equal time" burdensome for most stations.

Supporters of the doctrine claim that the relative scarcity of usable airwaves persists. The "scarcity of frequencies should not be measured by the number of stations allowed to broadcast, but by the number of individuals or groups who wish to use the facilities, or would use them if they were more readily available."[10] They point to the economic value of government licenses as a measure of the relative demand: Independent VHF licenses have sold for as much as $700 million in New York. Also, the number of stations has not increased in isolation, but in proportion to the growth in the nation's population. The broadcast medium continues to be more inaccessible to the private citizen than the print medium because the government must allocate the use of airwaves. Finally, the increase in stations does not necessarily correspond to any local increase in availability of diverse views on issues.

The Fairness Doctrine has been the *only* mechanism providing for public response that has any teeth. The House Committee on Energy and Commerce Report on the Fairness Doctrine points out that "numerous case histories demonstrate that the Fairness Doctrine promotes carriage of views that would otherwise not be available to the American public."[11] Charles Ferris, former Chairman of the FCC, testified before the Subcommittee on Telecommunications and Finance that "in 1979, during [his] watch, the Commission explicitly found that the Fairness Doctrine enhanced, not reduced, speech."[12] The congressional committee questioned the authority of the 1985 FCC report because it was based solely on broadcasters' accounts of the effects of the doctrine.

The Supreme Court has traditionally interpreted the viewer's right to a balanced presentation as correlative to First Amendment freedoms. The Fairness Doctrine has been considered an effective measure in controlling journalistic abuses and preventing biased broadcasting. The Committee on Energy and Commerce similarly found that "without the Fairness Doctrine, it is far from certain that many broadcasters would even discuss reasonable requests from individuals or groups seeking to present their view."[13] The 1985 FCC report makes mention of several

[10] T. Emerson, "The System of Freedom of Expression," as quoted in Report on Fairness in Broadcasting Act of 1987, p. 13.

[11] Report on Fairness in Broadcasting Act of 1987, p. 19.

[12] Charles Ferris at hearing on Fairness in Broadcasting Act of 1987 before the Subcommittee on Telecommunications and Finance on April 7, 1987, as quoted in Report on Fairness in Broadcasting Act of 1987, p. 19.

[13] Report on Fairness in Broadcasting Act of 1987, p. 19.

cases in which groups have used the doctrine to obtain advertising time that would have otherwise been denied.

Opponents argue that the Fairness Doctrine violates constitutional principles by allowing the government to intervene and to define how freedom of expression is to be used and practiced. The doctrine, they say, provides a dangerous potential for government abuse. They point to the FCC's statement that federal law permits government agencies to file Fairness Doctrine complaints against the media. This ruling (in July 1985) resulted in a complaint filed by the CIA charging that ABC's "World News Tonight" had three times distorted the news in broadcasting allegations that the CIA had tried to arrange the assassination of Ronald Rewald, a Honolulu businessman who was under indictment for several crimes. These CIA complaints would reverse past precedents and require greater accountability of the media to the government.

Two days later an editorial in the *Washington Post* expressed the press's opposition to government regulation: "Allowing one agency to haul a broadcast news organization before another (one capable of extracting huge financial costs) is a formula, intended or not, to intimidate the press and dry up the free flow of news."[14] (Ironically, ABC had been the only major network to oppose elimination of the Fairness Doctrine.) In November 1987, the National Association of Broadcasters mounted a major effort to defeat Senator Hollings' new bill in the Senate.[15]

The courts and Congress face a challenge in deciding the fate of the Fairness Doctrine. As members of a democratic nation, typical U.S. citizens are wary of government intervention in the private sector; but the Fairness Doctrine has traditionally been considered a justified exception. Although it is a measure that will inevitably intrude upon freedoms of the broadcaster, its intent is the protection of the individual's right to the presentation of differing views on important issues.

[14] Editorial, "CIA and FCC (Cont'd)," *Washington Post*, July 16, 1985, p. A14; and "FCC Turns Down Fairness Complaint Lodged by CIA against ABC," *Broadcasting* (January 14, 1985) p. 65.

[15] Bob Davis, "Hollings Again Tries to Revive Fairness Doctrine, Abolished by FCC, but Faces Maelstrom of Static," *Wall Street Journal*, November 18, 1987.

Manufacture and Regulation of Laetrile

> It has been estimated that consumers waste $500 million a year on medical quackery and another $500 million annually on some "health foods" which have no beneficial effect. Unnecessary deaths, injuries and financial loss can be expected to continue until the law requires adequate testing for safety and efficacy of products and devices before they are made available to consumers. (President John F. Kennedy in a message to Congress)[1]

> "Let me choose the way I want to die." It is not your prerogative to tell me how. (Glenn Rutherford, cancer patient and Laetrile supporter at FDA hearing)[2]

These two quotations express the essence of an acrimonious conflict that raged over the better part of the 1970s in the scientific and popular press, in courtrooms and hearing rooms, in prestigious research institutions, and among drug manufacturers. This debate emerged over the regulation, manufacturing, and marketing of Laetrile, a drug said to be a cure for cancer by its supporters but denounced as worthless by much of the scientific community.

The Food and Drug Administration (FDA) has been given responsibility for determining both the *safety* and the *efficacy* of a drug before allowing it to be marketed in the United States. The FDA's responsibility for drug licensing dates from the passage in 1906 of the Pure Food and Drug Act, which was primarily addressed to safety abuses among purveyors of patent medicines. In 1962, new laws were passed (partly in response to the Thalidomide tragedy involving malformed fetuses) that

---

[1] President quoted by David A. Smith, "The Laetrile Dilemma," *Pennsylvania Medicine* 80 (August 15, 1977), p. 15.

[2] Quoted by James C. Peterson and Gerald A. Markle, "The Laetrile Controversy," in Dorothy Nelkin, ed., *Controversy: Politics of Technical Decisions* (Beverly Hills, Calif.: Sage Publications, 1979), p. 175.

required the FDA to assess the efficacy of a drug as well as its safety before the drug could be approved for marketing.[3]

The FDA examined a drug known as Laetrile for safety and found no significant problems. However, the FDA could not find evidence of the effectiveness of the drug, and became convinced that Laetrile was worthless for the treatment of cancer. Consequently the drug was banned from the U.S. market.

Laetrile supporters reacted with fury when the drug was banned. Cancer victims demanded the right to use it; state legislatures who opposed the FDA's decision legalized it on their own; and others felt the FDA was denying the American people their Constitutional right to freedom of choice. Many argued that since the drug had not been proven *unsafe*, people should be allowed to use it while further tests were conducted. But many in the medical field opposed this "laissez-faire" attitude. They argued that patients were drawn toward an inexpensive, painless cure for their disease but failed to realize its ineffectiveness until too late. Critics claimed that numerous deaths had resulted although most victims could have been helped by legitimate alternative forms of treatment if caught in time.

The ferocity of this debate was new, but Laetrile was not. Amygdalin, the chemical name for Laetrile, has been known since the first half of the eighteenth century. Modern proponents of Laetrile therapy attribute the beginning of the movement to Ernst Krebs, who began experimenting with the extract of apricot pits in the 1920s, and to his son, Ernst Krebs, Jr., who refined the extract to produce the drug Laetrile in 1952. Since then Laetrile researchers have experimented with a variety of methods and techniques for using Laetrile in the treatment of cancer, and they claim that Laetrile is in fact effective in this cause. According to Krebs, Laetrile is effective because cyanide, which is an active ingredient, attacks the cancerous cells while an enzyme called rhodanese protects the normal cells.[4]

Initially Krebs' supporters claimed that Laetrile not only cured or controlled existing cancers but could also prevent cancers from forming. Their claims for the effectiveness of Laetrile were based primarily on patients' case histories (some published in a volume called *Laetrile Case*

[3] Two arguments were advanced in favor of the efficacy requirement. The economic argument had to do with consumer protection, *i.e.*, consumers were wasting their money on drugs that were not benefiting them. The second argument had to do with health and safety, namely, that reliance on ineffective drugs could be dangerous when effective alternatives were available. The FDA held that although Laetrile appeared "harmless," it had not been proven effective and therefore should not be approved for manufacture and sale in the United States.

[4] Thomas Donaldson, "Case Study—Laetrile: The FDA and Society," in Thomas Donaldson and Patricia Werhane, eds., *Ethical Issues in Business: A Philosophical Approach* (Englewood Cliffs, N.J.: Prentice-Hall, 1979), p. 208.

Histories) and on personal testimonials of "cured" cancer victims. However, the medical and scientific communities on the whole were not impressed with this form of "proof." The reported case histories were viewed as too sketchy and the follow-up times too short to support the claims. Moreover, few patients took Laetrile without first undergoing more traditional forms of cancer therapy. It is therefore virtually impossible to determine which treatment or treatments should receive credit for improvements. Also, the natural history of cancer is not totally understood, and spontaneous remissions can and do occur.[5]

In 1962, the FDA charged Krebs with violating the Federal Food, Drug and Cosmetic Act, on grounds that he could not prove the effectiveness of his drug. In 1963 Laetrile was banned because it was not found to be an effective treatment of cancer or any other health problem. Since then, proponents of Laetrile have revised their claims; they no longer proclaim Laetrile an independent *cure* for cancer, but instead emphasize its role in the prevention and control of the disease. However, supporters of Laetrile maintain that the standards of proof for Laetrile research have been higher than for other cancer drugs and that pro-Laetrile results have been obtained but suppressed.[6]

The controversy surrounding Laetrile turned largely on the drug's efficacy *and* on one's right to *manufacture, market,* and *purchase* the product. During the 1970s the FDA suffered criticisms that it was a "paternalistic" agency after it attempted to ban the manufacturing and marketing of the popular artificial sweetener saccharin. The Laetrile problem immediately followed this unpopular FDA policy. By mid-1977, FDA head Donald Kennedy found increasing evidence of the inefficacy of Laetrile. However, criticism of the FDA was also increasing and efforts were mounting either to allow free choice of the drug or to test for inefficacy in a public trial using human subjects. A number of state legislatures and judges were calling the FDA's findings into question.[7] Some states had legalized its manufacture and sale, and some courts had criticized the FDA record and policies. Even prestigious physicians and newspapers such as the *New York Times* endorsed the right of individuals to choose the drug even if it turned out to be inefficacious.

According to pro-regulation partisans, it is desirable and necessary to protect uneducated risk-takers who are vulnerable to unsubstantiated medicinal claims. "The absolute freedom to choose an effective drug is properly surrendered in exchange for the freedom from danger to each

---

[5] John M. Yarbro, "Laetrile 'Case Histories': A Review and Critique," *Missouri Medicine* 76 (April 1979), pp. 195–203.

[6] Peterson and Markle, "The Laetrile Controversy," p. 170.

[7] See, for example, *Rutherford* v. *United States*, 438 F. Supp. (1977), and John F. Cannizzaro and Madelon M. Rosenfield, "Laetrile and the FDA: A Case of Reverse Regulation," *Journal of Health Politics, Policy and Law* (Summer 1978), pp. 181–195.

person's health and well-being from the sale and use of worthless drugs."[8] From this perspective, regulation is not irreconcilable with freedom of choice. If a regulation promotes situations under which more informed and deliberative choices are made, it does not constrict freedom; and a choice cannot be free if the product is a fraud.[9]

By contrast, advocates of the freedom of choice claim that the simple restriction of Laetrile violates the individual's right to autonomous choice and the manufacturers' rights to market a product. Advocates of this view resent the characterization of cancer victims as people who are not capable of making rational or free decisions because of the stress of illness. They believe that most of these individuals are able to make well-founded personal decisions and should be allowed to do so.

The economic implications of banning Laetrile have also introduced a significant controversy in which each side has accused the other of economic exploitation of cancer victims. Until now Laetrile has primarily been manufactured and marketed in Mexico. It has been estimated that in 1977 alone, approximately 7,000 patients were treated in two Mexican clinics at an average cost of $350 per day.[10] Proponents of Laetrile counter that traditional cancer treatments represent an enormous and profitable industry, and a cost savings for patients would be achieved if Laetrile were marketed in the United States. For instance, the American Cancer Society estimated that as early as 1972 the direct costs of cancer treatment totaled over $3 billion (for hospital care, nursing home care, physicians' and nurses' fees, drugs and other treatments, and research).[11]

The United States potentially presents a growing market for Laetrile and for clinics that might provide it. Although the FDA does not control *intrastate* commerce, it would not be profitable for any one state to manufacture Laetrile in all its stages—that is, from the farming of apricot trees all the way to the laboratory synthesis of the finished drug. Approval of the drug for *interstate* U.S. manufacture and sale would not only be a boon to some businesses, but would also enable customers to avoid the enormous markup now paid for black market Laetrile. Moreover, Laetrile is extremely cheap on the retail market—a small fraction of the cost of conventional cancer therapies.

[8] HEW Release, Aug. 4, 1977, as quoted by Marion Smiley, "Legalizing Laetrile," in Amy Gutman and Dennis Thompson, eds., *Ethics and Politics: Cases and Comments* (Chicago: Nelson-Hall Publishers, 1984), p. 198.

[9] See Arthur L. Caplan, "When Liberty Meets Authority: Ethical Aspects of the Laetrile Controversy," in Gerald Markle and James Peterson, eds., *Politics, Science and Cancer* (Boulder, Col.: Westview Press, 1980), Chap. 6, pp. 133–150; and Smiley, "Legalizing Laetrile," p. 200.

[10] Donaldson, "Case Study—Laetrile," p. 211.

[11] Peterson and Markle, "The Laetrile Controversy," p. 172.

The courts as well as the press have provided the arena for the conflict over the rights of a patient to choose a treatment and the rights of manufacturers to market a product. While it was not the intent of Congress to impose such restrictions on choice, the patient's choice is in fact restricted as a result of the 1962 drug amendments. Because these amendments restrict the market to industry-tested and FDA-approved products, treatment by and manufacturing of alternatives are inevitably constricted,[12] at least until New Drug Applications for them are filed. Several of these applications for Laetrile have been filed with the FDA by manufacturers, but no application has been approved. Consequently, the status of Laetrile remains that of an unapproved new drug.

A series of lawsuits have challenged the FDA restrictions, and a number of states have passed laws "legalizing" its use. The judicial and legislative challenges are not, however, without opponents. Lawyer William Curran, for instance, has deplored the action of certain courts in allowing the use of Laetrile for the terminally ill. "It is understandable," he writes, "that judges have had trouble dealing objectively with the legal pleas of plaintiffs who are dying a painful death and whose only wish is to indulge in a harmless, although ineffective, gesture of hope. The courts have tried to dispense mercy. Their error has been in abandoning the protection of law for these patients."[13]

As the arguments have developed, the issues of choice and fraudulent representation by business have moved to the forefront. Franz Inglefinger, the distinguished former editor of the *New England Journal of Medicine* and himself a cancer victim, was convinced that Laetrile was "useless." In 1977 he wrote, "I would not take Laetrile myself under any circumstances. If any member of my family had cancer, I would counsel them against it. If I were still in practice, I would not recommend it to my patients." On the other hand, he said, "Perhaps there are some situations in which rational medical science should yield and make some concessions. If any patient had what I thought was hopelessly advanced cancer, and if he asked for Laetrile, I should like to be able to give the substance to him to assuage his mental anguish, just as I would give him morphine to relieve his physical suffering."[14] Inglefinger thus did not view truthful marketing of the drug as involving a fraudulent misrepresentation.

In January 1987 a Laetrile bill was introduced into the House of

[12] See Don G. Rushing, "Picking Your Poison: The Drug Efficacy Requirement and the Right of Privacy," *UCLA Law Review* 25 (February 1978), p. 587.

[13] William J. Curran, "Laetrile for the Terminally Ill: Supreme Court Stops the Nonsense," *New England Journal of Medicine* 302 (March 13, 1980), p. 621.

[14] Franz Inglefinger, "Laetrilomania" (Editorial), *New England Journal of Medicine* 296 (May 19, 1977), p. 1167.

Representatives. It provided that the controversial efficacy requirements of the Food, Drug, and Cosmetics Act would not be applied to Laetrile if a patient were under a physician's care (see Appendix).

The National Institutes of Health and most other health care institutions still discourage the use of Laetrile, preferring conventional methods of cancer treatment. The National Cancer Institute's official policy is to encourage conventional methods with the explanation that testing has always shown "evidence of Laetrile's failure as a cancer treatment."[15] Americans wishing treatment using Laetrile must travel outside the country. The FDA describes the issue as dormant, but not dead. As long as cancer remains "incurable," Laetrile (and many other unapproved methods) will be tried by those seeking relief.

APPENDIX: *Exhibit 1:* H.R. 651

A BILL

To provide that the effectiveness requirements of the Federal Food, Drug, and Cosmetic Act shall not apply to Laetrile in certain cases.

Be it enacted by the Senate and House of Representatives of the United States of America in Congress assembled, That in the administration of section 505 of the Federal Food, Drug, and Cosmetic Act, the effectiveness requirement of such section shall not be applicable to Laetrile when used under the direction of a physician for the treatment of pain.

[15] "Statement of the National Cancer Institute on Laetrile Tests with Patients," Vincent T. De Vita, Jr., M.D., Director, April 30, 1981.

The OSHA-Benzene Case

BACKGROUND

In May of 1977 the Occupational Safety and Health Administration (OSHA) of the U.S. government issued an emergency temporary standard (ETS) ordering that worker exposure to the chemical benzene be reduced from the regulated level of 10 parts per million (ppm) to 1 ppm [time weighted average (TWA)]. In addition, OSHA proposed to make this a permanent standard for benzene exposure in all industries except gasoline distribution and sales, pending a hearing (as required by section 6 of the Occupational Safety and Health Act).

Benzene is a colorless, sweet-smelling gas. It has a high vapor pressure that causes rapid evaporation under ordinary atmospheric circumstances. Benzene has long been recognized as a potentially dangerous substance capable of causing toxic effects and diseases. Over 70 percent of the benzene manufactured in the United States is eventually released into the air.[1] It is used in the processing and manufacturing of tires, detergents, paints, pesticides, and petroleum products. Ninety-eight percent of all benzene produced is used in the petrochemical and petroleum refining industries. In 1976 total production of benzene was 1.4 billion gallons; by 1980 production had increased to 2 billion gallons. Production declined by 30 percent in 1981 and by 20 percent in 1982, but as economic conditions improved, production increased in 1984 and again in 1985.[2] Over 270,000 employees are exposed to benzene in product-related industries.[3]

[1] Carl F. Cranor, "Epidemiology and Procedural Protections for Workplace Health in the Aftermath of the Benzene Case," *Industrial Relations Law Journal* 5 (1983), p. 394.

[2] 50 Fed. Reg. 50540 (1985).

[3] "Benzene, Formaldehyde: Workplace Exposure Limits Proposed," *Chemical and Engineering News* 63 (December 9, 1985), p. 5.

OSHA's decision to lower the 10-ppm standard was precipitated by a report to the National Institutes of Health in 1977 of excessive leukemia deaths related to benzene exposure. These deaths occurred in two rubber pliofilm plants in Ohio, both of which had benzene exposure levels in excess of 10 ppm. In addition, no animal or human test data was available for lower levels of exposure. However, OSHA determined that benzene is a leukemogen (leukemia-causing agent) and ruled that worker safety demanded reduction of exposure to the lowest technologically feasible level. OSHA based its decision to drop the standard exposure level on two assumptions: (1) Adverse health effects were evident at certain exposure levels, and thus a reduced exposure was necessary to maintain a customary factor of safety; and (2) there is no safe level of exposure to carcinogens, suggesting that exposure should be reduced to the lowest level that can be easily monitored.

At the time the ETS was issued, little medical evidence existed of a relation between benzene and cancer at any level found in the industry. The oil industry therefore questioned the wisdom of OSHA's regulation, which would demand large public and private expenditures, because there was considerable scientific evidence indicating there are no-effect exposure levels (*i.e.,* harmless levels). OSHA and the affected industries both determined that compliance costs would be large, with considerable uncertainty about the number of workers likely to be protected from cancer. Estimated *per employee* compliance costs ranged from $1,390 to $82,000, depending on the size and type of industry. The total cost for all industries was projected to surpass $500 million for the first year alone.[4]

OSHA'S AUTHORITY

The fact that benzene has been identified as a carcinogen, and that workers can be seriously affected by it, gives OSHA a legitimate interest in the regulation of its industrial manufacture. Regulatory authority is given to the Secretary of Labor under the Occupational Safety and Health Act, which provides that:

> The term "occupational safety and health standard" means a standard which requires conditions, or the adoption or use of one or more practices, means, methods, operations, or processes, reasonably necessary or appropriate to provide safe or healthful employment and places of employment.[5]

If the Secretary seeks to promulgate a standard involving toxic materials, such as benzene, Section 6 (b) (5) provides:

[4] R. Jeffrey Smith, "A Light Rein Falls on OSHA," *Science* 209 (August 1, 1980), p. 568.

[5] 20 U.S.C. § 652 (8).

The Secretary, in promulgating standards dealing with toxic materials or harmful physical agents under this subsection, shall set the standard which most adequately assures, to the extent feasible, on the basis of the best available evidence, that no employee will suffer material impairment of health or functional capacity even if such employee has regular exposure to the hazard dealt with by such standard for the period of his working life. Development of standards under this subsection shall be based upon research, demonstrations, experiments, and such other information as may be appropriate. In addition to the attainment of the highest degree of health and safety protection for the employee, other considerations shall be the latest available scientific data in the field, the feasibility of the standards, and experience gained under this and other health and safety laws.[6]

Mainly under study throughout 1978–79 was the level at which the chemical would be allowed in the environment, not whether its use and manufacture should be regulated. A 1978 study at Dow Chemical Corporation (by Dante and Picciano) found that 12 out of 52 workers exposed to low levels of benzene showed an abnormally high level of damaged chromosomes in their blood cells, as compared to 1 out of 44 in the control group, who were not exposed to benzene. A series of measurements taken over the course of the two-year study found the TWA exposure to have been below 10 ppm. While damaged chromosomes do not inherently produce injury, they have been linked to an increased risk of cancer.[7]

SUPREME COURT ACTION

Into this atmosphere of controversy stepped the U.S. Supreme Court, which reached a decision about certain aspects of this problem on July 2, 1980. In a case brought by the AFL-CIO (Industrial Union Department) and others against the American Petroleum Institute (the Trade Association of American Oil Companies), the Supreme Court ruled that the proposed OSHA standard was unjustifiably strict. However, the court was divided on the issues. Four justices agreed with the judgment and the reasoning, while one justice concurred in judgment only. The plurality agreed with the U.S. Circuit Court of Appeals (5th Circuit, New Orleans), which concluded that OSHA had exceeded its standard-setting authority because it had not shown that the new benzene exposure limit was "reasonably necessary or appropriate to provide safe or healthful employment" as required by the act, and because the act does not "give OSHA the unbridled discretion to adopt standards designed to create absolutely risk-free workplaces regardless of the costs."[8]

[6] 29 U.S.C. § 655(b) (5).

[7] "Research That Clouds the Benzene Issue," *Business Week* (June 26, 1978), p. 43.

[8] *Industrial Union Department, AFL-CIO* v. *American Petroleum Institute et al.,* 100 Sup. Ct. 2884 (1980).

Some central findings of the plurality in this case, as written by Justice John Paul Stevens, are as follows:

> As presently formulated, the benzene standard is an expensive way of providing some additional protection for a relatively small number of employees. According to OSHA's figures, the standard will require capital investments in engineering controls of approximately $266 million, first-year operating costs (for monitoring, medical testing, employee training and respirators) of $187 million to $205 million and recurring annual costs of approximately $34 million. [43 Fed. Reg., at 5934] The figures outlined in OSHA's explanation of the costs of compliance to various industries indicate that only 35,000 employees would gain any benefit from the regulation in terms of a reduction in their exposure to benzene. Over two-thirds of these workers (24,450) are employed in the rubber manufacturing industry. Compliance costs in that industry are estimated to be rather low with no capital costs and initial operating expenses estimated at only $34 million ($1,390 per employee); recurring annual costs would also be rather low, totalling less than $1 million. By contrast, the segment of the petroleum refining industry that produces benzene would be required to incur $24 million in capital costs and $600,000 in first-year operating expenses to provide additional protection for 300 workers ($82,000 per employee), while the petrochemical industry would be required to incur $20.9 million in capital costs and $1 million in initial operating expenses for the benefit of 552 employees ($39,675 per employee). [43 Fed. Reg. 5936–5938]
> Although OSHA did not quantify the benefits to each category of worker in terms of decreased exposure to benzene, it appears from the economic impact study done at OSHA's direction that those benefits may be relatively small. Thus, although the current exposure limit is 10 ppm, the actual exposures outlined in that study are often considerably lower. For example, for the period 1970–1975 the petrochemical industry reported that, out of a total of 496 employees exposed to benzene, only 53 were exposed to levels between 1 and 5 ppm and only seven (all at the same plant) were exposed to between 5 and 10 ppm. . . .
> Any discussion of the 1 ppm exposure limit must, of course, begin with the Agency's rationale for imposing that limit. The written explanation of the standard fills 184 pages of the printed appendix. Much of it is devoted to a discussion of the voluminous evidence of the adverse effects of exposure to benzene at levels of concentration well above 10 ppm. This discussion demonstrates that there is ample justification for regulating occupational exposure to benzene and the prior limit of 10 ppm, with a ceiling of 25 ppm (or a peak of 50 ppm) was reasonable. It does not, however, provide direct support for the Agency's conclusion that the limit should be reduced from 10 ppm to 1 ppm.[9]

The court held that OSHA must make a "threshold determination" of significant risk at the standard's present level before moving to a lower level. To the court a safe work environment is not necessarily a

---

[9] This material is quoted directly from the Supreme Court of the United States, *Industrial Union Department, AFL-CIO* v. *American Petroleum Institute et al.*, 448 U.S. 607 (1980).

risk-free work environment. Unsafe means the workplace has a *substantial* or *significant* health risk. OSHA must adequately prove that there will be significant health benefits at the lower level. The ruling stated OSHA had established a risk at levels above 10 ppm, but the agency failed to prove that any substantial benefit would result from dropping the level. In the past OSHA had required industries to prove that exposure to certain levels of a chemical in the air did not pose significant risk to employees. The court indicated that the finding of significant risk should not be viewed as a "mathematical straitjacket" as long as their standard has the support of "reputable scientific thought."[10]

Nonetheless, the ruling forces OSHA to place more reliance on scientific and quantitative data. The agency can no longer promulgate standards based purely on policy decisions. The dissenting justices believed that the Occupational Safety and Health Act had intentionally provided the Secretary of Labor with broad powers. They regarded these powers as necessary and justified in the face of scientific uncertainty. When lives are at risk, they held, the secretary should be able to promulgate strict standards given reasonable estimates of risk. While the court refused to uphold the 1 ppm standard, they in no way rejected the legitimacy of OSHA's right to regulate such industrial manufacture on a less strict standard. OSHA had no choice but to reinstate the previous 10-ppm standard.

RESPONSES TO THE COURT DECISION

The court decision produced mixed reactions. Industrial unions argued that too great a burden had been placed on "scientific data." They expressed concern that a "body count" would have to be produced before action could be taken.[11] Too many employees might be exposed to industrial chemicals at dangerous levels while OSHA was waiting for research to be completed and data to be interpreted.

Company spokesmen supported the court's ruling. The industries had long since criticized OSHA for promulgating standards that they believed were based upon speculation. Now they believed that some rational boundaries had been set for OSHA. They hoped that OSHA would be forced to regulate and set standards on quantitatively significant risk rather than theoretical risk and that new regulations would have to contain clear benefits.[12]

Officials at OSHA were left in a quandary. The burden of proof

[10] Smith, "A Light Rein," p. 568.

[11] "The Court Leaves OSHA Hanging," *Business Week* (July 21, 1980), p. 68.

[12] "High Court Overturns OSHA Benzene Rule," *Chemical and Engineering News* 58 (July 7, 1980), p. 4.

that a certain level of chemical was dangerous was shifted to their shoulders. Yet, they believed that they were not given any clear guidance in determining the level at which a standard should be set. The court required weighing costs and benefits, but the ruling did not say which method to use or at what level a standard should be abandoned as unreasonable.

The research community expressed concern that OSHA would be overly restricted by the need for quantitative data, which is difficult and costly to produce. There are many expenses—for facilities, personnel, and so forth—involved in financing a research project. There are also questions about the method of testing to be used—particularly concerning the use of animal data as opposed to human-based research. Animal testing is less costly. The results can be obtained more quickly, due to a shorter incubation time for diseases in animals, and use of a higher level of exposure. However, the process is still lengthy; a typical project takes six years. The applicability of animal test results to humans is questionable.[13] Researchers cannot be sure that a substance that is not carcinogenic in animals will not be carcinogenic in humans.

The most accurate results are obtained by studying human exposure to the chemical. There are two approaches used in human studies, the after-exposure case study and the ongoing exposure study. The former involves subjects who have developed a disease after a known exposure to a chemical. The latter requires following persons currently exposed to the chemical. There are inherent practical and ethical problems with both available methods. The potential for errors is great in any type of research, and it could be years before the errors are discovered. Moreover, the International Agency for Research on Cancer estimates that 92 percent of known or suspected carcinogens have not been tested adequately to identify them as safe or unsafe for human exposure at *any* level.[14] It could be a long time before discussion of safety at particular levels is taken up.

However, less than 5 percent of all cancer deaths result from occupational or environmental exposures to industrial chemicals, about 12,000 deaths annually.[15] Some cancer researchers fear that a disproportionate amount of cancer-research resources will now be focussed on industrial chemicals as a result of the court ruling. They note that the average cost of animal testing on one industrial chemical is approximately $500,000.[16]

---

[13] Cranor, "Epidemiology and Procedural Protections," pp. 380–385.

[14] *Ibid.*, p. 394.

[15] Milton Weinstein, "Cost Effective Priorities for Cancer Prevention," *Science* 221 (July 1, 1983), p. 17.

[16] *Ibid.*, p. 19.

FURTHER RESEARCH

In October of 1981 the World Health Organization (WHO) met to discuss chemicals in the workplace. They concluded that benzene is a leukemogen and that lifetime exposure to benzene at low levels would increase by a factor of three the chances of developing leukemia. They further predicted that exposure to 10 ppm over a lifetime could produce 17 additional leukemia deaths per 1,000 laborers.[17]

The epidemiological studies available in 1980 were updated and expanded and several new studies were completed. A 1984 study sponsored by the Chemical Manufacturers Association (CMA) produced mixed results. Researchers found a positive link between cancer and cumulative benzene exposure. In the study-group of 4,000 exposed workers, there was a higher rate of lymphatic and hematopoietic cancer. However, the higher rate was not statistically significant when compared to the general population. The study group experienced no leukemia deaths. The researchers concluded that there were too few deaths and illnesses to reach definite conclusions.[18]

Animal studies have shown benzene to be carcinogenic. A study conducted by the National Toxicology Program revealed excess risk of several types of cancers in both sexes of rats and mice. Other studies have indicated that benzene causes multiple site-specific cancers in animals and chromosomal damages to both human and animal cells. Scientific studies have established a causal relation between benzene exposure and the incidence of leukemia, of aplastic anemia (a bone marrow disease), and "suppression of various cellular elements of the peripheral blood, such as decreases in white cells or leukocytes (leukopenia), red cells (anemia), platelets or thrombocytes (thrombocytopenia) and all three of these cellular elements (pancytopenia)."[19]

FURTHER PROPOSALS

The regulatory battle over benzene continued amid scientific inquiries into its effects. In April 1983, OSHA was petitioned by labor unions and public advocacy groups, including the Industrial Union Department, AFL-CIO; the International Union of Allied Industrial Workers; the United Steelworkers of America; the Public Citizen Health Research Group; and the American Public Health Association, requesting an Emergency Temporary Standard lowering the permissible benzene exposure

---

[17] Marjorie Sun, "Risk Estimates Vanish from Benzene Report," *Science* 217 (September 3, 1982), pp. 914–915.

[18] "Benzene Study Details Cancer Risks," *Chemical and Engineering News* 62 (January 2, 1984), p. 21.

[19] 52 Fed. Reg. 34468 (1987).

level to 1 ppm. At the time, OSHA had not completed the necessary risk assessments to call for a new standard.

In December 1984, six unions and a consumer advocacy group filed a petition for a writ of mandamus in the U.S. Court of Appeals for the District of Columbia Circuit as *United Steelworkers of America* v. *Raymond J. Donovan, Secretary of Labor et al.* The motion asked the court to order OSHA to propose and take steps to put new benzene standards into effect. OSHA, in December 1985, proposed a *new* rule for occupational exposure to benzene. Once again OSHA proposed that the standard be dropped to 1 ppm. In proposing this new rule, OSHA adhered to the standards set by the Supreme Court in its 1980 ruling. First, quantitative risk studies were done to assess whether benzene exposure posed a threat to workers. OSHA's studies showed that benzene is definitely linked to leukemia. Both animal and human case studies were examined to make this determination.

OSHA then assessed whether the new standard would provide significant benefits to exposed workers. Few studies are available using exposure levels at or below 10 ppm, so OSHA extrapolated from studies involving higher levels of exposure. For this extrapolation they used a simple linear model that assumes that development of leukemia is directly related to dose. Several experimental studies have demonstrated a linear relationship between benzene and chromosomal damage associated with an increased risk of cancer. In addition, the linear model has been generally accepted by regulatory agencies in the United States and abroad for the study of chemical carcinogens. When questioned as to whether it was correct to assume a direct link, researcher Dr. Charles Brown replied, "The correct model is unknown, and will remain so until we know the mechanistic relationship between benzene exposure and leukemia; however I do not believe that the data warrant more sophistication than the simple linear model. . . ."[20]

Finally, OSHA looked at available data to set an exposure limit that was technologically and economically feasible. Even though the 1 ppm standard was proposed back in 1977 with substantial industry opposition, changes in the industry have made the proposed rule more feasible and palatable to the industry. The EPA imposed some pollution standards that caused industries to install some technologies that reduced airborne benzene levels as well. Also, surveillance and maintenance standards have been improved by industries in anticipation of a new standard. As a result, current average exposure levels are below 10 ppm, with most close to 1 ppm. Thus, the initial costs of the new standard promise

[20] 50 Fed. Reg. 50533 (1985).

to be much lower. The total initial capital expenditures for all sectors have been estimated to be approximately $38 million.[21] Annual costs are projected to remain near the same levels as those proposed for the 1977 1-ppm standard.

OSHA conducted public hearings on the proposed benzene exposure rules in March 1986. Assistant Labor Secretary John A. Pendergrass, head of OSHA, announced the final rules for benzene exposure in all industries on September 1, 1987. The final standard was based on a complete assessment of the proceedings. The new standard, which had to be met by February 1988, reduces the permissible exposure limit (PEL) from 10 ppm to the proposed eight-hour TWA of 1 ppm and a short-term exposure limit of 5 ppm, and establishes an action level of 0.5 ppm, to encourage lower exposures for employees and to reduce administrative burdens on employers.

The rules also establish "industrial hygiene" requirements including provisions calling for monitoring, engineering controls, respiratory protection, medical surveillance, and hazard communication.[22] "The basis for promulgation of this regulation is a determination by the Assistant Secretary that employees exposed to benzene face a significant health risk and that this standard will substantially reduce that risk."[23]

OSHA established a "significant risk" at existing benzene exposure levels based on scientific studies:

> The lifetime occupational risk of death from accident or acute illness is 20 to 30 per 1,000 in high risk occupations like mining and fire fighting, and 2 to 3 in occupations of average risk (all service and all manufacturing). . . . Based on the best supported estimates of 95 excess deaths [from leukemia] per 1,000, the risk from exposure to benzene at 10 ppm is clearly greater than that in the riskiest occupations and greater than the risk of one in 1,000 which the Supreme Court found a reasonable person might find significant.[24]

To further substantiate the significant benefit to be received by lowering the standard, the agency claims that the reduction to 1 ppm (decreasing exposure by 90 percent) is expected to save approximately 882 lives of workers who otherwise would have contracted cancer.

---

[21] *Technological Feasibility and Economic Impact Study of Alternative Standards for Benzene* (McLean, Va.: JRB Associates, 1984), pp. 5–129. (This study was done at the request of OSHA to aid in setting the PEL for benzene.)

[22] 52 Fed. Reg. 34460 (1987).

[23] *Ibid.*

[24] *Ibid.*, p. 34463.

Air Bags and Automobile Manufacturers

In 1966 the U.S. Congress passed the National Traffic and Motor Vehicle
Safety Act and established the National Highway Traffic Safety Administration (NHTSA) to administer the act. The purpose of the act was to
develop a coordinated national safety program. One of the major thrusts
of the legislation and the subsequent regulations and directives issued
by the administration was the development and enforcement of safety
performance standards for motor vehicles.

One of the NHTSA's first notices, entitled "Inflatable Occupant Restraint System," was published in 1969. It emphasized use of the controversial "air bag." It required that the air bag be installed in all vehicles
manufactured in the United States. This notice, Motor Vehicle Safety
Standard (MVSS) 208, was opposed by the automobile industry. Detailed
questions were raised about safety research, engineering designs, financial burdens, and possible legal violations in order to postpone required
implementation from 1972 yearly for a decade. By 1981, MVSS 208
(see Appendix for the history of this standard) appeared doomed. During
the period from 1969 to 1981, millions of dollars had been spent by
the automobile industry, automobile insurance companies, public interest
groups, and the government to promote their various views and to fight
those of the opposition.

What, then, are air bags, and why all the controversy? Judith Reppy
has described their attraction as a means of reducing the mortality and
morbidity associated with automobile accidents:

> Air bags are passive restraints in that they deploy automatically in a crash
> without any action by the automobile's occupants. They thus represent
> the ultimate in a "technological fix"—a technical solution of the social
> problems of traffic death and injuries. The bag, which inflates within a

This case was prepared by Martha W. Elliott and Tom L. Beauchamp and revised by
Linda Kern and Joanne L. Jurmu. **Not to be duplicated without permission of the holder
of the copyright,** © 1989 Tom L. Beauchamp.

few milliseconds of impact, acts as a cushion to reduce the deceleration forces on the occupants and to protect them from colliding with the interior of the automobile. When worn, seat belts perform much the same function. Except for the new passive seat belts, however, they have required the active participation of the occupant to be effective, and the extent of seat belt use in the United States has been very low (approximately 20 percent).[1]

Reduction of deaths and injuries is a major public policy problem in the United States, where approximately 50,000 persons die every year in automobile accidents. As automobiles have become more fuel efficient, their size and weight have been reduced, and with this reduction passengers are afforded less protection in an accident. Various air-bag systems have been designed that are keyed to deceleration rates and bumper contact. The bags are designed to inflate in less than $\frac{1}{28}$ of a second and also have been designed so that a driver's vision is not unduly impaired.[2] Although the basic design of the air bag is essentially the same as when first developed, it has been improved to better accommodate the needs of small children, to decrease the weight of the system, and to prevent accidental deployment. (The air-bag system was first designed in the 1960s by automobile industry researchers.)

Initial research done for NHTSA by the Cornell Aeronautical Laboratories has shown that air bags would be effective in preventing injuries and fatalities to adults in frontal crashes, but would be less effective in protecting (1) smaller passengers, (2) persons involved in angled crashes, and (3) persons involved in crashes preceded by panic braking.[3] Safety research conducted by the major auto makers supports the NHTSA contention that air bags would reduce fatalities in crashes and has identified the combination of active and passive restraints most effective in different types of crashes.

General Motors evaluated a series of traffic fatalities involving 706 men, women, and children and concluded that:

> If a person wears his lap belt, his potential for fatality reduction is 17 percent. If he wears his lap and shoulder belt, his potential for fatality reduction is 31 percent. If his car is equipped with air cushions his potential for fatality reduction is 18 percent. If his car is equipped with air cushions and he wears his lap belt, his potential for fatality reduction is 29 percent.[4]

---

[1] Judith Reppy, "The Automobile Air Bag," in Dorothy Nelkin, ed., *Controversy: Politics of Technical Decisions* (Beverly Hills, Calif.: Sage Publications, 1979), pp. 145–146.

[2] *Ibid.*, p. 147.

[3] Richard M. Hodgetts, "Air Bags and Auto Safety," in *The Business Enterprise: Social Challenge, Social Response* (Philadelphia: W. B. Saunders Co., 1977), pp. 130–131.

[4] General Motors Study, as quoted in Hodgetts, "Air Bags and Auto Safety," p. 131.

Further GM research showed that particular combinations of active and passive restraints were most effective in particular types of crashes. This data is summarized in Table 1.

The Ford Motor Company analyzed the protection that would have been offered by the various combinations of active and passive restraints in a series of several thousand accidents. Ford found that "the air bag and lap belt combination was the restraint system most likely to save the greatest number of lives, followed by the lap and shoulder belt combination,"[5] a conclusion similar to that reached by General Motors.

The U.S. Department of Transportation has stressed the air bag's role as a complement rather than an alternative to safety belts. The department has estimated that air-bag use could save approximately 7,000 lives every year. Former Secretary of Transportation Elizabeth Dole noted that air bags with seat belts "provide protection at higher speeds than safety belts [alone] do, and they will provide better protection against several kinds of extremely debilitating injuries (e.g., brain and facial injuries) than safety belts." Air bags would be especially protective for the many drivers who do not wear seat belts.[6]

Critics of this research point out, however, that air bags have never been adequately field tested. They argue that attempts to simulate actual crash conditions using human-like dummies and attempts to extrapolate from what happens in actual crashes to what would have happened had restraints been in use are inexact and may be misleading. General Motors produced approximately 10,000 cars equipped with air bags

TABLE 1. POTENTIAL FATALITY PROTECTION (IN PERCENTAGES)

	Restraint System			
Crash Mode	Lap Belt Only	Lap and Shoulder	Air Cushion Only	Air Cushion with Lap Belt
Frontals	14	37	38	40
Sideswipes	9	21	10	18
Sides	12	12	3	14
Rollovers	36	48	9	40
Rear	14	20	0	14

Source: Adapted from Richard M. Hodgetts, "Air Bags and Auto Safety," in *The Business Enterprise: Social Challenge, Social Response* (Philadelphia: W. B. Saunders Co., 1977), p. 132.

[5] *Ibid.*, p. 133.

[6] U.S. Department of Transportation study, as quoted in Anne Fleming, *About Air Bags* (Washington, D.C.: Insurance Institute for Highway Safety, 1987), p. 10.

during 1974, and the federal government purchased 5,000 similarly equipped Ford Tempos in 1985. These cars represent the nearest approach to a field test. Between 1974 and 1978 the GM cars had been involved in only 200 crashes in which the air bag had inflated, an insufficient number of crashes to constitute an adequate trial.[7] The 1985 cars produced little additional evidence.

Since the auto industry and NHTSA were in agreement concerning the effectiveness of air bags in reducing fatalities and injuries in at least some kinds of crashes, what fueled the controversy? Reppy sees the controversy as follows:

> The traditional view of automobile safety has taken the "nut behind the wheel" approach, stressing individual responsibility. This view is challenged by those who wish to focus responsibility on highway design and on the manufacturers' responsibility to make changes in the vehicle to reduce both the probability of a crash and the severity of injury if a crash occurs.[8]

Reppy points out that each side of the controversy has attracted a variety of proponents who have differing interests and arguments:

> The technical disagreement reached its most striking expression in the cost/benefit studies sponsored by the opposing sides, which, based on conflicting assumptions, yielded opposite conclusions. On a more philosophical level, participants in the controversy have debated the proper role of government and the morality of compelling an individual to protect himself from the risk of injury.[9]

Proponents of air bags cite research on the effectiveness of passive restraints and the desirability of reducing fatalities by whatever means available as reason enough for requiring air bags; automobile manufacturers and their allies, by contrast, contend that there are many unresolved problems in the implementation of this technology. While air-bag critics agree with the desirability of reducing traffic fatalities, they see the increased use of seat belts, through either public education or legislation, as the preferred means of achieving that goal. Historically, seat-belt usage in the United States has been low. In 1974, 26 percent of all motorists used seat belts. The level dropped to 14 percent in 1983.[10] Supporters of air-bag legislation cite a DeLorean Corporation study that found "[b]elt usage is, and may be expected to be . . . inade-

---

[7] Reppy, "The Automobile Air Bag," pp. 150–151.

[8] *Ibid.*, p. 146.

[9] *Ibid.*, p. 147.

[10] NHTSA study as quoted in Robert W. Crandall, *Regulating the Automobile* (Washington, D.C.: Brookings Institution, 1986), p. 54.

quate to allow benefits or payoffs equal to those predicted for air cushion–lap belt systems."[11]

Opponents of air bags have claimed that air bags could be a hazard and a potential *cause* of accidents in the case of accidental inflation. Research on this problem under test conditions has shown, however, that while people do demonstrate a "startle" reaction to unexpected bag inflation, "drivers retained good control of the test vehicle" and "were able to see to guide their car in spite of the minimal obstruction of vision produced by the inflated air bag."[12] General Motors experimented with inflating air bags without warning as test subjects drove on straightaways and turns at speeds up to 45 mph. General Motors reported that "without exception, the subject retained control of the automobile."[13]

Some concern also has been expressed over the propellant used to inflate the air bags. It is the chemical sodium azide, a class B poison (in the same category as insecticides). In solid form it is toxic, but the process of firing it involves a chemical reaction that causes it to become nontoxic hydrogen. Passengers do not in theory come into contact with sodium azide at any time, but critics fear that damage to the container or residual particles in the bag after firing might endanger passengers. The NHTSA firmly believes the current propellant container can be used without fear due to its strength and inaccessibility.[14]

Industry opposition to the air bags as revealed in Congressional hearings, court testimony, and lobbying efforts has focused on the cost of the system, the costs and difficulties in retooling the industry for this addition, the performance of the bag in real-life situations, and has complained about government "paternalism" and overregulation. Industry representatives see such government behavior as an unwarranted restriction on their freedom to design and produce automobiles.

The automakers consistently cite cost-of-production changes required to make and install the air bags. This argument gained force in 1973–74 when the energy crisis shifted public and government focus from safety to fuel economy. Redesigning and retooling to make smaller and more fuel-efficient cars took precedence for auto makers over redesigning and retooling to make automobile air bags. As the decade wore on, the increasing competition from fuel-efficient foreign cars, coupled with a general recession and the automobile industry's increasingly dismal

[11] Hodgetts, "Air Bags and Auto Safety," p. 138.

[12] H. Haskell Ziperman and G. R. Smith, "Startle Reaction to Air-Bag Restraints," *Journal of the American Medical Association* 233 (August 4, 1975), p. 440.

[13] General Motors study, as quoted in Fleming, *About Air Bags*, p. 7.

[14] U.S. House Committee on Interstate and Foreign Commerce, "Department of Transportation Automobile Passive Restraint Rule," *H. Rpt. 502-35* (Washington, D.C.: Government Printing Office, 1977).

economic situation, supported the auto manufacturers' contention that (1) they could not afford to absorb the cost of retooling for air bags and (2) they could not pass the additional cost on to consumers and remain competitive.

Driver-side air bags were offered as standard equipment in all Mercedes Benz autos for the 1987 model year. This feature added roughly $1,350 to the price of each car.[15] Ford simultaneously offered driver-side air bags as optional equipment in two of its lines for approximately $815.[16] The cost to the consumer should be much less if mandatory legislation were passed requiring installation in *all* cars, because production levels would be substantial if air bags were produced for every automobile.[17] The U.S. Department of Transportation has estimated the cost of full front-seat systems to be around $350.[18] Although the auto makers maintain that seat belts are the best safety feature, they have recognized that there is a market for air bags and passive belts. Consequently, the auto makers, especially Ford, plan to make passive restraints available for voluntary purchase on virtually all models.

Air-bag regulations have been supported by the automobile insurance industry, which is convinced that the bags save lives and health and insurance costs. The Insurance Institute for Highway Safety provided funds and technical expertise to counter auto industry arguments. Allstate Insurance Company was particularly active in support of air bags, providing favorable advertising and support before Congressional committees, and offering discounts on insurance premiums for air-bag equipped cars. A pamphlet issued by Allstate in 1976 stated, "Allstate advocates the use of lap belts, used in conjunction with air bags. This system offers the best protection feasible now and within the foreseeable future in most types of crashes—air bags to reduce injury and lap belts to prevent ejection in rollovers."[19]

Allstate was joined by a number of consumer interest groups. They maintain that air-bag technology is adequate, affordable, and lifesaving. These groups contend that the government's duty to protect the public interest entails required passive restraints. They point out that there is more at risk than the consumer's personal safety. The safety of passengers not directly involved in the purchase decision is clearly at risk.

There is also some evidence that the public supports air bags. The

[15] Gary Williams, Manager, Owner Services, Mercedes-Benz of North America, personal interview, Washington, D.C., October 1, 1986.

[16] Dave Zoia, "Some Wait to Decide on Passive Restraints," *Automotive News* (September 15, 1986), p. 1.

[17] Hodgetts, "Air Bags and Auto Safety," p. 142.

[18] U.S. Department of Transportation statistic adjusted for inflation, as quoted in Fleming, *About Air Bags*, p. 8.

[19] Quoted by Hodgetts, "Air Bags and Auto Safety," p. 136.

results of a 1976 national telephone survey indicated that interested car buyers preferred cars with passive restraints and that they were willing to pay extra for this feature: "For improved protection in crashes, 77 percent of new car buyers expressed a preference for [passive restraint] protection . . . —39 percent exclusively and 38 percent in combination with protection that has to be activated by driver or passenger."[20]

Potential car buyers polled were willing to pay an additional $12 per month for 36 months ($432) on new car payments to save 6,000 lives and $17 per month to save 12,000 per year. This is considerably more than the $4 per month ($103 total) estimated by NHTSA as the actual cost of the air bags that would save an additional 8,800 lives per year.[21] (This $432 installation cost is apparently based on more conventional estimates between $300 and $1,100, depending on quality and production volumes.)

Newsweek magazine conducted a survey in 1986 of people who purchased automobiles in November or December of 1985. When asked whether "air bags should be standard equipment on all new cars" the response was 34 percent strongly agree, 53 percent somewhat agree, 8 percent disagree, and 5 percent strongly disagree.[22] A 1983 poll taken by the Insurance Institute for Highway Safety revealed that 90 percent of car buyers believe that passive restraints should be required on new cars as standard or optional equipment. Only 4 percent of those polled responded that auto makers should be free to decide on the availability of automatic restraints.[23]

There is some consumer dissent concerning mandatory passive restraints. Some consumers resent being forced to purchase safety devices. While most agree that the government has some responsibility to the public to make sure that they purchase well-made automobiles, they do not think they should be unwillingly burdened with costs. Consumers suggest that insurance companies bill drivers according to the automobile safety devices they purchase. These consumers feel the freedom to choose also includes the freedom to make a wrong choice.

Strong political support for air bags has nonetheless proven difficult to arouse. With increasing financial difficulties for automobile manufacturers and the United Auto Workers Union, with a climate favoring governmental deregulation, and with increasing concern about tradeoffs in controlling traffic safety, the controversy had begun to fade by the end of 1981 and has since faded in and out.

[20] As reported in Leon S. Robertson, "Study Shows Public Willing to Pay for Motor Vehicle Crash Protection," *National Underwriter* (September 3, 1976), pp. 15–18.

[21] *Ibid.*

[22] "1986 Buyers of New Cars: Summary Report," research report, *Newsweek* (New York, 1986), Table 67.

[23] Fleming, *About Air Bags*, p. 13.

In October 1981, the NHTSA issued a final rule calling for the complete rescission of passive restraints and amended Modified Standard 208 accordingly. The end result was a standard identical to the 1968 standard, requiring manual seat belts in all motor vehicles. Within a month, on November 25, 1981, the National Association of Independent Insurers (NAII), representing 509 insurance companies, filed suit in a federal court seeking to overturn this order, which would repeal all rules requiring either air bags or automatic seat belts. The insurance companies were particularly upset by the way the matter had been handled in the Transportation Department (DOT): Raymond Peck, administrator of the NHTSA, said that the opposition of U.S. automobile companies had killed the air-bag policy. Peck said his decision was based on the fact that all of the major auto companies intended to comply with detachable, automatic seat belts, coupled with his firm belief that most motorists would simply disconnect the activating systems. He preferred a voluntary seat-belt campaign, but said he would try to revive interest in the development of better air bags. Mr. Peck's decision had been unanimously opposed by his senior staff, but it was praised as professionally sound by the three leading U.S. automobile manufacturers.[24]

The NAII suit challenged the claim that air bags and belts would be disconnected by owners, and argued that Mr. Peck did not understand the several different designs well enough to appreciate that it would be extremely difficult to dismantle properly engineered systems.[25] The suit also charged that the seat-belt systems are cost effective, especially considering that the insurance industry may have to increase premiums (perhaps by 30 percent) on cars not equipped with such systems. The NAII was joined in this suit by State Farm Insurance and the Automobile Owners Action Council.[26]

The case, *State Farm Mutual Automobile Insurance* v. *Department of Trans-*

---

[24] "Insurers Sue for Return of Passive Restraint Rule," *Baltimore Sun*, November 26, 1981, and Peter Behr, "U.S. Halts Effort to Require Use of Car Air Bags," *Washington Post*, October 24, 1981, sec. A, pp. 1, 24.

[25] *Ibid.*

[26] *Ibid.* In early spring of 1982, the Reagan administration announced a publicity campaign in conjunction with private industry to persuade motorists to "buckle up" voluntarily. As part of this effort, Goodyear Tire & Rubber Company's blimps were used throughout the summer to display messages urging drivers to use their safety belts; Warner Communications gave the government permission to use its superhero comic book characters (*e.g.,* Superman) in seat belt promotions; and Lorimar Productions featured safety belt use in its television series "Knots Landing." The Reagan administration's decision to pursue a vigorous, but voluntary course followed on the heels of a late 1981 Department of Transportation study showing that traffic deaths could easily increase by approximately 16,000 per year by 1990 if no major safety improvements on highway designs are made. The NAII argued that air bags and mandatory seat belts are essential to prevent this increase in fatalities. "Reagan Enlists Business to Cut Highway Deaths," *Washington Post*, April 15, 1982, sec. C., pp. 1, 5, and Peter Behr, "Traffic Deaths Surge Feared in DOT Study," *Washington Post*, October 14, 1981, sec. D, pp. 7, 10.

portation, was argued in the U.S. Court of Appeals on March 1, 1982. The petitioners sought review of the NHTSA's final order rescinding automatic crash protection requirements ten months before the standard's effective date. They challenged the move as being "arbitrary, capricious, an abuse of discretion, and a violation of law as defined by Section 10 of the Administrative Procedure Act."[27] The Circuit Court ruled on June 1, 1982, that the NHTSA had acted outside of its legislative mandate. Circuit Judge Mikva explained:

> An administrative agency, possessing power delegated by the legislative branch of government, must comply with the legislative requirement that its decisions be reasoned and in accordance with the purposes for which power has been delegated. NHTSA's rescission of the safety standard presents a paradigm of arbitrary and capricious agency action because NHTSA drew conclusions that are unsupported by evidence in the record and then artificially narrowed the range of alternatives available to it under its legislative mandate. NHTSA thus failed to demonstrate the reasoned decisionmaking that is the essence of lawful administrative action.[28]

The court found that the NHTSA's reasons for rescinding Modified Standard 208 were insufficient. However, the agency was given thirty days to present a schedule for resolving the questions raised in the case leading either to an ultimate rescission or to implementation of the standard. The standard was not rescinded.

In July of 1984, then Secretary of Transportation Dole added a new twist to the struggle. She announced that if states representing two thirds of the population pass mandatory seat-belt laws that meet predetermined federal standards, she would rescind the passive restraint requirement. States were given five years, until April 1989, to get these laws on their books. In the interim, auto makers were to begin phasing in passive restraints (air bags or automatic seat belts on the driver's and the passenger's sides) in the following percentages for each model year: 10 percent in 1987, 25 percent in 1988, 40 percent in 1989, and 100 percent in 1990. This phase-in could be stopped by the secretary at any time after the mandatory seat-belt law coverage attained the two-thirds level. A special incentive was given to the auto manufacturers to use air bags. One car equipped with air bags would count as 1.5 cars towards the requirement.[29]

After this announcement, interest groups changed their focus. They

---

[27] U.S. Court of Appeals, District of Columbia Circuit, No. 81–2220, *State Farm Mutual Automobile Insurance Co.* v. *Department of Transportation, National Highway Traffic Safety Administration*, p. 4.

[28] *Ibid.*, pp. 4–5.

[29] Zoia, "Some Wait to Decide on Passive Restraints," p. 1.

mobilized to influence state legislatures. Auto companies formed "Traffic Safety Now," whose express purpose was to lobby state legislatures to pass mandatory seat-belt laws. Proponents of air bags were left in a quandary. Should they lobby for strong mandatory seat-belt legislation and risk rescission of the passive requirements? Or should they lobby against seat-belt legislation, knowing that seat belts decrease deaths and injuries in all types of crashes, with the hopes of getting federal passive restraint regulations in place eventually?

The insurers went to court a second time. This time they challenged the secretary and the DOT on three issues: (1) safety standards must be uniform, (2) state laws are not substitutes for federal regulation, and (3) the secretary does not have the authority to influence state legislation. In September 1986, a three-judge panel of the U.S. Court of Appeals ruled the issues were "not ripe for decision" at this time. In essence, they decided not to decide. The judges found that of the twenty states currently with mandatory seat-belt laws, none met federal standards. With this evidence, they concluded that the two-thirds level would not be met by 1989, and the passive restraint standard would not be rescinded. However, the judges stated at several points that insurers would have new recourse if states modify seat-belt legislation to meet federal standards and/or states presently not covered by mandatory seat-belt legislation pass laws that comply with federal standards (achieving the two-thirds level by 1989). Under these circumstances, the insurers could file suit again and the court would make a definite ruling on each of the issues. Should the plaintiffs find the conditions about to be met they could refile and the judges would decide on the issues at that time.[30]

Because the required level of coverage of state seat-belt laws was not met, the phase-in procedure for the passive restraint rule began as of September 1, 1986. After that date an increasing number of automobiles must be equipped with passive restraints on both the driver and the passenger sides of the vehicle. Passive restraints could be air bags, passive seat belts, or protective interiors (padded dashboards, shock-absorbent steering columns, etc.).

In November 1986, the Department of Transportation proposed to delay the full front-seat automatic restraint systems requirement until model year 1994 in response to a petition from the Ford Motor Company. However, in May 1988 the Chrysler Corporation announced that it had started putting driver-side airbags as standard equipment in six of its car lines (24 percent of total sales). The corporation projected that it would meet the federal standard in all of its passenger cars by 1990.

---

[30] U.S. Court of Appeals, District of Columbia Circuit, No. 84-1301, *State Farm Mutual Automobile Insurance Co.* v. *Elizabeth Dole, Department of Transportation.*

APPENDIX: The History of Standard 208

1966:   National Traffic and Motor Vehicle Safety Act passed
1967:   Original Standard 208 passed
            Seat belts required
1970:   Standard 208 revised
            Passive restraints required
1972:   "Final" form of Standard 208
            Complete passive protection required
1974:   Amendments passed
            Entire standard of passive belts rejected by Congress
              1. Ignition interlock banned
              2. DOT's discretion to modify 208 in the future reduced
1976:   Passive requirements suspended altogether (under the adminis-
            tration of Secretary of Transportation Coleman)
1977:   Modified Standard 208 passed (under the administration of Secre-
            tary of Transportation Adams)
            Passive restraint regulation mandated on a phase-in basis
1981:   April: Rulemaking reopened due to automobile industry's eco-
            nomic difficulties (under the administration of Secretary of
            Transportation Lewis)
            MS 208 delayed for one year
            Possible rescission of entire standard proposed by NHTSA
            October: Notice 25 issued; NHTSA called for a complete rescis-
            sion of passive requirements and amended MS 208 accordingly
1982:   NHTSA Notice 25 ruled arbitrary and capricious by the United
            States Court of Appeals and remanded for further investiga-
            tion.
1984:   DOT issues ruling on remanded Notice 25
            State mandatory seat belt laws required by April 1, 1989, in
            order to avoid passive restraint requirements
1986:   First cars with required passive restraints produced by auto mak-
            ers
            Twenty states passed mandatory seat belt laws, but none met
            federal standards
            DOT proposes to delay the requirement of automatic restraint
            systems until model year 1994

Peer Review at Shamrock-Diamond Corporation

The Shamrock-Diamond Corporation was founded by an entrepreneur in 1895 as a manufacturer of cutting, drilling, and grinding instruments. By 1912 the company had begun to build overseas plants. Then, as the oil industry grew, Shamrock-Diamond grew further. In 1965 sales first exceeded $300 million, and in this same year the corporation's status passed from privately held to publicly held. Today it consists of seventy-two distinct firms employing 18,600 workers at ninety-six plant sites in fifteen countries. The company specializes in cutting tools, drilling equipment, grinding machines, sealants, and safety products.

Mr. Mario Pellegrino has been Chief Executive Officer of this corporation for twelve years. The company has been profitable and has increased its dividends and number of employees every year it has been under his direction. Mr. Pellegrino has for the past week been preparing a presentation and proposal for a meeting of his Board of Directors. After he calls the meeting to order, he gives his explanation of an additional agenda item. (Although the agenda for the meeting had been mailed, this item was not listed. He considered the matter too touchy, and instead selected this occasion to approach his board with his strong views. He does not expect these views to be fully shared by his board members.)

Mr. Pellegrino begins his presentation to the board as follows:

> You know that we have always been keen on a high standard of ethics in this corporation. Over the years we have developed separate codes of ethics to govern problems of "questionable payments" abroad, acceptable advertising of our products, and nondiscrimination in employment. We were out front of others with these proposals in the late 1960s, and we are still way out ahead of other American corporations.
>
> Two years ago, as some of you know, I took part of my vacation and attended a two-week seminar on Ethics and the Business Corporation at Dartmouth College. To my surprise, the focus of the discussion among the participants in this seminar was on employee discontent and the respon-

sibilities of management to ameliorate this discontent. I discovered that only a tiny minority of American corporations have institutionalized ethics programs directed at employee-management relationships. These include ethics committees and management development programs that have ethics units in their curriculum. Many corporations, of course, have so-called "open-door grievance" policies, but these are intimidating to employees and rarely eventuate in truly objective grievance hearings.

One idea that has met increasing acceptance but also increasing resistance is the use of Peer Review Panels to resolve employees' complaints and grievances. This idea was constantly discussed at Dartmouth, and I was deeply impressed with the idea while I was there.

Mr. Pellegrino pauses to measure the reaction from his Board, which is composed of successful businesspersons, none of whom had reflected very much on the ethics of management-employee relationships. He then proceeds to explain that when he returned from the Dartmouth seminar he immediately set up a meeting with his Council of Managers at a large plant site in Worcester, Massachusetts, for the purpose of implementing a small-scale two-year test period of peer review at the plant.

Under his insistent guidance, the managers agreed to the experiment. During the planning stages they reached the conclusion that one of the potential advantages of having a more explicit personnel policy was that formal rules would protect good managers and good employees alike. Before they began to implement their ideas, the managers established more explicit standards for firing, merit evaluation, retirement, and participative management by workers. The first decision they reached was that they would no longer permit a manager to fire an employee under any conditions without a stated reason or an explanation of the employee's right to an independent hearing.

Working closely with the most influential managers, Mr. Pellegrino quickly implemented his—and now their—ideas for peer review of grievance cases. They appointed four peer employees and three managers to hear each case, and ruled that the conclusions of this group were absolutely binding, with no further appeal open to a losing party. They also devised an intentionally informal arrangement for receiving evidence. No representation by lawyers was permitted for any party, and the hearings were conducted in a room having only eight chairs arranged in a circle. The manager, the grievant, and individual witnesses were each called into the room separately. Coffee was served during the "interview," and the discussion proceeded on the model of a conversation among friends.

Their first case involved a five-year employee who had received only modest raises for three straight years, whereas her male colleagues had received raises almost twice as large. The employee had prepared a massive pile of exhibits to show that the manager had a history of downgrading women and upgrading men. Upon review, it was established to the satisfaction of all seven members of the review committee that the manager did indeed have a history of favoring men, at least for promotion and raises. Although this manager at first insisted on his objectivity and fairness, even he came to see that his record did not support his claim. The employee was given her full raise, retrospective for three years, and her performance ratings were upgraded.

Everyone was buoyed by the success of this first case. Even the manager who lost praised the fairness of the process. But as time wore on, the managers became less satisfied with the experimental procedure. Over the full two-year period, management decisions were upheld in 59 percent of the cases, but managers came to view this statistic as more a failure than a success. Most of their victories were won in cases in which the employees were desperate and had no real opportunity to win. Virtually every manager had been overruled in a case in which he or she was certain an unfair decision had been reached. The managers had lost 86 percent of the cases in which they had *fired* an employee. These employees were generally reinstated under the same manager's supervision, leading to hostility and tension. Even the reinstated employees disliked working under someone whose authority they had undermined by filing and winning a grievance.

Managers came to believe that a system of four peers and three managers was unbalanced and unfair. They felt embarrassed by many of the decisions, and felt that their authority was undermined by a procedure that could overturn any decision at any time. Most concluded that they had been asked by the company to be supervisors, but that the authority that permitted them to supervise was then denied. They were now leery of firing any employee, no matter how poor the person's performance. Almost anything was preferable, they thought, to another grievance hearing. The plant manager who had most closely monitored the hearings admitted that after the end of the two-year experiment the morale of the managers was at an all-time low.

Mr. Pellegrino is fully aware of this history as he stands before his board. He has repeatedly interviewed the managers in the plant, 85 percent of whom would like to see the peer review process either dismantled or its composition changed so that managers are in the majority. But Mr. Pellegrino disagrees. He wants to insert more objectivity into the process by adding one *outside* member to the committee, a person from neither labor nor management. Although his managers are highly skeptical of the adequacy of this third party, Mr. Pellegrino is firm in his convictions. He now concludes his presentation to the board with the following statement of what are for him truly heartfelt views:

Business firms have typically been organized hierarchically, with production line employees at the bottom and the CEO at the top—with the interests of the stockholders given supremacy. However, there are now many reasons to challenge these arrangements. Employees want to make an essential contribution rather than serve as means to the end of profit. They want decent salaries and job security, and they also want appreciation from supervisors, a sense of accomplishment, and fair opportunities to display their talents. Many employees are also interested in participating in the future of the company, defining the public responsibilities of the corporation, and evaluating the role and quality of management.

Although it will be expensive, I want to give our employees all these opportunities. If we can implement this plan for grievance hearings and peer review in all our plants, I am confident we will be a much happier family. I also believe that the corporation as a whole will be better off. We will be more attractive to potential employees, our plants will be built on trust, unions will find no reason to organize our labor forces, and costly lawsuits by employees will not arise.

I want to assure you that if we do successfully implement this program, I will be back asking for more in the way of programs to protect the employment rights of our employees. These policies will cover maximum-hour work weeks, rights against discharge and discipline, privacy rights, severance pay, and standards for pensions. I simply want you to know now what the implications are of your approval of this plan.

At this point Mr. Pellegrino turns to his board and asks the members to approve his plan without modification and without further experimental testing at other plants. He notes, however, that there may be room for compromise, despite his strong preference that the package be implemented as a whole.

Consulting for Jones and Jones Pharmaceutical

Mr. Ricardo D'Amato is a high-salaried executive who has for four years been on the payroll of a large international pharmaceutical company, the Jones and Jones Company. He is located in the Swedish office, the company's European headquarters, where he is in charge of certifying that new products are ready for the approval and registration process and for subsequent marketing. His office is responsible for sending new products to the relevant government authorities in European countries, each of which has an organization similar to the U.S. Food and Drug Administration (FDA), where drugs are tested for safety and effectiveness.

Although Mr. D'Amato's relations with his peers have always been without significant strain, he now suddenly finds himself enmeshed in controversy and crisis. He has refused to authorize a $15,000 payment on a contract the company has with a consultant in Switzerland. The contract calls for the company to pay the specified fee to a distinguished pharmacologist, Dr. Helmut Koenig, for giving advice on how to obtain approval from the Swiss regulatory authorities. Dr. Koenig is uniquely qualified for this work because he is also employed by the Swiss Drug Regulatory Agency, the same agency that is responsible for approving all Swiss drug products for marketing.

Sitting on Mr. D'Amato's desk is an internal memo written by the most powerful vice-president at Jones and Jones, who arranged and then signed the contract with Dr. Koenig. The memo has a section on credentials that says, "Dr. Koenig is a vital influence and creator of opinion in the approval of drug applications in Switzerland."

Mr. D'Amato was alarmed to discover both Dr. Koenig's position of influence and his contractual arrangement with Jones and Jones. He believes it is unethical to make such payments to a man who is currently directly involved with the approval of five to ten pending product registrations for Jones and Jones. In particular, Dr. Koenig is involved with the application for Lotriprox, a drug believed by those who have tested it for the company to be more effective in the treatment of psoriasis than its main competitors. The original application for approval of this drug had been submitted and rejected twice by the Swiss Drug Regulatory Agency, each time cited for lack of evidence of its effectiveness. Jones and Jones officials view the receipt of Swiss approval as vital because regulatory agencies in other countries often follow the Swiss lead.

Mr. D'Amato is an American working in Europe, but most of his fellow executives in Sweden come from various European countries. Almost all have given him their opinion on the matter. They all concur that the practice of hiring regulators as consultants is a common and accepted practice in Switzerland. They point out, correctly, that other companies that market similar products have been hiring these consultants for years. They deny that this practice involves the use of devious or special influence to get applications approved, and they emphasize Dr. Koenig's ability to properly advise pharmaceutical companies on how to proceed.

Dr. Koenig has responded in a terse letter directly to Mr. D'Amato that he knows as well as anyone how to keep his consulting work separate from his work at the regulatory agency. He notes in the letter that he has many times been in this position and that there are clear advantages to both the company and the regulatory agency in his dual role. For example, he is able to keep on top of every aspect of a drug and of the approval system. He points out that the reason Jones and Jones has not previously obtained approval for Lotriprox is the company's "terrible testing" of the drug, which is precisely his professional domain.

Nonetheless, Mr. D'Amato does not accept these arguments. He has tried to make it clear to those with whom he has discussed his views that he is not disputing the history of the Swiss consulting process, but rather is questioning the practices of his company, Jones and Jones. He sees it as a willing and in fact devious violation of practices that are unacceptable in the United States—and in his company, which is, after all, an American one.

On his own accord, without anyone's advice or approval, Mr. D'Amato wrote the Intercantonal Office of Medicaments in Switzerland asking for an investigation. To his surprise they sent a detailed and reasoned response. They said that, upon investigation, they did find that Jones and Jones pharmaceutical products had been consistently approved for marketing after the hiring of well-placed consultants, but they found no indication that these approvals were made under fraudulent circumstances. Unless Mr. D'Amato could submit additional evidence to the contrary, the investigators concluded there was no reason why an educated and experienced advisor could not separately render his services to an outside company. In fact, they asserted that it makes good practical sense for Jones and Jones to obtain evaluations prior to submitting products for approval. As they see it, a safer and more effective product is produced, and it spares both the company and the regulatory agency wasted time considering inferior products.

Mr. D'Amato maintains that even if these payments do not openly constitute bribery, Jones and Jones has still abused its position of influence. Furthermore, he believes that Dr. Koenig is locked in an untenable conflict of interest. D'Amato is adamant in his view that under this system any corporation of sufficient size and financial backing could wield unfair advantages over less powerful companies.

Mr. D'Amato's supervisor, Raymond Freymaster, has now intervened in a process that he believes cannot be allowed to stalemate any longer. He has told Mr. D'Amato that the contract with Dr. Koenig is proper and therefore must be paid. Mr. Freymaster has increased the pressure by saying that if Mr. D'Amato does not authorize payment within ten days he will be fired, and Mr. Freymaster will then authorize it himself. Mr. D'Amato now sees no way to both keep his integrity and his job.

CHAPTER 6

The Multinational

INTRODUCTION   Multinational corporations often find themselves perplexed by the laws, rules, and customs of a host country in which they do business or have subsidiaries. They wonder whether they should do as the locals do or conform to the different and even conflicting cultural guidelines of their home nations. For example, should a Canadian firm follow the rules of financial disclosure required in Canada or rather the rules in certain Arab countries in which it has subsidiaries? Should payments for services that are encouraged in Japan but legally prohibited in the United States be sanctioned by a U.S. firm that does business in Japan? Should a company liquidate its stock of artificially sweetened fruit by selling to customers in West Germany, Spain, or third-world countries when it has been declared hazardous and outlawed in the home country?

No international body has answered these questions authoritatively, and there is at present no uniform agreement about the measure of control that governments and corporations should introduce for circumstances in which standards or expectations vary. The multinational setting presents a new level of complexity in addition to the complexities of ethics encountered in the cases in previous chapters. In this chapter, the cases presented cover three general areas of multinational dilemmas: (1) differences in the treatment of employees, (2) different products and practices for consumers and clients, and (3) different government and cultural expectations.

In the first area, the employer engaged in manufacturing or marketing in a foreign culture cannot simply assume that workers should be governed by the same salary standards, grounds for dismissal, workplace standards, requirements of company loyalty, and promotional standards as those found back home. An example of this problem of fair and equal treatment involves the use in a foreign workplace of hazardous chemicals such as benzene (see Chapter 5) that would not be permitted in the workplaces of a corporation's home country. If a foreign nation does not require masks to be worn by workers or does not stipulate permissible dose levels of the chemical in the environment, should a multinational adopt more stringent standards than those required locally?

Several other issues are presented in this chapter by the cases of John Higgins in Japan and Polaroid in South Africa. The Higgins case raises issues about fairness to employees who have different traditions and expectations from those of a foreign owner or supervisor. Generally such employment arrangements do not involve the voluntary consent of workers to standards to which they are not accustomed. Rather, they arise almost unnoticed from the different presuppositions supervisors and employees bring with them to the workplace. The Polaroid case raises issues about the responsibilities to employees in a country with extraordinarily different race-relation policies than those found in the multinational's home country. This case raises problems of alleged exploitation of workers and also questions profoundly whether a multinational corporation can develop and maintain adherence to moral policies in a country whose policies are immoral.

The latter problem has led some to argue that morality has no place in a country that demands immoral actions for a business to survive, but others take the position that some moral values transcend any policy imposed by another country and that these values may not be set aside.

In the second area of multinational dilemmas, the consumer of a company's product in a foreign country or a client from a foreign country may not be subject to the same government requirements or have the same concerns about a product or policy that persons in the home nation have. The infant formula case in this chapter illustrates how the highly restrictive rules on drugs and food that operate in the home country may be absent or starkly different in another country. Similarly, the Swiss Bank Corporation case illustrates the problems inherent in an international market for wealthy clients who prefer to keep their investments in the sophisticated financial climate of a country like Switzerland that has stringent rules of confidentiality.

Regulatory controls on foods, drugs, and financial markets in the United States are probably more stringent than those found in any other nation. These rules are framed for a culture with established views about acceptable risk, adequate testing, and fairness that do not exist in some nations in which multinationals operate. A product that is banned in the United States may be welcomed by authorities in another nation; and nothing illegal is done by marketing these items. These authorities may be ignorant or too loose in formulating standards, but nevertheless, the existence of these variations presents the multinational corporation with both a ready market and a problem about whether to satisfy that market.

American companies that market internationally generally believe that requirements of the FDA and other government agencies are too cautious, require too much testing, and are too stringent when applied to other cultures. American government officials, however, tend to see these standards as reasonable protections for all consumers, irrespective of their cultural affiliation. The implicit view seems to be that if there are good reasons for banning a product or restricting sales in the United States, then it would be immoral not to conform to these standards when marketing elsewhere. This is another example of the principle that some values transcend territorial and statutory boundaries.

Sometimes risks are worth taking, and risks may be more acceptable in one culture than another. As the infant formula case indicates, some countries may not see a product as harmful at all, even when they are aware of the product's alleged problems. These countries may be right or at least may have an acceptable viewpoint, but any corporation that markets a product banned at home and accepted abroad seems placed in a burden-of-proof situation: The firm should be able to offer good evidence that it is not intentionally releasing a harmful product and that there is a valid local need for the product.

An alternative possibility is to *warn* consumers about possible harms when they purchase a product. As long as all parties understand the terms of a transaction and have agreed to it, according to certain principles of valid consent, a company cannot be faulted for marketing a product with risks and consequences. However, warnings have proved no less controversial than marketing bans.

In the third area, if moral standards, professional codes, and criteria of acceptable prudential judgments in dealing with a government vary from society to society, which system of values, if any, is binding on the multinational? This question is raised in the cases already mentioned, but perhaps the best-known problem of this type is the facilitation of business transactions through so-called "grease payments," either to government officials or to influential members of a society. These payments have been defended by some corporations on the grounds that they are not illegal (often in either the host or the home country), are in the best interests of the corporation, are harmless, provide new employment opportunities for persons at home and abroad, and provide stimulation to the economies and to the technological capacities of both nations. The business community has also tended to view these "sensitive payments" as extortion, or at least as demands placed on their enterprise in order to do business. The nature of these justifications and possible problems with them are explored in the case study in this chapter on the bribery business.

Opponents have viewed grease payments and the like as simple bribery (though the U.S. Foreign Corrupt Practices Act does distinguish the two). In defense of their viewpoint, they do not simply cite laws and moral views about the unacceptability of bribery in their culture. Rather, they look to a broader set of social consequences they believe will result from the practice of special payments. For example, government mismanagement is promoted; those who take the money are placed in a more favorable economic position than are other members of their society who have no source of special payments; quality products become less important to manufacturers and government officials; competing firms with quality products may be ignored; and competition is weakened. In general, critics say, the public interest of the foreign nation is not promoted.

Critics also argue that crucial questions surround sensitive payments and other clandestine practices. For example, if bribery is condoned or is a "way of life" in another nation, does this practice persist because it is approved or consented to in that culture, or only because those in power have institutionalized the practice? Even if it has become customary, would it be regarded as scandalous if it were to come to public attention in the foreign nation—as, for example, occurred some years ago in Japan when Lockheed Aircraft's payments ultimately brought down the government of Prime Minister Kakuei Tanaka? These questions and many more are raised in the final two cases in this chapter.

John Higgins: An American Goes Native in Japan

In the fall of 1962, Mr. Leonard Prescott, Vice-President and General Manager of the Weaver-Yamazaki Pharmaceutical Company, Ltd. of Japan was considering what action, if any, to take regarding his executive assistant, Mr. John Higgins. In Mr. Prescott's opinion, Mr. Higgins had been losing his effectiveness as one who was to represent the U.S. parent company because of his extraordinary identification with the Japanese culture.

The Weaver Pharmaceutical Company was one of the outstanding concerns in the drug field in the United States. As a result of extensive research it had developed many important drugs and its product lines were constantly improved, giving the company a strong competitive advantage. It also had extensive international operations throughout many parts of the world. Operations in Japan started in the early 1930s, though they were limited to sales activities. The Yamazaki Pharmaceutical House, a major producer of drugs and chemicals in Japan, was the franchise distributor for Weaver's products in Japan.

Export sales to Japan were resumed in 1948. Due to its product superiority and the inability of major Japanese pharmaceutical houses to compete effectively because of lack of recovery from war damage, the Weaver company was able to capture a substantial share of the market for its product categories. In preparing for increasingly keen competition from Japanese producers, the company undertook local production of some of the product lines.

From its many years of international experience, the company had learned that it could not hope to establish itself firmly in a foreign country until it began manufacturing locally. Consequently, in 1953

This case was prepared by Dr. Michael Yoshino under the direction of Professor J. S. Ewing, in Tokyo, as a basis for class discussion rather than to illustrate either effective or ineffective handling of an administrative situation. Copyright © 1963 by the Board of Trustees of the Leland Stanford Junior University. Reprinted with the permission of Stanford University. **Not to be duplicated without permission of the authors and publisher.**

the company began its preliminary negotiations with the Yamazaki Company Ltd., which culminated in the establishment of a jointly owned and operated manufacturing subsidiary. The company, known as the Weaver-Yamazaki Pharmaceutical Co. Ltd. of Japan, was officially organized in the summer of 1954. . . .

The subsidiary was headed by Mr. Shozo Suzuki, as President, and Mr. Leonard Prescott as Executive Vice-President. Since Mr. Suzuki was Executive Vice-President of the parent company and also was President of several other subsidiaries, his participation in the company was limited to determination of basic policies. Day-to-day operations were managed by Mr. Prescott as Executive Vice-President and General Manager. He had an American Executive Assistant, Mr. Higgins, and several Japanese directors who assisted him in various phases of the operations. Though several other Americans were assigned to the Japanese ventures, they were primarily concerned with research and development and held no overall management responsibilities. . . .

Mr. Leonard Prescott arrived in Japan in 1960 to replace Mr. Richard Densely who had been in Japan since 1954. Mr. Prescott had been described as an "old hand" at international work, having spent most of his 25-year career with the company in its international work. He had served in India, the Philippines, and Mexico prior to coming to Japan. He had also spent several years in the international division of the company in New York. He was delighted with the challenge to expand further the Japanese operations. After two years of experience in Japan, he was pleased with the progress the company had made and felt a certain sense of accomplishment in developing a smooth-functioning organization.

He became concerned, however, with the notable changes in Mr. Higgins' attitude and thinking. Mr. Higgins, in the opinion of Mr. Prescott, had absorbed and internalized the Japanese culture to such a point where he had lost the United States point of view and orientation. He had "gone native," so to speak, in Japan, which resulted in a substantial loss of his administrative effectiveness as a bi-cultural and -lingual executive assistant. . . .

In the summer of 1961, Mr. Higgins married a Japanese girl whom he had met shortly after he returned to Japan. His wife was an extremely attractive and intelligent woman by any standard. She had been graduated from the most prominent women's college in Japan and had studied at a well-known Eastern university in the United States for a brief period of time. Shortly after their marriage, Mr. Higgins filed a request through Mr. Prescott with the personnel director of International Division in New York, asking to extend his stay in Japan for an indefinite period of time. The personnel director approved the request upon consultation with both Mr. Densely and Mr. Prescott. Mr. Prescott noted that marriage was a big turning point for Mr. Higgins. Until that time, he was merely interested in the Japanese culture in an intellectual sense, but since his marriage he was observed to have developed a real emotional involvement with it.

He and his wife rented an apartment in a strictly Japanese neighborhood and he was often seen relaxed in his Japanese kimono at home. He was also observed using the public bath, a well-known Japanese institution. His fluent Japanese combined with a likeable personality and interest in the Japanese culture won him many friends in the neighborhood. Everyone, including small children, greeted him with a big smile and friendly gestures, addressing him as "Higgins-san" whenever they saw him.

His mode of living was almost entirely that of a typical Japanese. He seemed to have completely integrated himself with Japanese life. He was invited to weddings, neighborhood parties, and even Buddhist funerals. On these occasions, he participated actively and fulfilled whatever part was required by the customs and traditions.

The Weaver Pharmaceutical Company had a policy of granting two months home leave every two years with transportation paid for the employee and his family. When Mr. Higgins' turn came, he declined to go home even on vacation on the grounds that his parents were already dead and his brothers and sisters were widely scattered throughout the United States. Consequently, he did not feel he had many home ties in the United States. Instead he and his wife took his two months leave and visited many of the remote historical sites throughout Japan.

None of these points by itself disturbed Mr. Prescott greatly. However, he was afraid that accumulations of these seemingly insignificant factors would tend to distort Higgins' cultural orientation and identification, thereby losing his effectiveness as a bi-lingual and -cultural representative of the American parent company. In administrative relationships, there had been a number of incidents that tended to support Mr. Prescott's anxiety. A few of the specific examples were these.

In performing his responsibilities as executive assistant, Higgins had taken on many of the characteristics of a typical Japanese executive. For example, Mr. Higgins was reported to spend a great deal of time in listening to the personal problems of his subordinates. He maintained close social relationships with many of the men in the organization and he and his wife took an active interest in the personal lives of the employees. They even had gone as far as arranging marriages for some of the young employees.

Consequently, many of the employees sought Mr. Higgins' attention to register complaints and demands with the management. For example, a group of middle management personnel approached Mr. Higgins concerning the desirability of more liberal fringe benefits. These were particularly in the areas of company-sponsored recreational activities such as occasional out-of-town trips and the acquisition of rest houses at resort areas.

On another occasion, the middle management personnel registered their objections concerning a recent company policy of promoting personnel based upon merit rather than length of service and education, the two most important criteria in the traditional Japanese approach. Shortly after Mr. Prescott took over the Japanese operations, he was appalled with Japanese promotion practices and decided to change these to a merit system. In the process, he consulted with Mr. Higgins as to its applicability in Japan.

The latter objected to the idea, saying that the Japanese were not quite ready to accept what he considered a radical approach. Since Mr. Prescott did not see it as a radical concept, he went ahead and announced the policy. At the same time, he installed an annual review system, whereby every one of the management personnel would be evaluated by his immediate superior and this would constitute an important basis for promotion.

The Japanese objections were primarily based upon the ground that their traditional personnel practices were so different from those of the United States, that a mechanical imposition of the U.S. method would not work in Japan. The system had, as Higgins expected, created many undesirable problems. The Japanese group contended that Mr. Prescott, who did not understand the language, was not aware of the magnitude of the anxiety and insecurity the policy had caused. Because of the traditional superior-subordinate relationship characterized by distance, fear, and obedience, they were not willing to take these problems directly to Mr. Prescott. Therefore they asked Mr. Higgins to intercede on their behalf by reporting their feelings to Mr. Prescott.

Mr. Prescott felt that though it was helpful to have Mr. Higgins report back to him the feelings and opinions of the middle management personnel, which otherwise might never come to his attention, he did not appreciate Mr. Higgins' attitude in so doing. In these cases, Mr. Higgins' sympathy was with the Japanese group, and he usually insisted that these demands were reasonable and well justified according to the Japanese standard and traditions. Mr. Prescott found it necessary to deal with Mr. Higgins on these demands instead of being able to work with him as it had been in the past. His perception had been so colored that Mr. Prescott became hesitant to ask Mr. Higgins' opinions on these matters. Lately, whenever Mr. Prescott proposed a change in administrative procedures that might be contrary to Japanese traditions or culture, Mr. Higgins invariably raised objections. In Mr. Prescott's thinking, there were dynamic changes taking place in traditional Japanese customs and culture, and he was confident that many of the points Mr. Higgins objected to were not tied to the cultural patterns as rigidly as he thought they might be. Besides, Mr. Prescott thought that there was no point for a progressive American company to copy the local customs and felt that its real contribution to the Japanese society was in bringing in new ideas and innovations.

To substantiate this point, he learned that some of his Japanese subordinates were much more susceptible to new ideas and more willing to try them out than Mr. Higgins. This fact had convinced Mr. Prescott that Mr. Higgins was too closely identified with the traditional pattern of the Japanese culture, not sensing the new and radically different development taking place in Japan.

Moreover, two recent incidents raised some doubts in Mr. Prescott's mind as to the soundness of Mr. Higgins' judgment, which he, heretofore, had never questioned. The first incident was in connection with the dismissal of Mr. Nonogaki, Chief of Subsection in the Purchasing Department. In the opinion of Mr. Prescott, Mr. Nonogaki lacked initiative, leadership, and general competency. After two years of continued prodding by his superiors, including Mr. Prescott himself, he had shown little interest in self-improvement. As a result, Prescott had decided to dismiss him from the organization. Both Higgins and Takahinshi, Personnel Manager of the subsidiary, objected vigorously on the ground that this had never been done in the company. Besides, in Japan the management was required to live with a certain amount of incompetent executives as long as their honesty and loyalty were not questioned. They further claimed that the company was partially responsible for recruiting him initially and had kept him on for the last ten years without spotting his incompetency, thus it was not completely fair to require Mr. Nonogaki alone to take the full burden. Mr. Prescott, unimpressed by their arguments, dismissed him after serving proper notice.

A few weeks later, Mr. Prescott learned quite accidentally that Mr. Nonogaki was re-employed by one of the other subsidiaries of the Japanese parent company, the Yamazaki Pharmaceutical Co., Ltd. Upon investigating, he found, to his surprise, that Messrs. Higgins and Takahinshi had interceded and arranged for him to be taken back without informing Mr. Prescott. For understandable reasons, Mr. Prescott did not appreciate their action and confronted Mr. Higgins with this, who in turn told Mr. Prescott that he had only done what was expected of a superior in any Japanese company.

Another incident was in connection with his relationship with the government. In Japan, the government plays a substantially greater part in business and economic activities than it does in the United States. It is important for companies to maintain a good working relationship with government officials of those agencies that have control over their activities. This is particularly true of foreign subsidiaries. Because of many complicated intricacies, government relations had been entrusted to Mr. Higgins and his two Japanese assistants.

Mr. Prescott had observed a basic difference in the view with which he and Higgins looked upon practices of this sort. Prescott, knowing the differences in business ethics in various countries, accepted some of these activities as a necessary evil but felt that they had to be kept to a minimum in order to preserve the overall integrity of the company; whereas Mr. Prescott felt Mr. Higgins had become a willing participant in the system without much reservation or restraint.

Mr. Prescott believed these problems to be quite serious. Mr. Higgins had been an effective as well as efficient executive assistant and his knowledge of the language and the people had proved invaluable. On numerous occasions, his American friends envied Prescott for having a man of his qualifications as an assistant. He also knew that Mr. Higgins had received several outstanding offers to go with other American companies in Japan.

Prescott felt that Higgins would be far more effective could he take a more emotionally detached attitude toward the Japanese people and culture. In Mr. Prescott's view, the best international executive was the one who retained a belief in the fundamentals of the U.S. point of view while also understanding foreign attitudes. This understanding, of course, should be thorough or even instinctive, but it also should be objective, characterized by neither disdain nor strong emotional attachment.

He was wondering how he could best assist Mr. Higgins to see his point of view, so that they could collaborate more effectively in fulfilling their administrative responsibilities.

Polaroid In and Out of South Africa

American companies operating in South Africa have become increasingly sensitive to charges that their activities bolster a regime that practices apartheid—a legal system of racial segregation and oppression judged immoral.

Apartheid is an Afrikaans term meaning "apartness," in this case racial apartness. This policy of white domination has been the cornerstone of social policy in South Africa since the beginning of the Union of South Africa in 1910. According to the classification scheme implementing this policy, South Africa's population is composed of 17 percent white, 70 percent African, 10 percent Coloured (mixed descent), and 3 percent Asian. Whites alone may be members of Parliament and the cabinet, and only whites may possess firearms or be arms-carrying members of the police and military forces. Organizations doctrinally opposed to apartheid are banned. There has also been a history of political involvement by indigenous industry aimed at promoting apartheid because industrialists have worked to keep labor both cheap and unorganized.

Despite these modes of enforced segregation, most nonwhites reside in white-owned urban territory or on white-owned farms whose economies depend upon their labor. Under this system, blacks are allowed to own only 13 percent of the land surface. These lands are designated "native reserves." Though whites constitute 17 percent of the population, they control 87 percent of the land. Whites also control all major business activities, and the system is constructed so that black workers are paid less than white workers for comparable work.

AMERICAN INVESTMENT

About 240 U.S. companies currently have operations in South Africa. These include such blue chip companies as Mobil Oil, R.J. Reynolds,

This case was prepared by Tom L. Beauchamp, with assistance from R. Jay Wallace and Barbara Humes and revised by Joanne L. Jurmu. **Not to be duplicated without permission of the holder of the copyright,** © 1989 Tom L. Beauchamp.

Goodyear, and Xerox. South Africa is a financially attractive country for American investments. Part of the attraction derives from the economic benefits of South Africa: Profits are substantial, labor is remarkably cheap, and capital was not threatened until recently by the political insecurity created by unstable governments. The market is thriving; currency is hard and convertible; and South Africa is rich in natural resources, especially minerals. The United States is the second largest direct foreign investor in South Africa, a nation of 30 million people, 5 million of whom are whites. U.S. investments in South Africa were approximately $1.3 billion in 1986,[1] down from $1.7 billion in 1976. U.S. companies control substantial portions of South Africa's petroleum, auto, and computer markets and are easily the main suppliers of many major consumer products. Thus the U.S. presence in South Africa is not an insignificant factor in the country's economic health.[2]

U.S. corporations began to trade in South Africa around 1880, when the white South African community alone was involved in commerce and employment. Whites at that time held all available jobs, even in factories. There were no black employees. Gradually the South African economy became so spectacularly successful that there were not enough whites to fill available positions, and blacks began to move into factories and other low-paying jobs. Though salaries have always been extremely low, blacks have made enough money to purchase goods and become a factor in the South African economy. The more they interacted in the economy, the more repressive apartheid laws became, and this in turn presented dilemmas for U.S. corporations about participation in the immoral activities required by the South African government.

U.S. corporations have become increasingly sensitive to charges of immoral exploitation and opportunism in South Africa. Between 1984 and 1986 over sixty companies took the initiative to withdraw from South Africa.[3] Companies withdrawing included General Motors, IBM, Coca-Cola, AT&T, Procter & Gamble, and General Electric. They pulled out for a number of reasons, ranging from declining market share to shareholder political pressure. However, Polaroid was one of the leaders in pulling operations from South Africa as an expression of corporate social responsibility. Polaroid has had a long history of sharply criticizing the South African government and—as we shall see—has now withdrawn completely from all entanglement in South Africa. Not surprisingly, Polaroid was one of the first U.S. firms to condemn apartheid publicly

---

[1] "U.S. Stake: $1.3 B," *U.S. News and World Report* 100 (June 30, 1986), p. 29.

[2] See Richard DeGeorge, "U.S. Firms in South Africa," in his *Business Ethics*, pp. 253–255, and Dharmendra T. Verma, "Polaroid in South Africa" (Bentley College, 1978), distributed by Harvard Business School, HBS Case Services, p. 6.

[3] *Ibid.*, and Harry Anderson, "Big Business Pulls Out," *Newsweek* 108 (November 3, 1986), p. 44.

and to assume responsibility for the uses that government made of Polaroid technology. Polaroid views itself as a "corporation with a conscience" and has been a pacesetter in both race-relations policies and community-relations programs in the United States.[4] In February 1987, Polaroid was given a special award by the Council on Economic Priorities for exhibiting social responsibility by "its decision to pull out of South Africa a decade before it was chic" for businesses to withdraw.[5]

POLAROID IN SOUTH AFRICA

Nonetheless, in 1970 Polaroid found itself embroiled in a controversy over its involvement in South Africa. The events in this controversy began when a few of Polaroid's black American employees formed a group called Polaroid Revolutionary Workers Movement (PRWM). They were outraged because they believed Polaroid products were being used in South Africa's repressive pass book system. The hated pass laws were designed by the South African government to control the movement of blacks in urban areas. This practice has been described by Bishop Desmond Tutu, head of the South African Council of Churches, as ". . . among the most humiliating of the dehumanizing laws and regulations applied to this country."[6] In brief summary form, these laws require: (1) that all African citizens over sixteen carry a pass book that gives such details as where the person is permitted to be and personal items such as the person's place of work and payment of taxes; (2) that Africans may not remain in a white urban area longer than seventy-two hours without a permit unless special permission has been granted or the person has a long history of approved residence and work in the area.[7]

PRWM employees at Polaroid in the United States distributed leaflets that charged in their title, "Polaroid Imprisons Black People in 60 Seconds." These leaflets were also placed on company bulletin boards. This campaign intensified and came to a point of confrontation in October 1970. The general charge by the employees was that Polaroid was (like other U.S. companies) exploiting cheap black labor in South Africa, and (unlike other U.S. corporations) was actually having its technology

[4] C. L. Suzman, "Polaroid Experiment in South Africa" (Johannesburg, South Africa: Graduate School of Business Administration, University of Witwatersrand, 1974, revised 1977), distributed by Harvard Business School, HBS Case Services, p. 2.

[5] Janice E. Simpson, "Here's the Newest Top 10: Companies with a Conscience," *Wall Street Journal*, March 3, 1987, p. 18.

[6] Marjorie Chan and John Steiner, "Corporate America Confronts the Apartheid System," in George A. Steiner and John F. Steiner, eds., *Casebook for Business, Government, and Society,* 2d ed. (New York: Random House, 1980), pp. 86 f.

[7] See Muriel Horrel, *South Africa: Basic Facts and Figures* (South African Institute of Race Relations, 1973).

used to support the more repressive aspects of the apartheid system.[8] The above-mentioned pamphlet and this last charge refer to the use of film and cameras involved in implementing the South African government's pass book system. At least one Polaroid executive (Tom Wyman, Vice-President of Sales) admitted an awareness that Polaroid products were being used at that time in the pass book identification program. The supply source was Frank and Hirsch, Polaroid's (independent) South African distributor.[9]

On October 27, 1970, some large demonstrations organized by PRWM were held in Boston, and the more activist-minded members of PRWM called for a worldwide boycott of Polaroid products. In this same month Polaroid officials denied that the company's equipment was being used in the pass law program. Polaroid's director of community relations was authorized to make the following statement in response to PRWM charges: "We have a responsibility for the ultimate use of our product. . . . In response to the charge we articulated a very strict policy of refusing to do business directly with the South African government. . . . We as a corporation will not sell our products in instances where its use constitutes a potential abridgement of human freedom."[10] Mr. Edwin Land, then owner and manager of the corporation, also reiterated his "personal ban" on the sale of Polaroid products to the South African government, a ban originally instituted in 1948, but less than diligently enforced in some years.[11]

Instead of yielding to PRWM demands to have Polaroid put an end to all activities in South Africa, Polaroid management determined that it would rather investigate less radical alternatives. Management at Polaroid then formed a committee of fourteen employees, representing a cross section of the company's work force. This group was mandated to make a final withdraw-or-stay decision. This committee recommended:

1. That a four-member fact finding group be sent to South Africa to review the feeling of blacks in South Africa first hand. The four-man team was to report on the use of Polaroid products in South Africa, conditions at Frank and Hirsch, and the use of Polaroid film in the Pass Book Program, and was to give recommendations on the engagement-disengagement decision.

[8] David Vogel, *Lobbying the Corporation: Citizen Challenges to Business Authority* (New York: Basic Books, 1978), p. 173; Chan and Steiner, "Corporate America Confronts," pp. 86 f; and Suzman, "Polaroid Experiment," p. 6.

[9] See accounts in the *Boston Globe*, October 18, 1964, p. 64, and Suzman, "Polaroid Experiment," p. 7.

[10] As quoted in Vogel, *Lobbying the Corporation*, p. 173.

[11] H. Landis Gabel, "Polaroid Experiment in South Africa" (Charlottesville, Va.: Colgate Darden School of Business Administration, University of Virginia, 1981), distributed by Harvard Business School, HBS Case Services, p. 1, and Suzman, "Polaroid Experiment," p. 7. See also *Business Week* (November 14, 1970), p. 32.

2. That the committee would consult outside experts in economics, African history, politics, and other fields in order to assist them in making recommendations about Polaroid's future in South Africa and Polaroid's future business in "free Black Africa."[12]

THE POLAROID EXPERIMENT

This travel group had a reasonably free hand to assemble data and conduct interviews while in South Africa. Their final recommendation was that Polaroid should not pull out of South African operations, but instead should initiate a program that would come to be known as "The Polaroid Experiment." The program had four main points:

1. Sales to the South African government were to be discontinued, but the company would not disengage from the Republic and would set up an experimental program for one year.
2. Polaroid's local distributor and its suppliers were going to improve salaries and other benefits for black employees.
3. The company's South African associates were to be obliged to start a training program for blacks so as to enable them to take up important posts.
4. A proportion of Polaroid's South African profits was to be devoted to encouraging black education.[13]

The South African government agreed to permit these employment practices by a U.S. company as long as no law was violated. The government specified, however, that any promotion of nonwhites into positions of authority over whites would not be permitted.

One year later Polaroid evaluated the effects of this experiment and found that significant improvements had been made in the salaries, advancement, and benefits of its nonwhite employees. The average monthly salary for blacks had increased 22 percent (including a "bonus" for black employees). The principle of the same pay for the same job had been accepted. Eight black employees were promoted to supervisory positions. Three programs were designed to improve the education of black employees' children, to establish a foundation to support black students and teachers, and to promote black leadership. Polaroid also contributed $75,000 in grants to black educational groups in South Africa.[14]

This program continued successfully for six years. However, the actual measure of "success" is debatable. Frank and Hirsch noted at the time,

---

[12] Suzman, "Polaroid Experiment," p. 10.

[13] *Ibid.*, p. 12; see also Gabel, "Polaroid Experiment," p. 2.

[14] Chad and Steiner, "Corporate America Confronts," p. 89.

and Polaroid knew, that it would be extremely difficult to enforce a complete ban on the sale of all products to the South African government. It was easy to stop direct sales, but indirect sales through private photographers and retailers in other countries would be difficult to stop. Thus the effectiveness of the ban on the sale of Polaroid products during these years was questionable. Nonetheless, for six years both Polaroid and Frank and Hirsch expressed virtually complete satisfaction with the program. The managing director of Frank and Hirsch noted that it was a period when racial discrimination was attacked and virtually eliminated at Frank and Hirsch. Blacks and whites came to share the same offices and have the same working hours. The racial balance of Frank and Hirsch employees grew to be almost 50 percent black, and the company donated money to upgrade the education of black African children.[15]

"EXPERIMENT" DISCONTINUED

In November 1977 a dramatic new development occurred in Polaroid's "Experiment." On November 21 the *Boston Globe* ran a front-page story claiming that Frank and Hirsch had been clandestinely selling Polaroid products to the South African government in violation of its 1971 standing agreement not to permit such sales. This story emerged through the whistle-blowing efforts of a former employee in the shipping department of Frank and Hirsch—a South African Indian named Indrus Naidoo. He had made photostatic copies of invoices documenting the delivery of Polaroid products to the Bantu Reference Bureau on September 22, 1975. This is an agency that issues pass books for nonwhites. Naidoo passed on this photostatic copy and other information to Paul Irish, a staff member of the American Committee on Africa in New York. Irish then released the copy to the *Boston Globe* after a time when Naidoo was able to leave South Africa (as an exile, after discharge from his job). Naidoo's documentation showed that Frank and Hirsch had for years billed all its shipments to the South African government through a drugstore in Johannesburg. These shipments of film and cameras were packed in unmarked cartons. Deliveries had also been made to the military, including a large shipment of Polaroid sunglasses. Since all billing was done through the pharmacy, there was no record of direct sales.[16]

---

[15] Suzman, "Polaroid Experiment," p. 14.

[16] George M. Houser, "Polaroid's Dramatic Withdrawal from South Africa," *Christian Century* (April 12, 1978), pp. 392–392. Mr. Houser was then Executive Director of the American Committee on Africa, located in New York. See also Verma, "Polaroid in South Africa," p. 3; Vogel, *Lobbying the Corporation,* p. 173; and Gabel, "Polaroid Experiment," p. 1.

Polaroid had been informed by the *Boston Globe* of these charges five days prior to the appearance of the story in their newspaper. The company immediately sent their export sales manager to South Africa to investigate the charges. The sales manager was able to document several deliveries to the South African government, and to interview Mr. Hirsch (the owner of Frank and Hirsch), who expressed shock and complete ignorance of these sales. (Polaroid officials indicated at the time that they had long had suspicions about Frank and Hirsch, and had periodically attempted investigations.) Polaroid then immediately announced—on the day the story appeared in the *Boston Globe*—that it was terminating its distributorship and all involvement in South Africa. Polaroid issued an official statement saying it "abhorred" the policy of apartheid and that it was largely the recommendations of black Africans that had led to continued sales in 1971. The statement also mentioned that Polaroid's contributions to black African scholarships during this period amounted to approximately half a million dollars, that there was considerable evidence that Polaroid had had a positive effect on black employees and on foreign investors, and that they would not establish a new distributorship in South Africa.[17] Polaroid's South African annual sales were then between \$3 and \$4 million. The company's universal 1977 sales were over \$1 billion.[18]

According to Harry Johnson, Manager of Public Relations, all contracts in South Africa expired five weeks after the announcement of Polaroid's withdrawal. There has been no new business in South Africa since that time. He states emphatically that "our practice is our policy."[19] As of 1988 Polaroid has not constructed an official policy statement on investment on South Africa.

[17] Letter from the Polaroid Corporation, November 21, 1977.

[18] Verma, "Polaroid in South Africa," p. 104, and Houser, "Polaroid's Dramatic Withdrawal," p. 392.

[19] Telephone conversation, Harry Johnson, Manager of Public Relations, Polaroid Corporation, Cambridge, Mass., March 18, 1987.

Marketing Infant Formula

On May 21, 1981, the Thirty-fourth World Health Assembly of the World Health Organization (WHO) passed a resolution adopting the International Code of Marketing of Breastmilk Substitutes, urging all member states "to give full and unanimous support to the implementation of the recommendations made by the joint WHO/UNICEF Meeting on Infant and Young Child Feeding."[1] The code is designed to regulate marketing practices related to prepared infant formula and other products designed as partial or total substitutes for breastmilk, but specifies that it is a recommendation and not a requirement for member nations. Article 5 of this code states:

> There should be no advertising or other form of promotion to the general public of products within the scope of this Code.
> Manufacturers and distributors should not provide, directly or indirectly to pregnant women, mothers or members of their families, samples of products within the scope of this Code. . . .
> There should be no point-of-sale advertising, giving of samples, or any other promotion device to induce sales directly to the consumer at the retail level, such as special displays, discount coupons, premiums, special sales, loss-leaders and tie-in sales, for products within the scope of this Code. . . .
> Manufacturers and distributors should not distribute to pregnant women or mothers of infants and young children any gifts of articles or utensils which may promote the use of breastmilk substitutes or bottle-feeding.
> Marketing personnel, in their business capacity, should not seek direct or indirect contact of any kind with pregnant women or with mothers of infants and young children.[2]

[1] Thirty-fourth World Health Assembly, "International Code of Marketing of Breastmilk Substitutes," World Health Assembly 34.22 (May 21, 1981), p. 1. Passed under Article 23 of the WHO Constitution.

[2] *Ibid.*, p. 7.

These limitations on the marketing of breastmilk substitutes are designed to apply generally in all WHO-member countries. They evolved from a specific controversy that has raged over the past decade regarding the marketing of prepared infant formulas in Third World countries.

Annual sales of infant formula, as marketed by approximately twenty multinational corporations, amount to roughly $2 billion. Figures in the Third World were estimated in 1981 to be no less than $690 million.[3] Abbott Laboratories, through its Ross Laboratories nutritional division, is the largest domestic manufacturer of infant formula in the United States, with 65 percent of the market. In the Third World the market is dominated by the Swiss conglomerate Nestlé, S.A., with 60 percent of total sales. Chicago-based Abbott/Ross has approximately 6 percent of the remaining Third World market, while the other 34 percent is shared by several companies, including Mead Johnson (Bristol-Myers), Wyeth Laboratories (American Home Products), and numerous foreign competitors.[4]

Since 1970 the Abbott/Ross and Nestlé companies have been involved in a controversy over the ethical responsibilities of marketing infant formula in Third World countries. Critics have questioned both the morality of *any* infant formula marketing in the Third World and the morality of specific promotional claims and marketing techniques. The controversy has been sustained in various health organizations (*e.g.*, UNICEF, the World Health Organization, and the Pan American Health Organization), the popular press, consumer boycotts organized primarily by religious groups, the annual meetings of the corporations involved, the SEC, the courts, and federal and international hearing rooms.

The basic charges against these corporations are that in the Third World countries: (1) prepared infant formula is likely to be a dangerous product because it will be improperly used; (2) the "aggressive" marketing tactics used by certain companies encourage women to choose bottlefeeding and thereby cause a decline in breastfeeding; and (3) infant formula is unnecessary because breastfeeding is "free and available for all." In Third World countries the use of prepared infant formulas often is complicated by ignorance and consequent failure to understand the instructions and by poverty. Poor sanitation, lack of adequate water supplies, and improper facilities for cleaning and storing supplies lead to improperly cleansed bottles and to mixing the formula with impure water. Due to the high cost of infant formula (which can cost 25 to 40

---

[3] David O. Cox, "The Infant Formula Issue: A Story in Escalation and Complication," a paper delivered at the Conference on Business Environment/Public Policy and the Business School of the 1980s, College Park, Md., July 12–17, 1981, p. 5.

[4] Earl A. Molander, "Abbott Laboratories Puts Restraints on Marketing Infant Formulas in the Third World," in his *Responsive Capitalism: Case Studies in Corporate Social Conduct* (New York: McGraw-Hill, 1980), p. 265.

percent of a family's income), mothers sometimes over-dilute the preparation in order to make it "go further." Over-dilution coupled with bacterial contamination leads to malnutrition, diarrhea, and increased susceptibility to infectious disease.

Marketing strategies to sell infant formula in Third World countries have included direct mass media advertising by radio, television, newspapers, and billboards. Free samples are also distributed through health professionals in hospitals and clinics. The provision of free samples of formula is detrimental to breastfeeding because formula use may irreversibly suppress lactation, leaving the mother with no choice but to continue with the formula. The samples have, in many cases, been distributed by "milk nurses," company employees dressed like nurses who visit prospective and new mothers at home and in hospitals. The use of the "milk nurses" has been denounced as a deceptive practice because these company employees may be easily confused with bona-fide nurses. These promotional strategies have been viewed by critics as a major cause of the decline of breastfeeding in some Third World countries.

Infant formula is considered unnecessary by many critics who point out that breastfeeding is a free and available resource. Although prepared infant formulas do provide adequate nourishment if properly used, it is almost universally agreed that from a medical, nutritional, and psychological standpoint breastfeeding is the superior way to feed infants (assuming a healthy mother).

It is important, however, not to overgeneralize complex situations by use of the term "Third World countries." These countries have substantially different situations, and within each the mothers using the formula vary dramatically in socioeconomic background. Perhaps three fourths of the women in the Third World are not in the cash economy in their country, and could not purchase formula even if they wanted to. For example, socialist Algeria permits no advertising whatsoever, but the Algerian government purchases yearly in excess of 20 million pounds of infant formula, which it then distributes. Breastfeeding rates remain high in this country.[5]

The controversial history of infant formula is marred by lack of clarity and disagreement about all of the relevant cause-and-effect relationships and about the importance of related cultural practices. Health and nutritional experts disagree as to the exact relationship between bottlefeeding and infant mortality and morbidity and as to the continuing decline of breastfeeding. It is, however, agreed that these relationships are complex and multicausal.

In 1970 the problem of "bottle illness" was brought to the attention of Abbott/Ross, Nestlé, and other infant-formula manufacturers by Dr.

[5] Based on data supplied in correspondence by Tom McCollough of Ross Laboratories.

Derrick B. Jelliffe, then head of the Caribbean Food and Nutrition Institute in Jamaica, who charged that "infant morbidity and mortality in general were linked in a significant way to the promotion and use of commercial formulas." Jelliffe recommended that prepared formulas be entirely withdrawn from the developing countries.[6] Jelliffe was joined by other medical and nutritional experts in favoring the complete "demarketing" of infant formula and the regulation of the industry as part of a more comprehensive plan of government control.

In 1971 an *ad hoc* committee of the United Nation's Protein Advisory Group observed that "the extensive introduction and indiscriminate promotion of expensive processed milk-based infant foods in some situations may constitute a grave threat to the nutritional status of the infants for whom they are intended." In 1974 the governing body of the World Health Organization (WHO) passed a resolution that stressed the problems caused by advertisements promoting the superiority of bottlefeeding over breastfeeding. The resolution urged member countries to "review sales promotion activities on baby foods and to introduce appropriate remedial measures, including advertisement codes and legislation where necessary."[7]

However, other medical and nutritional experts disagreed with these views. A group led by Dr. Fernando Monkeberg of the Institute of Nutrition and Food Technology at the University of Chile maintained that even more serious health and nutrition problems would exist if prepared infant formulas were *not* available. The group argued that the decline in breastfeeding ". . . was largely independent of prepared infant formula promotion," and insisted "that data on morbidity and mortality had to be examined as part of a much larger picture that included maternal nutrition, sanitation, access to health care, purchasing power, education, lactation failure due to family disruption, urbanization with subsequent life-style changes," and so on. The UN's Protein Advisory Group modified its earlier position on the basis of a series of international meetings on infant nutrition. While still critical of industry *promotional* practices, the group's report included the recommendation that "infant formulas be developed and introduced to satisfy the special needs of infants who are *not* breast fed."[8]

A study done by Jose Villar of the Johns Hopkins School of Hygiene and Public Health and Jose M. Belizan of the Institute of Nutrition of Central America and Panama can be viewed as supportive of the availability of prepared infant formula when used properly in the poorer countries:

---

[6] Molander, "Abbott Laboratories," p. 266.

[7] David Vogel, "Infant Formulas," in his *Lobbying the Corporation: Citizen Challenges to Business Authority* (New York: Basic Books, 1978), p. 189.

[8] Molander, "Abbott Laboratories," p. 267.

Unsupplemented human milk from a well-nourished, well-motivated mother is all that a baby in optimal nutritional condition may require to sustain growth and good nutrition during the first 4 to 6 months of life. To have a healthy, well-nourished, and well-developed infant, the mother must have laid down adequate nutritional reserves during pregnancy, including subcutaneous fat, and must remain well-fed throughout lactation. Unfortunately, in developing countries poorly nourished women give birth to infants of low birthweight (LBW) in bad environmental and sanitary conditions. The frequency of low birthweight (<2500g) is, on the average, three times greater in underdeveloped (17 percent) than in developed countries (6 percent). In some areas 30–40 percent of birthweights may be below 2500g with 75 percent of the infants intrauterine-growth-retarded (IUGR). IUGR infants are the ones most at risk of perinatal death, illness, and subsequent handicap. . . .

A healthy, well-nourished woman must be prepared for successful lactation in two ways:

a) By the physiological changes of pregnancy, especially the accumulation of fat reserves (an average of 4 kg during a normal gestation period). This represents an additional 36,000 kcal.

b) By an increased dietary intake during lactation (600–800 additional kcal/day) to give a total daily intake of 2800–3000 kcal. Greater consumption of all essential nutrients, including an additional 20 g of protein/day, is also necessary for adequate lactation. . . .

Neither of the two physiological processes required for successful lactation is found in poorly nourished mothers from developing countries and these women are, from their first pregnancy, in a state of general "maternal depletion," characterized by progressive weight loss and/or specific nutritional deficiencies.[9]

Villar and Belizan conclude that in the case of malnourished children born to already malnourished mothers, breastfeeding alone neither corrects "malnutrition nor modifies its basic courses. When the infant is already malnourished at birth, as are about 40 percent in developing countries, breastfeeding alone during the first four months of life is unlikely to provide adequate nutrition."[10]

Drs. Villar and Belizan do not take a general position on the controversy surrounding economic and sanitation factors or about marketing practices in the Third World. Like most scientific studies on this topic, theirs supports the contention that infant formula is not inherently dangerous, yet its abuse may be unavoidable in the face of consumer misuse. Breastfeeding cannot be considered a "free and available" resource in light of the insufficient milk syndrome associated with maternal malnutrition in Third World countries. *Some* forms of supplemental feeding, they say, continue to be needed for Third World infants. Studies have failed

---

[9] Jose Villar and Jose M. Belizan, "Breastfeeding in Developing Countries," *Lancet* (September 19, 1981), pp. 621–622.

[10] *Ibid.*, p. 623.

to answer questions concerning the kind of maternal and child supplements that should be used (prepared formula or selected foods), who should pay for the supplements (government or family), and the permissible marketing tactics. There is also no conclusive evidence to establish a causal link between infant formula advertising and the decline in breastfeeding. Dr. William Foege, then Director of the Centers for Disease Control in Atlanta, examined this relationship and found that significant declines in breastfeeding could be measured in only three countries—Taiwan, Malaysia, and Singapore—which all had comparatively low infant mortality rates.[11]

THE ABBOTT/ROSS RESPONSE

David Cox, Chairman of Ross Laboratories, agrees with many of the criticisms leveled at some of the companies that market infant formula in the Third World. He disagrees, however, with both the notion that infant formula sales are responsible for the decline in breastfeeding and the across-the-board condemnation of infant formula producers (by the press, the public, and specific action groups). Cox points out that infant mortality is closely related to the general level of a country's economic and technological development, to the health status of the population, to child spacing, to the nutritional and educational status of the mother, and to the availability of adequate supplies of pure water. He also notes that "infant mortality is often highest in areas where lactation is universal and extended, for example, in the rural areas of the Third World."[12] Cox agrees, however, that breastfeeding is the desirable means of infant feeding and should not be *unnecessarily* replaced by substitutes. "Breast milk is a relatively inexpensive, nutritionally ideal first food for infants. As a natural fertility regulator, exclusive breastfeeding tends to increase the spacing between births; additionally, its immunological properties can be passively transmitted to the newborn, offering some protection from environmental insult."[13]

Tom McCollough, Director of Business Practices Research for Ross Laboratories, takes issue with the tendency of the critics of infant formula sales to lump all Third World mothers together, "implying that infant formula is widely used by the poor and that all Third World women and their situations are alike."[14] And Cox holds that, despite accusations to the contrary, Abbott/Ross has consistently demonstrated responsible "stewardship" in this matter:

[11] Carol Adelman, "Closing the Book on Infant Formula Fears," *Wall Street Journal*, June 19, 1986, p. 30.

[12] Cox, "The Infant Formula Issue," p. 2.

[13] *Ibid.*

[14] McCollough correspondence.

In 1972, we published our first Marketing Code of Ethics in Developing Countries; it was later strengthened in 1977.

We were the first member of industry to develop such an ethical regulation and believe it remains the most stringent one in the industry. For the most part, our code development was but a clarification of policies already in place and based on the following three marketing philosophies:

(1) Breastfeeding is superior and the preferred method of feeding;

(2) Our marketing practices should in no way discourage the adoption of breastfeeding; and

(3) Promotion of our product is limited to the health professional community.

It is our belief that health professionals are best qualified to evaluate and recommend the appropriate use of our products for babies in their care. It is our policy, that where no health care counseling is available, the use of our product is inappropriate.

New labels stress the importance of breastfeeding as the most desirable feeding for infants. The labels also include written and graphic instructions for use, emphasize that the product should only be used under the supervision of a qualified health professional, and warn against the dangers of improper preparation.[15]

(In (3) above Cox is referring to a policy and organizational difference between Abbott/Ross and some competitors. Abbott/Ross manufactures pharmaceuticals and health care products, not food products, as do some competitors. Abbott/Ross therefore has marketed its products by calls on professionals, rather than through mass marketing practices.)

Other Abbott/Ross measures initiated to control infant formula abuses include: (1) placing an insert in each carton of formula asking Third World distributors to limit the product to consumers who can afford and properly prepare the product; (2) a similar request to Third World health professionals; (3) the limitation of samples to health professionals; (4) the reduction of sample size from 250 grams to 125 grams to preclude the chances of interference with the establishment of lactation; (5) the elimination of bonuses to employees based on sales; and (6) the banning of nurses' uniforms for nurses and midwives hired as company representatives.

Abbott/Ross has also undertaken an extensive program to promote maternal and child health in the Third World, and in 1976 formed a permanent team that includes a nutritionist, an anthropologist, a medical education specialist, and a pediatric consultant to study infant nutrition, formula, and breastfeeding in the Third World. Projects undertaken by the company as a result of this effort include the preparation of posters, sample radio announcements, and films advocating the merits of breastfeeding for distribution to Third World health ministries, and

---

[15] Cox, "The Infant Formula Issue."

the development of instructional material for training traditional birth attendants in the Arab world.[16]

THE NESTLÉ RESPONSE

A campaign against the Nestlé Corporation began in 1974 when a Swiss political organization published a United Kingdom report on infant formula marketing in developing countries under the title "Nestlé Kills Babies." In response the company filed a libel suit in a Swiss court. Nestlé won the suit on the point of libel in the title, but the court, in rendering its judgment, called on the company to adjust its marketing practices in Third World countries. Specific mention was made of their mass advertising and sales promotion techniques.[17] Nestlé was also the target of a worldwide boycott begun in 1977 by the Infant Formula Action Coalition (INFACT), which was joined by other church and local groups to form the International Nestlé Boycott Committee (INBC). INFACT called for Nestlé to stop mass-media advertising, distribution of free infant formula samples, use of milk nurses, and promotion through the medical profession.

While Abbott/Ross relies on health professionals for distribution and promotion of its products, Nestlé, which is basically a producer and distributor of foods rather than pharmaceuticals, relies on more commercial methods. Nestlé advertised its infant formula on billboards, posters, through radio and television messages, and in newspapers and booklets; and they provided free samples to hospitals and health professionals. Critics of Nestlé cite the following radio message as an example of its "aggressive advertising":

> Bring up your baby with love and Lactogen.
> Important news for mothers/Now Lactogen is even better, because it contains more proteins plus vitamins and iron, all essential for making your baby strong and healthy.
> Lactogen Full Protein now has an even creamier taste and is guaranteed by Nestlé.
> Lactogen and love.[18]

Because of criticism for using free gift schemes and premiums to promote its milk products, for the establishment of baby clubs,[19] and,

---

[16] *Ibid.*

[17] "Infant Formula: An Activist Campaign," reprinted from *Europe's Consumer Movement: Key Issues and Corporate Responses* (Geneva: Business International, S.A., n.d.), p. 9.

[18] Marjorie Chan, "Nestlé under Fire for Hyping Infant Formula," in George A. Steiner and John F. Steiner, eds., *Casebook for Business, Government, and Society*, 2d ed. (New York: Random House, 1980), p. 197.

[19] *Ibid.*

like the other infant formula manufacturers, for the use of milk nurses (or as the company prefers to call them, "mothercraft" nurses), Nestlé has made changes in its advertising and marketing tactics, suspending "all consumer advertising of infant formula products in developing countries in order to reevaluate the role of advertising in educating Third World peoples about the use of infant formula."[20] The company also has changed the outfits worn by the "mothercraft" nurses from white nurses' uniforms to colored company uniforms.

Nestlé agreed early to endorse "the principle" behind the marketing code recommended by the World Health Assembly. On March 16, 1982, the company agreed to abide strictly by the code in the 120 countries in which its product is marketed.[21] Nestlé created the Infant Formula Audit Commission, chaired by former U.S. Senator Edmund Muskie, to review the company's compliance with the WHO code and to investigate any charges of abuse. However, Nestlé executives have voiced concerns over the prohibition of contact between company representatives and consumers. The company holds that improvements in labelling are not adequate to fulfill often illiterate consumers' need for accurate information and that a "show and tell" approach is necessary.

> What we're talking about is not necessarily the *right* but the *responsibility* of industry to communicate with its consumers. . . . If consumers—mothers in this case—are not given adequate instructions which can help them to use a product correctly, there are certain circumstances under which a manufacturer could be held responsible. So if you say, "Treat it like lettuce and just put it on the shelves" you are neglecting what is seen as a manufacturer's basic responsibility to do everything in his power to ensure that the product he sells is used correctly and appropriately.[22]

In June 1981 Dr. Thad M. Jackson, Vice-President for Nutrition and Development, Nestlé Coordination Center for Nutrition, testified before subcommittees of the Foreign Affairs Committee of the House of Representatives on the WHO Infant Formula Code. In his testimony Dr. Jackson reviewed the company's past practices and stated its position on a number of elements in the ongoing controversy:

> The Nestlé Company's involvement in infant nutrition began in 1867 when Henri Nestlé, a Swiss chemist, developed and marketed a milk food that he used to nourish a premature infant who could not take any food and was in immediate danger of dying.

---

[20] John A. Sparks, "The Nestle Controversy—Anatomy of a Boycott," Public Policy Education Fund (Grove City, Pa.: n.d.).

[21] Philip J. Hilts, "Nestle to Comply with Tougher Code on Infant Formula," *Washington Post*, March 17, 1982, sec. A, p. 8.

[22] "Infant Formula: An Activist Campaign," p. 13.

Nestlé's concern for the quality of its products, especially infant and child nutrition products, has not diminished from its earliest history. And just as Henri Nestlé's first use of his milk food saved a baby's life in Switzerland more than a century ago, our products save thousands of lives today. For example, Nestlé infant food products have been used to fight famine and feed starving refugees in Thailand, Somalia, Nicaragua, Bangladesh and elsewhere. Our products have been used by the International Red Cross, the Save the Children Fund and the Baptists' Missions of Thailand to fight starvation and to save the lives of babies. . . .

The need for breastmilk supplements and substitutes is clearly supported by the World Health Organization and eminent pediatric authorities. We fully recognize our responsibility to market infant formula in ways that do not discourage breastfeeding. We have been conscious of the need to modify our policies to meet changing conditions and to maintain our commitment to breastfeeding.

In 1974, Nestlé's president, Dr. Arthur Furer, aware of changing social patterns in the developing world and the increased access to radio and television there, reviewed the company's marketing practices on a region-by-region basis. As a result, mass media advertising of infant formula began to be phased out immediately in certain markets and, by 1978, was banned worldwide by the company.

Nestlé then undertook to carry out more comprehensive health education programs so as to ensure that an understanding of the proper use of our products reached mothers, particularly in rural areas. . . .

Nestlé fully supports the aim of the Code of Marketing of Breastmilk Substitutes recently adopted by the World Health Assembly: the provision of safe and adequate nutrition for infants by the protection and promotion of breastfeeding and by ensuring the proper use of breastmilk substitutes, when they are necessary, on the basis of adequate information and through appropriate marketing and distribution.

Moreover, Nestlé welcomes the World Health Assembly's decision to adopt the WHO Code as a recommendation, rather than a regulation, so as to encourage individual countries to introduce, where needed, specific national codes most appropriate to their socio-economic, educational and cultural backgrounds, and best suited to protect the health of infants in each sovereign nation.

Many countries have already adopted individual national codes, and several more are in the process of doing so. Nestlé currently markets infant formula in ten nations that have their own codes, and it abides by all ten of the codes, as it will abide by new codes as they are developed and enacted if needed by individual nations. . . .

Nestlé continually refines its policies to meet the needs of individual nations, and it will continue to do so. We reviewed our infant formula marketing practices seven years ago and made significant changes. We have made many more changes since then. We will continue to review current marketing practices to ensure that they are in agreement with national codes.[23]

The International Council of Infant Food Industries, of which Nestlé is a founding member, has also issued a statement regarding the World

---

[23] Thad M. Jackson, "Nestlé Discusses the Recommended WHO Infant Formula Code."

Health Assembly Code of Marketing which holds that national rather than international codes would be preferable:

> ICIFI members firmly support this WHO/UNICEF principle that marketing should not discourage breastfeeding. At the same time, ICIFI members believe "it is essential to make formulas, foods, and instructions for good nutrition for their infants available to those mothers who do not breastfeed for various reasons."
>
> ICIFI members have criticized the proposed single, detailed, international code which does not take into consideration varied socio-economic and cultural differences and, therefore, does not help infant nutrition in specific countries.
>
> Instead, ICIFI members are convinced that national codes of marketing—adaptable as they are to the very diverse conditions of developed countries as well as the Third World—are a much better way to guide business practices.[24]

CONTINUING CRITICISMS

In spite of the above responses, Abbott/Ross and Nestlé have been sharply criticized by certain church, medical, and public health groups. One ecumenical agency of the National Council of Churches has argued that corporate "development" often means *creating* a market for a product (*i.e.,* creating a need that previously did not exist). They hold Abbott/Ross and Nestlé responsible for increasing the incidence of infant malnutrition and mortality. They are willing to agree that an infant formula product can be "benign" in developed countries, but they believe the same product can seriously endanger health and welfare levels in underdeveloped countries. This group has occasionally met with representatives of Abbott/Ross. The company believes it has done all it can to satisfy their proposed changes in marketing, but the church group cites two remaining problems: (1) the company continues to offer "large quantities of free formula" that flow through health professionals to mothers; and (2) the company continues to pay its representatives to *sell* its products. However, the church group has also cited Abbott's code of marketing ethics as making important strides in proper marketing. The group further holds that whether the code is or is not adequate will depend more on how progressively the company monitors its implementation, including the reporting of abuses, than on any literal wording of the code.

Numerous medical and public health groups remain critical of industry marketing practices, and some have arranged and joined a boycott of Nestlé products. The following official statement on the WHO Code

---

[24] International Council of Infant Food Industries, "Infant Formula Marketing in the Third World," *National Journal* (May 9, 1981), p. 854.

of Marketing of Breastmilk Substitutes by the Board of Directors of the Ambulatory Pediatric Association is representative of these concerns:

> Despite claims to the contrary, marketing of infant formula influences maternal feeding practices. In recent testimony before the House Subcommittee on International Economic Policy and Trade, Carl Taylor, Professor and Head of the Department of International Health at the Johns Hopkins School of Hygiene and Public Health, presented some evidence: Massive advertising and availability of formula have been associated with a decline in breastfeeding in oil-rich Arab countries so that only 15 percent of mothers are nursing their babies at 3 months of age. In 1977 in Papua, New Guinea, promotion of infant formula was banned and feeding bottles could only be obtained with prescriptions from health workers. Breastfeeding increased from 65 percent to 88 percent, and by 1980 there was a statistically significant association with decreased incidence of gastroenteritis and malnutrition. With the institution of practices to encourage breastfeeding in an area in rural Costa Rica, neonatal mortality from diarrheal infections decreased from 3.9/1,000 in 1976 to near zero in 1980. . . .
>
> Recent hearings by the House Subcommittee on Domestic Marketing, Consumer Relations, and Nutrition and an administrative petition by Public Advocates, Inc. to "alleviate domestic infant formula misuse" indicate growing public concern about the policies of infant formula manufacturers in the United States. The free distribution of formula within health facilities makes health professionals conduits for free advertising. . . .[25]

Abbott/Ross vigorously denies that these claims have been adequately validated in New Guinea, the Arab countries, or elsewhere. Both Nestlé and Abbott/Ross continue to insist they are providing a product vitally needed by *some* Third World infants in a way that is not detrimental to the ideal of breastfeeding. Furthermore, they believe that no solid evidence linking infant formula sales to the decline of breastfeeding has yet been produced.[26] Abbott/Ross argues that it has developed a good marketing code and is attempting to enforce it. Tom McCollough, of Ross Laboratories, argues in addition that this controversy is a "cover" for a number of other agendas that are less openly discussed. In particular he mentions the conflicts between private enterprise and centralized ownership and between conservative and liberal philosophies.[27]

Nestlé signed a joint statement with the International Boycott Committee (INBC) on January 24, 1984, ending the six-year boycott against Nestlé. The INBC had gradually narrowed its points of disagreement to four concerns: (1) the use of educational materials, (2) hazard warnings on bottle labels, (3) personal gifts to health professionals, and (4) distribution of supplies. Douglas A. Johnson, the National Chairperson of IN-

---

[25] "Statement," *Pediatrics* 68, no. 3 (September 1981), pp. 432–433.

[26] Cox, "The Infant Formula Issue," p. 7.

[27] McCollough correspondence.

FACT, explained, "The signing of the joint statement . . . represented the [WHO] Code's transition from an urgent moral mandate to the accepted business practice by the largest and singly most important actor [concerning infant formula] in the world."[28]

Despite the end of the Nestlé boycott, the controversy has continued. In a May 1986 WHO meeting, new WHO/UNICEF guidelines were endorsed. These stringent guidelines specify the conditions under which it is advisable to bottlefeed an infant and recommend the use of a wet nurse or a breastmilk bank.[29] Infant formula manufacturers face continuing criticism concerning their marketing practices. Governments have delayed consideration and passage of regulatory legislation, with approximately twenty-five of 157 member nations having passed the new WHO code.

In October 1988, Nestlé and American Home Products were criticized by a public interest group, Action for Corporate Accountability, for "documented" violations of the provisions in the prevailing codes. As a result, a new boycott was initiated. These two corporations denied all charges.

[28] Susan Jenks, "Nestle Boycott Ends, Firm Revises Tactics," *Washington Times*, January 27, 1984.

[29] Carol Adelman, "Closing the Book on Infant Formula Fears," *Wall Street Journal*, June 19, 1986, p. 30.

Confidentiality at Swiss Bank Corporation

Alan Adler is an investment adviser in Zurich, Switzerland. Educated at the London School of Economics, he set up his practice in Zurich because he saw an international market for wealthy clients who prefer to keep their financial transactions in the confidential and sophisticated climate of Switzerland. Alan trades in international currency, bonds, and stocks for his clients, each of whom keeps at least $1 million in his or her personal account. Most of his clients are from West Germany and the United States, with a smaller number from Britain and South Africa. He has no clients from Switzerland, but he often trades in Swiss currency.

Alan prefers the freedom with which investment counselors can deal with their clients in Switzerland, and he has always liked being able to assure his clients of absolute confidentiality. The official records of clients kept in his office are maintained by number rather than name. He makes annual reports to his customers by their number only; and his clients also do not use their names but only numbers in correspondence. He keeps the decoding system for names and numbers in a safe deposit box at the Swiss Bank Corporation. He makes no report to any government, as he is not legally required to do so.

The Swiss Bank Corporation is in fact pivotal to Alan's method of dealing with clients. All clients keep their money and securities in their own names in private accounts at the Swiss Bank. Alan has written authorizations allowing him to use the money in their accounts to buy stocks, bonds, or foreign currency to be placed in the account. Although all transactions are at his discretion, he cannot himself withdraw anything from any customer's account at the bank. Only the customer can request or make a withdrawal, and any request must be made directly to the bank. Alan receives no fees per transaction, as they come only from the annual net *gains* he is able to make for his customers.

Alan has become concerned about the extent to which his promises of confidentiality can be sustained. Tradition at Swiss banks seems to be changing so that secretive policies are becoming less so. The government has become more interested in avoiding local tax abuses, and pressure is being brought by foreign governments for further changes. Jean-Paul Chapuis, Managing Director of the Swiss Bankers' Association, had said recently, "There is no guarantee of secrecy if you are dishonest." Swiss banks can no longer stand aloof, as the bankers see it, because their own expanded operations in other countries have made them vulnerable to pressures from those countries. Local law of course applies in the countries where their branches are doing business.

Alan has always given his customers a booklet entitled *Profile,* published by the Swiss Bank Corporation, as an annual report and explanation of services offered by the bank. He urges his customers to read a section entitled "Switzerland's Advantages as a Financial Centre" which assures a "safeguarding of privacy." Two of the sections are the following:

7. Tax Morality

    Switzerland is one of the few countries in which voters can directly determine how heavy their tax burden should be. This prevents prohibitive tax rates and is an important precondition for tax morality. The principle of self-assessment is yet another reflection of the special relationship between the Swiss and their government. The safeguarding of privacy vis-à-vis the tax authorities is guaranteed by banking secrecy.

    The state concentrates its efforts on combatting the abuse of this relationship. In recent years, the measures to hinder tax evasion and tax flight have been substantially strengthened. Parliament and secondarily the people may amend existing fiscal disadvantages (Stamp Duty Act, double taxation of corporate earnings) at any time within the framework provided for statutory revisions.

8. Responsibility of the Individual

    In contrast to countries with a centralist political structure, Switzerland places great emphasis on the individual citizen's responsibility for himself. The State's role is to guarantee the impartial administration of justice as well as an environment propitious to economic activity.

Until recently Alan has felt comfortable with simply asking his clients to read these sections and telling them that his data and the bank's data are strictly secret and under a pledge of confidentiality. Several events in recent months have convinced him that the government and the banks are modifying their forms of cooperation with foreign requests. For example, the government just froze the Swiss bank assets of two former foreign dictators, Ferdinand Marcos and Jean-Claude Duvalier, at the request of the respective governments of the Philippines and Haiti. These events were striking because in the past Swiss banks had always refused to confirm even whether they held a deposed ruler's account. The U.S. government had tried for nearly twenty years to locate suspected Nazi bank accounts, but had gotten nowhere with Swiss officials.

As a second example, the banks cooperated with the Securities and Exchange Commission of the U.S. government in prosecuting Dennis B. Levine in a major insider-trading scandal. (Insider trading has not been illegal in Switzerland; however, a bill that would make the misuse of inside information a criminal offense has been debated in the Swiss parliament.) This case is particularly worrisome to Alan in that the Bank Leu divulged the name and records of customer Levine in return for immunity. The Swiss government shortly thereafter announced that it was helping the U.S. government investigate three cases of tax fraud.

Finally, two cases in American courts have shaken Alan's confidence to the core. In a case in Tampa, Florida, U.S. District Court Judge Ben Krentzman threatened two Swiss lawyers with contempt citations if they did not stop resisting efforts to obtain financial information on criminal suspects who were U.S. customers of Swiss banks. The threat was a clear intimidation of lawyers to stop a *legal* maneuver in defending their client, and the intimidation was successful. In a second U.S. case, Federal Judge Milton Pollack had threatened Banca della Svizzera Italiana—a Swiss bank—with a fine of $50,000 per day unless it disclosed the identities of traders in the common stock of St. Joe Minerals. Faced with the seizure of its assets in the United States, the bank "persuaded" one of its customers to waive his secrecy rights, and the bank then identified him.

Disconcerted by these developments, Alan requested further information from the Swiss Bank Corporation. He observed that the most recent edition of the bank's *Profile* booklet had been amended; the sections concerning banking secrecy had been *omitted*. Another booklet published by the bank entitled *Secrecy in Swiss Banking* explained banking policies in new and unnerving detail. The Bank affirmed the premium placed on individual liberty and privacy in Switzerland, but it recognized that banking secrecy was not absolute. Alan read a section entitled "Limitation of Banking Secrecy under Swiss Law." It stated the following:

> Where stipulated in the law, banks are required to furnish to public authorities pertinent information on clients' accounts. Such disclosures are mandatory in actions involving inheritance, bankruptcy and debt collection as well as in all criminal cases, but not in ordinary tax matters and when violating foreign exchange regulations.
>
> Switzerland is party to many bilateral and multilateral conventions for legal assistance with other countries. Where such treaties exist, Swiss authorities assist foreign countries in criminal cases under conditions provided by these treaties. To be prosecuted as a crime, however, the alleged offense must always be considered a crime under the terms of Swiss legislation.

Alan surmised that the legal shelter of secrecy in Switzerland was still as good as any other in the world—e.g., as good as that found in the Bahamas—but nonetheless was contracting in scope and certainty. He wondered what moral responsibility he had to his customers to inform them about these changes. Should he warn them of new risks? Of course he had no idea what his customers did in the way of reporting or not reporting their accounts to their governments, and he did not view it as his business to know. But he had always given his customers an absolute guarantee of secrecy and confidentiality. He was not concerned that he would ever violate confidentiality himself; yet his safe deposit box did contain the names, addresses, and account numbers of all clients.

Alan sat down before his word processor and drafted a letter informing his clients of these developments. But when he read it, the changes sounded ominous. He decided to try another draft tomorrow to see if they sounded less alarming.

Italian Tax Mores

The Italian federal corporate tax system has an official, legal tax structure and tax rates just as the U.S. system does. However, all similarity between the two systems ends there.

The Italian tax authorities assume that no Italian corporation would ever submit a tax return which shows its true profits but rather would submit a return which understates actual profits by anywhere between 30 percent and 70 percent; their assumption is essentially correct. Therefore, about six months after the annual deadline for filing corporate tax returns, the tax authorities issue to each corporation an "invitation to discuss" its tax return. The purpose of this notice is to arrange a personal meeting between them and representatives of the corporation. At this meeting, the Italian revenue service states the amount of corporate income tax which it believes is due. Its position is developed from both prior years' taxes actually paid and the current year's return; the amount which the tax authorities claim is due is generally several times that shown on the corporation's return for the current year. In short, the corporation's tax return and the revenue service's stated position are the opening offers for the several rounds of bargaining which will follow.

The Italian corporation is typically represented in such negotiations by its *commercialista*, a function which exists in Italian society for the primary purpose of negotiating corporate (and individual) tax payments with the Italian tax authorities; thus, the management of an Italian corporation seldom, if ever, has to meet directly with the Italian revenue service and probably has a minimum awareness of the details of the negotiation other than the final settlement.

Both the final settlement and the negotiation are extremely important to the corporation, the tax authorities, and the *commercialista*. Since the tax authorities assume that a corporation *always* earned more money

This case was prepared by Arthur L. Kelly, and is published here with the permission of the author. Copyright © Arthur L. Kelly. **Not to be duplicated without permission of the author and publisher.**

this year than last year and *never* has a loss, the amount of the final settlement, *i.e.*, corporate taxes which will actually be paid, becomes, for all practical purposes, the floor for the start of next year's negotiations. The final settlement also represents the amount of revenue the Italian government will collect in taxes to help finance the cost of running the country. However, since large amounts of money are involved and two individuals having vested personal interests are conducting the negotiations, the amount of *bustarella*—typically a substantial cash payment "requested" by the Italian revenue agent from the *commercialista*—usually determines whether the final settlement is closer to the corporation's original tax return or to the fiscal authority's original negotiating position.

Whatever *bustarella* is paid during the negotiation is usually included by the *commercialista* in his lump-sum fee "for services rendered" to his corporate client. If the final settlement is favorable to the corporation, and it is the *commercialista*'s job to see that it is, then the corporation is not likely to complain about the amount of its *commercialista*'s fee, nor will it ever know how much of that fee was represented by *bustarella* and how much remained for the *commercialista* as payment for his negotiating services. In any case, the tax authorities will recognize the full amount of the fee as a tax-deductible expense on the corporation's tax return for the following year.

About ten years ago, a leading American bank opened a banking subsidiary in a major Italian city. At the end of its first year of operation, the bank was advised by its local lawyers and tax accountants, both from branches of U.S. companies, to file its tax return "Italian-style," *i.e.*, to understate its actual profits by a significant amount. The American general manager of the bank, who was on his first overseas assignment, refused to do so both because he considered it dishonest and because it was inconsistent with the practices of his parent company in the United States.

About six months after filing its "American-style" tax return, the bank received an "invitation to discuss" notice from the Italian tax authorities. The bank's general manager consulted with his lawyers and tax accountants who suggested he hire a *commercialista*. He rejected this advice and instead wrote a letter to the Italian revenue service not only stating that his firm's corporate return was correct as filed but also requesting that they inform him of any specific items about which they had questions. His letter was never answered.

About sixty days after receiving the initial "invitation to discuss" notice, the bank received a formal tax assessment notice calling for a tax of approximately three times that shown on the bank's corporate tax return; the tax authorities simply assumed the bank's original return had been based on generally accepted Italian practices, and they reacted accordingly. The bank's general manager again consulted with his lawyers and tax accountants who again suggested he hire a *commercialista* who knew how to handle these matters. Upon learning that the *commercialista* would probably have to pay *bustarella* to his revenue service counterpart in order to reach a settlement, the general manager again chose to ignore his advisors. Instead, he responded by sending the Italian revenue service a check for the full amount of taxes due according to the bank's American-style tax return even though the due date for the payment was almost six months hence; he made no reference to the amount of corporate taxes shown on the formal tax assessment notice.

Ninety days after paying its taxes, the bank received a third notice from the fiscal authorities. This one contained the statement, "We have reviewed your corporate tax return for 19____ and have determined that [the lira equivalent of] $6,000,000 of interest paid on deposits is not an allowable expense for federal tax purposes. Accordingly, the total tax due for 19____ is lira____." Since interest paid on deposits is any bank's largest single expense item, the new tax assessment was for an amount many times larger than that shown in the initial tax assessment notice and almost fifteen times larger than the taxes which the bank had actually paid.

The bank's general manager was understandably very upset. He immediately arranged an appointment to meet personally with the manager of the Italian revenue service's local office. Shortly after the start of their meeting, the conversation went something like this:

GENERAL MANAGER: "You can't really be serious about disallowing interest paid on deposits as a tax-deductible expense."

ITALIAN REVENUE SERVICE: "Perhaps. However, we thought it would get your attention. Now that you're here, shall we begin our negotiations?"[1]

---

[1] For readers interested in what happened subsequently, the bank was forced to pay the taxes shown on the initial tax assessment, and the American manager was recalled to the United States and replaced.

The Bribery Business

On February 3, 1975, Mr. Eli Black, Chairman of United Brands, Inc., smashed the window of his forty-fourth-floor Manhattan office with his briefcase and jumped to his death on the street below. Mr. Black, who had been ordained as a rabbi in his youth, was widely respected as a business leader who had done much to try to make business corporations more responsive to the needs of American society. Since no explanation of his decision to commit suicide was found, there was a great deal of speculation about why this man of seemingly exemplary character had done so.

It is the practice of the Securities and Exchange Commission to make an immediate investigation of the financial affairs of any important corporation whenever one of its senior officers takes his own life. The SEC began such an investigation of United Brands shortly after Mr. Black's death and quickly discovered that the company had recently paid some $1.25 million into the Swiss bank accounts of government officials of Honduras. The major business of United Brands is the cultivation and sale of bananas, and the company owns 28,000 acres of banana plantations in Honduras. The Honduran government had announced its intention to double the export tax on bananas, but shortly after the payment by United Brands, the proposed tax increase was cancelled. Actual ownership of the Swiss bank accounts was never publicly identified, but shortly after the SEC announced its finding, General Oswaldo Lopez, the president of Honduras, was ousted. The record of payment had been falsified in United Brands' accounts.

This case was prepared from published sources by Professor Dwight R. Ladd, Dean of the Whittemore School of Business and Economics, University of New Hampshire, with the collaboration of Professor Blair Little of the University of Western Ontario. It is intended as a basis for classroom discussion and not to illustrate either effective or ineffective handling of an administrative situation. Copyright © 1975 by the University of New Hampshire, and reprinted with the permission of the authors. The Postscript was prepared by Tom L. Beauchamp, with the permission of Professor Ladd. **Not to be duplicated without permission of the authors and publisher.**

FURTHER DEVELOPMENTS

This disclosure, coming more or less on the heels of the resignation of Richard Nixon from the U.S. presidency amid, among other things, evidence of widespread illegal corporate payments to the Nixon campaign fund, caused a good deal of public clamor. Further investigations by the SEC and the opening of hearings by a Senate committee quickly followed. As a result, it has become clear that corporate payments to government officials, political parties, "influential persons," and so on in many parts of the world were well-established practice. Gulf, Northrop, Carnation, Johnson & Johnson, Goodyear, Phillips, and Lockheed are among the major corporations whose officials have admitted such activities.

The sums involved have not been trivial. Gulf, for example, admitted to the payment of $4.2 million to the party of President Park of South Korea. Lockheed has acknowledged payments of $22 million to various officials, mostly in the Middle East. In general these payments have not been recorded on the companies' books but were "laundered" in one way or another through overseas subsidiaries. Gulf, for example, created a Bahamian subsidiary which was used as a conduit for making political contributions that were unlawful in the United States. Perhaps the most notorious case was that of Lockheed. The notoriety was undoubtedly related to Lockheed's having been kept from bankruptcy by a loan guarantee from the government, to governmental crises in the Netherlands and Japan as a result of testimony that Prince Bernhard of the Netherlands and senior government figures in Japan had received Lockheed money, and to the continuing and rigorous arguments of Lockheed's Chairman Haughton that payoffs were just good business.

These events, and continuing disclosures of additional companies involved, have raised a number of rather troublesome issues and questions about the international business system. The balance of this case attempts to define and discuss these issues.

THE LEGAL SITUATION
BEFORE THE FEDERAL
CORRUPT PRACTICES ACT

In the United States, bribery of public officials is a criminal offense. The U.S. government and many state governments have strict rules against the taking of gifts of any value by purchasing agents, contract officers, and so on. Corporate contributions to political parties or candidates are also forbidden by law. Many business corporations have regulations against giving or receiving of gifts which could be construed as bribes or payoffs. While it is known that these rules and regulations are violated from time to time, it is clear that the practices described are considered to be improper in the United States and this is reflected in the laws and regulations which prohibit them. However, these laws did not apply to actions by Americans—individuals or corporations—outside the United States until the Foreign Corrupt Practices Act was passed in 1977. When an American company did business in country X it was (until this act was passed) exclusively governed by the laws of X, just as a company from X would be governed by U.S. law when it does business here. Thus, at least in those countries where payments to public officials or political contributions by corporations are (or were) not illegal, the described actions of the companies were not illegal until 1977.

Before 1977 there were two possible exceptions to the foregoing: The SEC has long assumed the power to require that American-based companies disclose any such material payments to investors and to penalize companies that fail to do so. A second possible exception involves the Internal Revenue Code which requires that expense deductions for tax purposes be "necessary and proper" business expenses. The courts could obviously hold that bribes and payoffs are neither "necessary" nor "proper," in which case companies making such deductions would be in violation of the tax code or perhaps would be misstating profits to investors. That is, bribing and paying off foreign officials were not until the Foreign Corrupt Practices Act *illegal.* The *ethical* issues were the truly troublesome and contentious ones, but this is probably no less true *after* passage of this act.

OTHER CUSTOMS

It is a fact that in many parts of the world some forms of what we call bribery or payoffs are not only legal, but are widely accepted ways of conducting affairs. "Baksheesh," as it is known in Arabian countries, or "La Mordida," as Latin Americans style it, is commonplace. Not only for sales of military hardware, but for such routine transactions as purchasing a railway ticket, getting a telephone installed, or customs clearances, one is expected to make some sort of payment to those empowered to further or complete the transaction. Simply getting an appointment in order to further one's business may be virtually impossible without "La Mordida."

In many countries, such things as beginning and operating a business or getting import or export licenses are not more or less simple matters of meeting a few uniformly applied regulations as is the case in the United States and most industrial countries. Some payoff to those officials who have virtually complete latitude to grant or withhold necessary approvals is both expected and accepted practice. The following paragraphs provide a 1975 description of such a situation.

> For 18 months Del Monte Corp. tried to buy a 55,000 acre banana plantation in Guatemala, but the government said no.
>
> Then the company hired an influence-wielding "business consultant" and agreed to pay him nearly $500,000. Suddenly, the Guatemalan government reversed itself. Now, Del Monte owns the profitable banana-growing properties, for which it paid $20.5 million.
>
> The California food packer declines to identify the Guatemalan consultant, citing his fear that disclosure of his relationship with the large U.S. company could diminish his influence in Guatemala and perhaps provoke left-wing threats against his life. For these reasons, he demanded and received company assurances of anonymity.
>
> To protect him, Del Monte paid him outside the country. It charged his fee to general and administrative expenses on the books of several Panamanian shipping subsidiaries. His fee was entirely contingent on his ability to influence the balky Guatemalan government. Del Monte hasn't publicly disclosed these facts, but it confirms them.
>
> The company says that the fat fee secretly paid to its agent was entirely proper. It concedes that the consultant, a wealthy businessman, frequently contributes to political parties in Guatemala. But the consultant has assured Del Monte that no corporate cash went to any government officials there, a company spokesman says. Thus, Del Monte says its payments to the consultant shouldn't be compared to foreign bribes paid by United Brands Co. and Northrop Corp. or to illegal political contributions made abroad by Gulf Oil Corporation.
>
> Still, Del Monte's experience suggests why many U.S. companies find it necessary to hire well-connected fixers—a practice that would seem irregular in the U.S.—to help swing foreign transactions. Sometimes a fat fee paid to the right intermediary can quickly produce a few crucial phone calls and a favorable decision. Whether or not things went that way in the Del Monte case, a company spokesman does recall: "For a year we pounded on doors and waited for meetings. Then we hired this guy and things started occurring."[1]

General political "contributions" are in a somewhat different category for they are usually not related to specific transactions, but rather are intended to foster a generally favorable climate for the companies' activities. In the most general case, they may simply be intended to preserve a favorable climate, as in the case of Exxon's openly accounted for gifts to Canadian political parties. "Obviously, Imperial (Exxon's Canadian subsidiary) doesn't contribute to such parties as the New Democratic Party (a Socialist party) whose ideologies would nationalize us or put us out of business."[2] In a time when governments are more and more involved in activities relating to business, there is a tendency to forestall

---

[1] *Wall Street Journal,* July 14, 1975.

[2] *Wall Street Journal,* May 19, 1975.

retaliation of a general sort. This was the motivation expressed by some of the companies "contributing" to the Nixon reelection fund. Then there is the rather specific payoff of protection money. In South Korea, for example, Chairman Bob Dorsey of Gulf Oil reported that the threats made by the financial chairman of President Park's party—threats against Gulf's $300 million investment—"left little to the imagination."[3] Mr. Dorsey claimed not to have learned until after having made contributions of some $4 million, that doing so might have been illegal under South Korean law, but since President Park was a dictator, this presumably made little difference.

Finally, it must be observed that forms of corruption such as bribery have long been neither legal nor tolerated in some countries in the world. In March 1975 Yuri Sosnovsky, head of a furniture-making organization in the Ministry of Timber and Wood Processing of the Soviet Union, was shot by a firing squad after being convicted of accepting a $150,000 bribe from Walter Haeflin, representative of an unidentified Swiss company. Mr. Haeflin was sentenced to ten years in prison.[4]

THE ISSUES

Most of the discussions resulting from these revelations of corporate practices have centered around the ethical issue, and around the question of what, if anything, should be done at the governmental level in the United States or elsewhere. The ethical discussions center on two closely related issues: First, are ethical considerations in any way involved, and, second, is it appropriate to attempt to transfer the ethical standards of one culture to another?

What Should Be Done?

If one argues that whatever local customs may be, the practice of bribery and payoffs should not be continued, one is faced with what to do to insure control. While there are obvious barriers to attempting to impose U.S. law outside the United States, some argue that if American-based corporations face strong sanctions for engaging in bribery overseas, and if everyone knows that to be the case, an individual company can refuse to go along with the practice without much fear of reprisal or economic loss. No one has suggested that Mr. Dorsey of Gulf or Mr. Haughton of Lockheed should have been shot like Mr. Sosnovsky of the Ministry of Timber and Wood Processing, but one may assume that with such a precedent, Russian businessmen can put up a pretty

---

[3] *Newsweek* (International Division), May 26, 1975.

[4] *International Herald Tribune*, May 19, 1975.

strong defense against demands for bribes or payoffs if they choose to do so. As Mr. Dorsey said in urging Congress to pass legislation outlawing bribes overseas, it would "make it easier to resist the very intense pressures which are placed on us from time to time."[5]

On the other hand, it is feared by some that American legislative initiatives inevitably put American-based corporations at a disadvantage vis-à-vis German, Japanese, French, and other competitors not facing similar sanctions. There is ample evidence that businessmen from other countries are not reluctant to make payoffs in order to obtain sales. Viewed in this way the specific issue of bribery merges into the broader question of overall control of multinational corporations. Some feel that if the United States were to act first it would be easier to push other governments—German, Japanese, Swiss, Dutch, British, French—to follow. Others argue that the issue is best tackled through existing mechanisms for regulation such as the Common Market, the OECD, the International Monetary Fund, and so on.

Others, notably the business press, have tended to argue against legislative solutions. *Business Week* argued editorially in 1975:

> It is time for top management of U.S. companies to establish a single standard of ethical behavior for their executives at home and abroad. Competition should be in terms of product quality, price and financing— not in the purchase of local politicians. Each company must look past short-term profit to the long-term results of corruption.[6]

The *Wall Street Journal* argued:

> It is easy for moralists on the side-lines to say that business executives should not buckle to pressures from politicians. No doubt it is a great deal harder to make such decisions when the price of a bribe must be weighed against a perceived threat to a large business and all the jobs and shareholder investments tied up in the enterprise.
>
> Nevertheless, we can't help feeling that executives who bend to illicit political pressures either in the U.S. or abroad are buying only short-term success. The whole history of extortion at any level suggests that a strong resistance to the first approaches is the most effective response. There is a great deal of bargaining strength to be gained from taking a position that is morally and ethically strong.[7]

What Has Been Done?

By mid-1976, the Securities and Exchange Commission had drawn up much more specific and sweeping regulations for the control and

---

[5] *International Herald Tribune*, May 23, 1975.
[6] *Business Week*, June 23, 1975.
[7] *Wall Street Journal*, June 1975.

disclosures of foreign payments, though it had been reported[8] that the SEC had considerable difficulty in doing so. One issue was whether or not the names of recipients of bribes and payoffs should be disclosed. Some argued that such disclosures could result in nationalization of companies, or cancellation of valuable business concessions. Another issue was how to distinguish, in regulations, between bribes and $5 tips. Some of the same issues were involved in legislation being considered by the Senate Banking Committee. This legislation was more directed towards elimination rather than disclosure and control and was opposed by the Ford administration, ostensibly because of enforcement problems. The OECD nations were also in the process of developing an international code to limit these practices, but the group as such had no enforcement power, depending, rather, on individual governments.

In February of 1976, the Conference Board published the results of a survey of seventy-three senior international executives. About three-quarters of the respondents did not think foreign payoffs or bribes were an important problem in their industries—though many of these felt they were a problem for other industries. Only one-quarter of the companies had any formal, written policy covering the matter. On the other hand, the directors of Gulf Oil, acting on the report of an investigating committee which they had created, rather pointedly discharged Chairman Dorsey and two other senior officials. As Table 1, a summary of the status of a number of corporate officials who had admitted to or been convicted of illegal payoffs by mid-1975, suggests, Gulf's example was not widely followed, and the practice of bribery and payoffs was not regarded as a very serious matter in the boardrooms of the United States.

POSTSCRIPT 1988

On December 20, 1977, President Jimmy Carter signed into law the Foreign Corrupt Practices Act. This act received its impetus from the aforementioned disclosures during the Watergate hearings of large slush funds maintained by a number of American corporations (at least 117 of the Fortune 500, by one SEC account). The act makes it a criminal offense for a representative of an American corporation to offer or transmit payments to the officials of other governments for the purpose of facilitating business. A number of reporting measures and fines are specified in the act, including up to five years in prison. The act does not, however, prohibit so-called "grease" payments to lower officials in foreign governments, the rationale being that these officials often will not perform their normal specified functions without such payments.

[8] *Wall Street Journal*, September 9, 1975.

The Foreign Corrupt Practices Act has been the focus of intense and ongoing debate, especially in the business community, since its initial voyage through Congress. Even some U.S. government officials have spoken publicly in opposition to the act, on grounds of its implications for the frustration of American business. The most common argument is that in many countries payments are a necessary condition of doing business and resemble an approved system of extortion more than bribery. Questions have also been raised about whether there is anything unethical or corrupt in making such payments.[9]

Such questions have been raised about many recent cases. For example, on June 30, 1982, the Boeing Aircraft Company pleaded guilty to making over $7 million in secret payments from 1973 to 1977 to middlepersons in foreign countries (Spain, Lebanon, Honduras, and the Dominican Republic). The money was intended to facilitate the sale of $343 million of passenger planes. These payments were not at that time illegal, although they would be now. Boeing pleaded guilty for illegally concealing the payments from the Export-Import Bank, which financed up to 45 percent of the purchases. Boeing and Judge John H. Pratt concurred, in a plea agreement, that Boeing would pay a fine of $450,000.[10]

Many U.S. businesses would like to have the Foreign Corrupt Practices Act repealed or at least amended. In a 1983 Louis Harris survey, 78 percent of the corporate officials polled agreed that the act makes it more difficult to do business in countries where bribery is common; and 20 percent claim to have lost business due to provisions of the act.[11] However, business executives were deeply divided in this poll over which amendments should be enacted, if any. For example, 46 percent favored elimination of criminal penalties for violations, but 44 percent preferred the criminal penalties.

Most business complaints cluster around three areas: (1) the amount of record-keeping required; (2) less than specific guidelines on who can legally receive payments in foreign countries; and (3) the inability to pay foreign officials to speed up routine government functions.

The Senate has attempted to amend the act several times since 1977. Attempts in 1981 and 1983 were not successful because the House did not take similar action. The House and Senate produced bills in 1987 with similar provisions, which included revisions to reduce the record-keeping requirements, to allow payments to facilitate quicker handling of routine government functions, and to permit the Attorney General

---

[9] For information on this act and the ethical issues that surround it, see Mark Pastin and Michael Hooker, "Ethics and the Foreign Corrupt Practices Act," *Business Horizons* (December 1980).

[10] Al Kamen, "Boeing Draws Fine for Secret Payments in Overseas Plane Sales," *Washington Post,* July 1, 1982, sec. A, p. 7.

[11] "The Antibribery Act Splits Executives," *Business Week* (September 19, 1983), p. 16.

to file civil suits against corporations to enjoin them from action deemed to be in violation of the act. These 1987 bills also stated that "it shall be an affirmative defense to any violation of the act that a payment, gift, offer, or promise of anything of value to a foreign official is lawful under the law and regulation of the foreign official's country."[12]

As of this writing there is only minor opposition to the bills in either body of Congress. If other provisions of attached measures do not forestall passage, the Foreign Corrupt Practices amendments will become reality. However, all previous attempts at modification have failed.

[12] S. 651 (March 3, 1987).

TABLE 1. What Happened to Convicted Watergate Donors?

Company	Person	Penalty	Outcome
American Ship Building	George M. Steinbrenner 3d	$15,000	Still Chairman at $50,000/yr.
Ashland Oil	John H. Melcher, Jr.	$2,500	Discharged. Practicing law in Cleveland.
	Orin E. Atkins*	$1,000	Still Chairman at $314,000/yr.
Associated Milk Producers	Harold S. Nelson	4 mos. prison $10,000	Resigned. Now in commodities exports.
	David L. Parr	4 mos. prison $10,000	Resigned.
	Stuart H. Russell	2 yrs. prison**	Resigned. Now in private law practice.
Braniff International	Harding L. Lawrence	$1,000	Still Chairman at $335,000/yr.
Carnation	H. Everett Olson	$1,000	Still Chairman at $212,500/yr.
Diamond International	Ray Dubrowin	$1,000	Still V.P. for public affairs.
Goodyear Tire & Rubber	Russell DeYoung	$1,000	Still Chairman of 2 committees at $305,000/yr. Also collecting pension of $144,000/yr.
Gulf Oil	Claude C. Wild, Jr.	$1,000	Consultant in Washington, D.C.
HMS Electric	Charles N. Huserman	$1,000	Still President.
IBC&W Inc.	William G. Lyles, Sr.	$2,000	Still Chairman.
Lehigh Valley Cooperative Farmers	Richard L. Albson	Suspended fine of $1,000	Discharged.
3M	Harry Heltzer	$500	Retired as Chairman, but does special projects at $100,000/yr.
Northrop	Thomas V. Jones	$5,000	Still Chief Executive at $286,000/yr.
	James Allen	$1,000	Retired as V.P. with pension est. at $36,000/yr.
Phillips Petroleum	William W. Keeler	$1,000	Retired with pension at $201,742/yr.
Ratrie. Robbins & Schweitzer	Harry Ratrie	1 mo. probation	Still President.
	Augustus Robbins 3d	1 mo. probation	Still Exec. V.P.
Time Oil	Raymond Abendroth	$2,000	Still President.

* Pleaded no contest
** Under appeal
Source: Data taken from *New York Times*, August 24, 1975. Not updated after 1975.